D1389172

KINGMAKERS

KINGMAKERS

HOW POWER IN
ENGLAND WAS
WON AND LOST
ON THE WELSH
FRONTIER

TIMOTHY VENNING

AMBERLEY

First published 2017

Amberley Publishing
The Hill, Stroud
Gloucestershire, GL5 4EP

www.amberley-books.com

Copyright © Timothy Venning, 2017

The right of Timothy Venning to be identified
as the Author of this work has been asserted in
accordance with the Copyrights, Designs and
Patents Act 1988.

ISBN 978 1 4456 5940 4 (hardback)
ISBN 978 1 4456 5941 1 (ebook)

British Library Cataloguing in Publication Data.
A catalogue record for this book is available
from the British Library.

Printed in the UK.

CONTENTS

INTRODUCTION

The society of the Welsh Marches, the sociopolitical and administratively distinct district of the Anglo-Welsh border after the Norman Conquest, was a region constructed from a mosaic of small and larger lordships under the new Norman government after the conquest of 1066. The latter date saw Duke William of Normandy and his followers take over the established state and society of Anglo-Saxon (and Anglo-Scandinavian) England and transform it into a French-speaking and partially 'Frenchified' 'European' state, based on the same lines of governance and culture as the new leadership elite's Continental homeland. This applied to the Anglo-Welsh frontier as it did across England, with the existing higher ranks of society marginalised and mostly replaced – with the irony that the incomers on this border faced a militarily advantageous situation recently created by King Harold's destruction of the threat of a unified Welsh state under Gruffydd ap Llywelyn ap Seisyll, king of Gwynedd and Powys and conqueror of Deheubarth, in 1063. This precariously reunited state, more of a 'union of crowns' than a viable long-term regime due to complex Welsh inheritance law and the multitude of potential heirs to the five main Welsh kingdoms, had indeed reconquered parts of western Herefordshire from the English in the 1050s and forced King Edward 'the Confessor' to recognise this – the Welsh were a serious military threat then and thus caused an English military reaction, which the arriving Normans later followed up. The private army/bodyguard of housecarls that Harold Godwinson relied on to lead his army at the Battle of Hastings, and which the Normans destroyed there, 'blooded' themselves under Harold (as Earl of Hereford) in fighting off the threat posed by Gruffydd in 1057–63 and had finally broken up his kingdom to install a group of new dynasts as Harold's nominees. Indeed, the experiment of using 'Norman' cavalry to defeat the Welsh infantry and castles to defend the landscape had already been tried out in the 1050s, with only limited success – King Edward was half-Norman and used to using French cavalry knights against infantry. But it was William and his new group of frontier lords who reaped the benefit.

The post-1066 frontier was governed as a part of the kingdom of England by a military-based ruling class almost entirely North French (mostly but not exclusively Norman) in ethnic origin and cultural orientation, though inter-married with local Anglo-Saxon and Welsh heiresses. It was not that different in its creation by the first King William from the lands governed by the elite in the rest of his new regime. As with the remainder of England, the pre-1066 ruling class (a mixture of Anglo-Saxon and Scandinavian nobility; in this region, probably mostly 'Anglian' rather than Saxon or Scandinavian as a part of the old Anglian kingdom of Mercia, not occupied by the Vikings in the late ninth century) were evicted by King William in the years from 1067 and replaced by a more trustworthy group of Normans from his invading army of 1066 and their later reinforcements. Indeed, we have more direct literary evidence than for most of England of the process of removing some native landholders, bringing in Normans who spoke French and formed a militarily coherent body of cavalrymen (able to move around the country faster than and usually defeat the English infantry), and their building a chain of new motte-and-bailey castles as defensive and administrative bases starting in 1067. Resentment at this resulted in a local revolt, led by members of the marginalised pre-1066 elite, headed by Earl Edwin of Mercia (brother-in-law to the late King Harold II) and the legendary guerrilla Eadric the Wild, which was crushed by force with more expropriations following. This resembled the situation across England and the 'Marches' – the word coming from the word 'Mark' for 'frontier', as with the former name of the Anglian kingdom of the midlands, Mercia – was thus not exceptional in origin. In due course the land-hungry and enterprisingly aggressive new warlords on the English side of the (flexible) border moved on into the Welsh kingdoms beyond to seize land and build castles, aided by the constant bickering and sporadic fratricide of the Welsh princes, and land that had been Welsh in linguistic and cultural (and largely ethnic) terms since the stabilisation of the Anglo-Welsh frontier in the eighth century became politically and militarily English. But in ethnic terms the lower ranks of vassals of the (now Anglo-Norman) great lords were decidedly mixed, with the farming lower classes still mainly Welsh, though some blocs of Anglo-Normans – and in Pembrokeshire Flemings – moved into the conquered regions.

Nowadays historians tend to play down the concept of a legally distinct system of feudalism created by the new Norman kings, as there was not so much an established and coherent North French system of law and government imported by King William to England and imposed on his new kingdom; but the word serves as a convenient shorthand for a clearly new system of a pyramid of landholders, each holding estates from a social and legal superior in return for military service and owing him some dues of monetary payment and subjection to his private legal court in various matters. At the top of this 'chain of command', above a smallish group of 'tenants in chief', was the king to whom all his subjects owed obedience as well as to their own direct lord. The middle ranks of society were usually classed as knights, holding land as 'knights' fees' in return for military service to their lord, though how much actual military service they did (and whether they did so as cavalry) depended on the state of local security or the personal ambitions of the great lords in terms of military campaigning against their enemies (both Anglo-Norman and Welsh). Parallel to this, the old Anglo-Saxon system of county government by the king's officials and subjection to his justice and financial demands also survived – weakest where the needs of a military frontier under threat of attack gave a de facto leadership role in military action to the local lords, as in both the Welsh Marches and on the border with Scotland.

The special status that the Marches were to come to hold in the medieval Anglo-Norman and Plantagenet kingdom of England through to the fifteenth century lay in the crucial fact that whereas the primacy of military needs began to fade across the more peaceful majority of the kingdom after the politico-military difficulties of the later eleventh century (occasional civil wars aside), it survived on the Welsh frontier. This was more acute than on the frontier with Scotland, which was mostly peaceful until the Wars of Independence from 1296 as Edward I, II and III attempted to conquer Scotland; in Wales the English king and his lords faced not one ruler but a group of small kingdoms/principalities, only rarely united, and a sporadic ongoing campaign of local conquest of native Welsh lords by adventurous and land-hungry Anglo-Norman warlords. The frontier was marked by language and ethnicity as well as a difference in political authority, with the Welsh regarding themselves correctly as the original Britons who the Anglo-Saxons had driven out of England; the incomers were constantly attempting to extend their power and landholding into the Welsh lands from the 1070s onwards until the final success of Edward I in 1277–83. This gave an unusual (for contemporary England) primacy to military authority and leadership, plus a constantly shifting dynamic as new lordships were created or old ones passed to new hands following peaceful or violent deaths and inheritance by heiresses, and as in the nineteenth-century American 'Wild West' the turbulence saw both opportunities for leadership skills and the adventurous careers of shrewd and charismatic – and often downright thuggish – warlords and chancers. This system was duly replicated in Ireland when the latter was partially conquered from 1170 onwards, often by the same men as in the Welsh Marches or their close allies, but there the invaders' military success and chances of politico-cultural domination were lower due to the scale of the challenge. (In due course many incomers were evicted by the revived local 'Celtic' Irish, which did not happen in Wales.) From the Welsh sources it seems that the overwhelming initial grass-roots attitude of the conquered locals – Welsh in particular – to their new lords and their roving warbands was that the latter were no better than brigands, who stripped the land like locusts, and certainly some of the early generations of lords were notorious and piratical adventurers. Robert de Belleme, third Earl of Shrewsbury, was a particularly bad example as an extortionist, looter, and political chancer, and even when the area had settled down after *c.* 1290 there were occasions when ambitious lords (mostly now dabbling in national politics) were unrepentant villains.

The new Marcher world post-1066 was a classic 'frontier society', which made its own contribution to legend, as with outlaws like Sir Fulk FitzWarin (fl. 1200), plus the exploits of ambitious men who used their resources on the national political stage such as the Marcher baron-turned-queen's lover, invader, and national regent Roger Mortimer in the mid-late 1320s. Indeed, the amount of resources in men and money available to great Marcher lords led time and again to the king having to keep a wary eye on them as they created a major impact on national affairs, as a group or as individuals, with their greatest warlords holding major earldoms among the kingdom's top 'tenants-in-chief'; the history of the Marches was thus often a crucial part of the history of England, as in the turbulence of the mid-1260s and 1320s. From the early 1170s onwards some Marcher lords indeed acquired substantial lands in newly conquered eastern Ireland and were able to challenge the king on two separate British islands at once, as King John faced with the de Braoses and Henry III from the Marshals dynasty, earls of Pembroke.

The continuing need for military readiness and expansion against the Welsh until the 1280s – when Edward I seized the conquered lands of Gwynedd and South-West Wales to make himself the greatest lord in the Marches – enabled the distinctive 'frontier' society to survive there longer than in the rest of England. The Marcher lords were constantly war-ready at the heads of their tenant armies, and so could keep on their authority and legal power over the latter longer than in most of England. Indeed, only the eastern parts of the Marches were part of the administratively English county system set up pre-1066, and the originally Welsh principalities and lordships to the west were legally separate from this and at their conquest fell either to Marcher lords or to the king (as part of his new 'Principality of Wales', usually held by the king's heir from 1301). Both regions were finally incorporated into the English county system only in 1536 by Henry VIII. There were a few embryonic counties in Wales held before that as one unit by the king and not by Marcher lords, for example Ceredigion/Cardigan. But all had a different legal and administrative structure to England, with governance and juridical power lying with their hereditary lords (usually Anglo-Norman barons in origin), appointed and removable by the English king as his 'tenants-in-chief', but if this did not happen descending hereditarily or by marriage. These lordships were thus 'family principalities' like the original Welsh states and sub-states in this region, with private armies of tenants raised by and loyal to their lords rather than the king – against whom they often rebelled. They had a complex and bloody history, with family feuds, long-running hatreds, endemic violence, 'gangster state' ethics in the case of the worst offenders but a 'harsh but just' rule in the case of the most conscientious lords, and a constant theme of autonomist struggle against the central state – involving the personal relationships between these lords and the various English kings.

The lordships were centred on the fortified residences of the rulers, many of which still survive as major regional tourist magnets. The stories of the castles and their rulers is a mixture of clan-like family history and the involvement of the personnel involved in central government politics, and touches on major events such as the civil war of King Stephen's reign (1135–54), the resistance to King John and the Magna Carta crisis plus the 1216 attempt to replace John with Prince Louis of France, the rebellion of Simon de Montfort and the establishment of Parliament, the overthrows of Edward II in 1327 and Richard II in 1399, and the Wars of the Roses. One of the most important of the castles and dynastic centres involved, Ludlow Castle, was the lordship of the rebel Roger Mortimer who had a relationship with Queen Isabella and helped her remove (and murder?) her husband Edward II; his family later claimed to be Richard II's heirs and transmitted their claim to the Yorkist dynasty. Edward IV and Richard III, plus Edward V, the elder of the 'Princes in the Tower', were brought up at their ancestors' Ludlow Castle, and crucial events in the Yorkist versus Lancastrian struggle took place there: Edward V left Ludlow for his journey to London and deposition in 1483. This study will trace the history of the main Marcher lordships and their interaction with the English state from the embryonic pre-1066 Norman activities in Herefordshire to the role of the Mortimers of Ludlow in late medieval politics, culminating with the assumption of the crown by the Mortimer heir Edward IV in 1461 and the showdown of his heir's entourage with the future Richard III, lord of Glamorgan, and the Duke of Buckingham, lord of Brecon, on the road from Ludlow to London in early May 1483.

The main Marcher lordships, which will feature in this study, were as follows:

NORTH
Earldom of Chester: later acquired by the Crown.
Oswestry; Chirk; Bromfield and Yale; Mold; Dyffryn Clywd (the last two were annexed Welsh lordships).

CENTRE
Earldom of Shrewsbury (early period).
Clun; Ludlow; Bishop's Castle; Montgomery; Builth; Maelienydd; Elfael; Ceri; Cedewain (the last four were annexed Welsh lordships).

SOUTH-EAST
Earldom of Hereford (early period).
Brecon (the former Welsh kingdom of Brycheiniog).
Hay; Clifford; Monmouth; Chepstow (a former seat of earldom of Hereford); Ewais Lacey; later Goodrich.
Glamorgan (former Welsh kingdom); its sub-lordships, traditionally twelve in number and headed by Newcastle/Bridgend (west), Coety/Oldcastle, Bridgend (east), Ogmore/Ogwr, Llanblethian, St Athan, Sully.
Abergavenny; Caerleon (former Welsh lordship), Newport.

SOUTH-WEST
Earldom of Pembroke.
Talacharn/Laugharne; Llansteffan; Cydweli/Kidwelly (usually held with Ogmore); Gower (usually held with Oystermouth Castle and Swansea); St Clears; Narbeth; Wiston; Haverfordwest; Pebediog and Cemaes (former Welsh lordships).

I

THE NORMANS IN THE MARCHES BEFORE 1066

A reunion of the Welsh kingdoms threatens the borders of pre-Norman England in the 1040s to 1066; Edward the Confessor responds by bringing in the first Norman knights and castles, before the Conquest, to fight them.

The first Norman warlords to be placed on the Welsh borders were not, contrary to usual assumptions, the post-1066 vassals of the new King William. In fact the danger of a reunified Wales raiding or even retaking border regions from England in the 1040s had already led to this policy, bringing in new men and methods of warfare, by King Edward, later known as 'the Confessor' (reigned 1042–1066) in the 1040s. The joint, North/Central Welsh kingdom of Gwyedd and Powys and the South-Western kingdom of Deheubarth had already been united briefly under the most successful ruler of the latter, Hywel 'the Good' (accession Deheubarth 905, Gwynedd/Powys 942) from 942–50. This then broke up under his successors, but both dynasties were descended from the earlier rulers of Gwynedd and the more successful of them at times imposed unity before their multitude of ambitious relatives reversed this again. The most sustained attempt at reunion followed the reign of Iago ap Idwal of Gwynedd/Powys (ruled 1023–39), who was succeeded by a distant cousin, Gruffydd ap Llywelyn, the son of Llywelyn ap Seissyll who had ruled both the kingdoms of North and South in 1018–23 (and the North from 1005). Possibly more strongly motivated than most of the dynasty by being an 'outsider' like his father (owing their claim to female not male descent), Gruffydd was the most successful of the Welsh dynasts since Hywel. He was strongly supported enough on accession to soon heavily defeat the English at Rhyd-y-Groes near Welshpool, killing Midlands 'strongman' Earl Leofric of Mercia's brother Edwin; Mercia would no longer be able to predate on Gwynedd/Powys as it had done through the ninth century when its attacks had forced the two states into a union in 853. By this date, the strong joint-kingship of England and Denmark created by the Danish intruder Cnut (ruled 1016–1035) had ended and Cnut's sons were fighting over his inheritance. The skilful and aggressive warlord Cnut, often overseas, had relied on a trio of senior 'earls' to act as his deputies in England – the Sussex 'thegn' Godwin in Wessex, the West Mercian Leofric (d. 1057) in Mercia, and the Dane or Danish Yorkshireman Siward in Northumbria – and where Cnut with his large army and fleet had been able to dominate these men, the same was not true of his weaker and less experienced successors. Indeed, at times the earls appeared stronger than the kings of England – and this was to 'impact' on the politics of the Welsh borders, too, giving able and adaptable rulers such as Gruffydd ap Llywelyn the chance to play one English magnate off against another and to expand their dominions. Cnut's feuding sons Harold 'Harefoot' (ruled 1036–1040) and Harthacnut (unsuccessful claimant 1035–1036, ruled 1040–1042) were succeeded by Aethelred's surviving son Edward, later known as 'the Confessor' (ruled 1042–1066), who had to be recalled from long exile in Normandy and had no experience of England or personal connections with its elite. The already middle-aged and not notably militaristic Edward relied heavily on his earls, especially Godwin, who became his father-in-law, and his French upbringing in Normandy (his mother Queen Emma's homeland) led to him importing not only Norman clerics and architecture but military innovations. These were Norman and other North French knights who, unlike the Anglo-Saxons, usually fought on horseback and governed from well-defended motte-and-bailey castles rather than wooded halls surrounded by easily burnt palisades. The fissiparous nature of a multitude of small and war-wracked principalities in northern France had led to the development of new defensive 'castles', firstly in wood and then in stone, in the tenth and eleventh centuries, and they were more difficult to take than wooden Anglo-Saxon halls that burned easily. Mobile horsemen could also shelter inside and ride out to harass attackers and loot their homes over a wide area. Edward sought to use this to combat the mobile bands of raiding Welsh, who could now cause less damage and be caught more easily – provided the new system was managed properly and men trained to fight and build expertly. His experiments with Norman military tactics, in conjunction with grants of land to Norman knights in return for defending it from his enemies, were first put into effect in the dangerous and deteriorating situation on the Welsh border nearly two decades before the 'Norman Conquest'. The first arrival of the Normans and their Continental way of life in England thus took place in the South of the lands that were to form the Marches, though as a limited and cautious experiment rather than as a new 'system' as such. It was done as a reaction to the advances made by Gruffydd ap Llywelyn, an overlooked figure in Anglo-Welsh history who (unlike the subsequent unifiers from Gwynedd in the thirteenth century) has suffered from a lack of surviving historical sources. As in the ninth and tenth centuries, we are mostly reliant on a limited number of English and Welsh annals who baldly state basic facts with little extra detail.

Gruffydd managed to drive his rival Hywel ap Edwin of Deheubarth in South-West Wales (ruled 1033–1044) out of his lands and sacked Llanbadarn in 1039, presumably in the flush of victory after his success at Rhyd-y-Gross, which attracted support to him. Hywel collected overseas troops (probably Irish Viking mercenaries from the ports of Dublin and Waterford) and was able to regain his kingdom later, but lost the Battle of Pen Cadeir in a second invasion in 1041 and even had Gruffydd carry off and marry his wife. In 1044 Gruffydd managed to impose a union by killing Hywel in battle at the mouth of the River Teifi as the

latter invaded after being driven out. He then faced Gruffydd ap
Rhydderch, son of the late King Rhydderch ap Iestyn (d. 1033)
of Deheubarth and probably ruler of the district of Glywysng in
Glamorgan (around Cardiff), in a war for Deheubarth. His foe
could call on overseas Vikings in Ireland for mercenary support, as
plotting contenders for Welsh thrones had done for a century; to
counter this, Gruffydd relied on his new ally Swein (*c.* 1020–1052),
recently appointed as the new Earl of Hereford and eldest son of
the English chief minister, Earl Godwin of Wessex (d. 1053). King
Edward had now set up a new earldom of this crucial Southern
district of the Welsh border where Gruffydd was advancing his
frontier and had designs on the lands around the middle Wye, and
the half-Danish Swein, probably still in his early or mid-twenties,
had energy and ambition (but was to turn out to be hot-headed
and very much a 'loose cannon', like many future Marcher lords
given extra powers and resources by their sovereigns). Swein
marched into Deheubarth to assist Gruffydd ap Llywelyn and
ravaged his enemy Gruffydd ap Rhydderch's lands in 1046, but got
into trouble with King Edward for seducing and running off with
the abbess of Leominster (possibly with her consent) on his return
from the campaign. He was exiled, the first instance of Edward
turning on the increasingly powerful Godwin dynasty. Despite
Edward's marrying Godwin's daughter Edith in 1045 and granting
earldoms to Swein and his next brother Harold (East Anglia, 1045)
and cousin Beorn, his relations with them were uneasy, not least
because of Godwin's part in betraying Edward's brother Alfred to
his death in 1036 at the behest of Harold 'Harefoot'. Rumours
were to spread about why Edward and the much younger Edith
had no children – was the king seeking to deny the 'kingmaker'
of 1042, Godwin, the chance of putting his grandchildren on
the throne? In place of Swein, Edward appointed his half-French
nephew Ralph of the Vexin, son of his sister Goda and a French
count whose lands lay on the Norman border in the Seine valley,
to rule Herefordshire. Ralph brought in northern French (Norman

or Vexin) knights to build motte-and-bailey castles, most notably Richard FitzScrob, who built the eponymous 'Richard's Castle' in northern Herefordshire, and Osbern Pentecost, who built what was then known as 'Pentecost's Castle' and was later renamed 'Ewias Harold' (after Ralph's son Harold who inherited it), at the southern end of the 'Golden Valley' south-west of Hereford. He also taught his levies to fight on horseback in the Norman fashion – before the 'Norman Conquest' made such actions routine – and may have built the first castle outside the county capital, Hereford.

The French knights and their fellow-countrymen, most notably Bishop Robert of London, who King Edward made Archbishop of Canterbury in 1051 instead of Godwin's candidate, were apparently unpopular in England – or at least in the London region, where they would have concentrated at court – and became mixed up in Edward's struggle for power with the overbearing Godwin and his sons. Swein was exiled to Denmark, and his ally Gruffydd's impressive rule of all Wales was interrupted by his rival Gruffydd ap Rhydderch's recapture of Deheubarth by invasion in 1047. In 1049 Swein returned to England and landed at Godwin's main estate, Bosham on Chichester Harbour, to seek the restoration of his earldom (possibly with Godwin's support or at his behest) as the king was dealing with a pirate squadron led by exile Osgod Clapa in the Channel and Gruffydd ap Rhydderch was attacking the Forest of Dean with the help of Irish Viking mercenaries. But plans for Swein's recall went wrong, as his brother Harold and cousin Beorn refused to return lands of his which they had been granted on his disgrace; he then turned pirate, too. He lured his land-seizing cousin Earl Beorn, whose dominions included Gloucestershire, onto his ship when the latter called on him at Bosham to mediate. He took him prisoner and sailed off down the Channel, and then beheaded him and had his body sent ashore at Dartmouth, for which he was exiled again. Was his crime premeditated, or a result of a sudden quarrel? In 1051 a confrontation developed between Edward and Godwin when the latter refused to punish the citizens of Dover for attacking the entourage of the king's visiting brother-in-law, Count Eustace of Boulogne, Earl Ralph's stepfather. Godwin refused to come to the royal court at Gloucester, and both sides called out their levies. A truce saw the dispute adjourned to a council meeting at London, but there the king proved implacable; he was backed up by earls Leofric and Siward with their earldom's armies (and presumably Ralph, too). Godwin and his sons were exiled, the queen was sent away from court, and Ralph was among the leaders of the new regime. He was to jointly command the royal fleet with Odda of Deerhurst (in Gloucestershire), now co-earl of Wessex, as Godwin and his sons returned from exile in summer 1052 with strong fleets. Harold and his younger brother Leofwine brought in the ubiquitous Scandinavian mercenaries from Dublin for an unsuccessful landing at the mouth of the River Parret in Somerset, and then joined Godwin at the Isle of Wight; the royal fleet had ventured out from Sandwich but could not stop Godwin, perhaps due to bad weather. The royal fleet broke up amidst poor morale, plus evident sympathy for Godwin among Wessex sailors and an unwillingness to be commanded by a Frenchman. Godwin sailed to the Thames and landed at Southwark, across the Thames from London, and as Leofric and Siward deserted the king's cause and demanded Godwin's restoration, Edward had to agree to this. The unpopular Frenchmen at court, including some holding office, who the Anglo-Saxon Chronicle says were accused of injustice, and presumably Richard and Osbern too, had to fight their way out of London in company with the hated Norman archbishop Robert and his countryman, the new Bishop William of London. Robert apparently took hostage Godwin's youngest son, Wulfnoth, and grandson. He transported them back to Normandy and handed them over to his master Duke William, whose propagandists were subsequently to allege that King Edward had promised him the succession to the English throne on a recent visit. It was probably partly the hostages' detention in Normandy that caused Harold to travel there in 1064/5 and end up being forced to swear an oath to aid William's accession, which he later broke – thus the pieces began to fall into place for the events of 1066. The Herefordshire knights rode back home safely to their castles, and Richard was able to keep his new lands, as did Earl Ralph (his rival Swein had died recently on pilgrimage to Jerusalem), while the fugitive Bishop William was invited back later. Not all the 'French' were expelled: the triumphant Godwin family did not insist on this – there was no clear 'anti-French' policy by the Godwin family, though Archbishop Robert no doubt denounced the family to William, and the Pope continued to recognise Robert as archbishop. Other knights fled back to Normandy or else to Scotland, where they entered the service of King Macbeth (ruled 1040–1057). A just and able ruler, not the tyrant of myth and Shakespearian drama, Macbeth saw the use of cavalry as Edward had done, and was to retain them in his army. Some of them were killed fighting for him and others expelled in the invasion from England of his rival Malcolm (III) mac Duncan, Siward's protégé, in 1054. Normans fighting on horseback for the Scots king met English infantry fighting for his challenger at the Battle of Dunsinane in Perthshire, near Dunkeld, which lost Macbeth control of Scotland south of the Forth, and after this defeat and Macbeth's later killing at Lumphanan in 1057 the Norman presence in Scotland ended until King David invited them back after 1100. Other French courtiers remained in England unmolested, such as the king's adviser Robert Fitz Wimarc, who built a new pre-1066 castle in Essex. The triumphant Godwin now died suddenly at Easter 1053, and Harold succeeded him as Earl of Wessex; Harold's former earldom of East Anglia passed to Leofric's son Aelfgar, who had held it during the Godwins' exile in 1051-2.

Gruffydd ap Llywelyn reconquered Deheubarth and killed his rival Gruffydd ap Rhydderch in summer 1055, reuniting all Wales except for the small kingdoms of Glamorgan/Gwent. This followed the controversial appointment of Harold's brother Tostig to become a rare non-local Earl of Northumbria after the death of Earl Siward, who had lost his elder son in battle with Macbeth and the Normans in Scotland in 1054. At a heated royal council meeting in March 1055 Earl Aelfgar opposed the appointment, thus placing the dynasties of Godwin and Leofric in direct opposition in a struggle to influence the militarily weakened and ageing king. He was almost immediately dismissed and possibly outlawed, in which Harold was the main actor, and fled to Ireland to recruit eighteen shiploads of Vikings to invade, as Harold had done earlier. But this time the exile also involved the Welsh, as Aelfgar sailed to North Wales and interested Gruffydd ap Llywelyn in his cause; at an unknown date (but possibly linked to this campaign or that of 1058) Aelfgar married his daughter Edith to Gruffydd. It appears that Aelfgar participated in Gruffydd's invasion of Deheubarth and killing of his eponymous rival; this may have been Gruffydd's terms for the alliance. The two armies then invaded Herefordshire, probably anticipating that Aelfgar's father, the neighbouring Earl Leofric, would stand aside and enable his son to confront Harold and demand his earldom back by armed force. The allies then defeated Earl Ralph in a clash outside Hereford on 24 October 1055. The English cavalrymen, unused to fighting on horseback, ran away from the Welsh, and Gruffydd won the battle and proceeded to a spectacular sack of Hereford, burning down the cathedral. As a result, Ralph was unable to stop Aelfgar – Leofric apparently did not intervene – and Harold had to bring the royal/ Wessex army to help; he probably outnumbered the invaders, who retreated west, but did not dare to pursue them into the hills where he could be ambushed. A treaty was patched up, Aelfgar had his earldom returned and was able to succeed Leofric to Mercia when the latter died in 1057, and Gruffydd regained some long-lost Welsh territory – probably Herefordshire south-west of the Wye as far as the Black Mountains, the ancient mini-kingdom of 'Ergyng' that the English called 'Archenfield'. The following year Gruffydd killed the new Bishop Leofgar of Hereford, a 'fighting bishop' used to commanding troops, who had formerly been chaplain to Earl Harold and was apparently his choice to succeed the venerable Bishop Athelstan and restore the demoralised local army, in battle at Glasbury on the middle Wye near Hay-on-Wye on 16 June 1056. Sheriff Aelfnoth was also killed, and the location of the battle just within Wales suggests that the English had taken the offensive in an attempt to recover nearby Ergyng but were driven back. Gruffydd was now able to force Earl Harold and King Edward to recognise him as king of all of Wales in return for his doing homage to Edward – the past year's events were the greatest Welsh military triumph for centuries and reflected on the threat posed to an admittedly disunited English elite. When King Edward's ineffective nephew Earl Ralph of Hereford died on 21 December 1057, Harold had to take over the earldom and its defence in person; Ralph's underage son (a ward of Queen Edith, Harold's sister), who if his father had been a military success might have had a chance of the throne, had to make do with scattered lands in the shire (including Ewias Harold and its castle) and later became the Conquest-era lord of Berkeley Castle in Gloucestershire. His family held this for centuries, and will appear again in the story of the Marches as captors of Edward II in 1327.

Gruffydd countered the House of Godwin by an alliance with their rival Earl Aelfgar, Leofric's son, ruler of East Anglia in 1051–2 and 1053–7 and of Mercia in 1057–?62, whose daughter Edith he married – probably in the late 1050s. He helped the exiled Aelfgar to force his way back into his earldom when he was exiled again in 1058. On this occasion, Aelfgar fled to Gwynedd and joined up with a fleet of Hebridean Vikings under their overlord King Harald of Norway's son Magnus, which aided him and Gruffydd in an invasion of Mercia. As a result Harold seems to have judged it wiser to avoid fighting, and Aelfgar had his earldom restored; no Welsh king had had such influence in the internal struggles of the English elite for four centuries. But then Gruffydd faced a sustained attack by Harold, started in midwinter 1062–3 with a raid on his headquarters at Degannwy in Gwynedd. The post was taken by a surprise assault and burnt, though he managed to flee into the Arfon hills. Given the lack of any intervention from his ally Mercia, his father-in-law Aelfgar had probably died and Harold was seeking to destroy him as a threat to the Godwinsson family. He was driven into the mountains by superior English numbers, with Harold's brother Tostig bringing Northumbrian troops into Gwynedd, too, and was killed in August 1063 by one of his followers, Cynan ap Iago (a dynastic rival?), as Earl Harold ravaged Gwynedd in a prolonged English campaign. His head was purportedly put on the prow of Harold's ship as it sailed back to the royal court at Gloucester. His widow Edith, probably not more than twenty at the time, was later married by his nemesis Harold in 1066 to cement an uneasy alliance between Harold, now King of England, and her brothers earls Edwin of Mercia and Morcar of Northumbria; Gruffydd and Edith's daughter Nest married a Norman baron around 1075. Edith had a son or twins by Harold, born posthumously after their father's death at the Battle of Hastings as Edith sheltered from the Norman invasion at Chester. Her subsequent fate is unclear but she may have died in Spain in the 1080s.

Gruffydd was the most successful Welsh ruler since the sixth century in territorial terms, but proved unable to resist English military superiority even under the pre-Norman kingdom. On his death, Earl Harold imposed the rule of his half-brothers Bleddyn and Rhiwallon to the joint kingdom of Gwynedd and Powys.

2

THE ESTABLISHMENT
OF THE MARCHES
1066–1135

The Norman Conquest, the Saxon revolts, and the establishment of the Welsh Marches as semi-autonomous Norman lordships; the failed attempt to overrun all Wales.

The Northern Marches, 1066–1135

The death of King Harold and most of his elite troops at the Battle of Hastings (or 'Senlac') on 14 October 1066 did not lead to the new King William immediately destroying the old English elite and setting up his countrymen in their lands, but this was not to last. Whether or not the hard-headed and suspicious 'William the Bastard' had intended a sociopolitical and military revolution in landholding from the start, many of his senior English subjects proved disloyal, and from 1068 revolt flared in the name of the dispossessed Edgar 'Atheling', great-nephew of King Edward. In 1069 the failure of a Mercian revolt against the Normans, who had been setting up unwanted new castles in a 'security network' staffed by their countrymen, led to King William marching northwards to secure control of the regional capital of Chester, which had strong Roman walls for defence. The last pre-1066 earl, Edwin, son of Aelfgar, had been involved in the revolt but was not a notable military leader – he had been routed by the Norwegians at Gate Fulford in 1066 – and fled to York to join other rebels. William imposed a new 'strongman' as its earl, his countryman Hugh d'Avranches (*c.* 1047–1101). The latter was nicknamed 'Lupus', 'the Wolf', and, less flatteringly, 'Le Gros', 'The Fat' – though the latter nickname had also been borne by his father, Richard 'Le Gros', viscount of Avranches in the Cotentin in Normandy, and may have been inherited. (It was supposed to have been the origin of his distant relatives' 'Grosvenor' name, 'from 'Gros Venour', 'Fat Huntsman'.) Hugh's mother was Emma, according to some accounts from the family of de Conteville who were related to the knight Herluin de Conteville, stepfather of the new King William and husband of his mother Arlette (daughter of a tanner from Falaise and mistress to William's late father Duke Robert). That would make Hugh a kinsman of Arlette and Herluin's sons, William's half-brothers and leading henchmen Count Robert of Mortain, since 1066/7 lord of Pevensey Castle in Sussex and also lord of Cornwall, and Bishop Odo of Bayeux, since 1066/7 Earl of Kent. Hugh had a sister, Margaret, who was married to Ranulf de Briquessart, viscount of the Bessin in Normandy, and probably did not marry until well after the Conquest, as his son Richard was not born until a couple of decades later. One of the younger Norman warlords on whom William now relied to take control of strategic positions, he now took control of the northern Marches as lord of Cheshire, with the potential to expand westwards across Flintshire into the fertile Clywd Valley and on towards the mountains of Arfon, and built a major new castle at Chester as the centre of his dominions. The struggle for the Welsh administrative districts between Dee and Conwy now began with the main tactical advantages – in terms of mobile cavalry and easily defensible motte-and-bailey castles – with the invaders.

Bleddyn ap Cynfyn of Gwynedd was the senior Northern Welsh ruler who the arriving Normans faced in the late 1060s, though his younger brother Rhiwallon was technically his co-ruler as installed by Earl Harold in 1063. He faced thwarted rivals from the large royal kindred, as had most of his predecessors, and his position was far from secure. He killed Gruffydd's two sons when they attempted to overthrow him at the Battle of Mechain in 1070, but was betrayed and defeated in battle (and either killed then or murdered later) by Rhys ap Owain, a claimant to Deheubarth, which he was attempting to add to his kingdom, in 1075. His eulogy remembered him as generous, just, and not self-seeking unlike most of the other current princes. The throne was seized by an 'outsider' of dubious lineage and no known close connections to the main line of Gwynedd, the princeling Trahaern of Arwystli. Trahaern faced a rival for Gwynedd – Gruffydd ap Cynan (born *c*. 1055), a descendant of Iago ap Idwal and son of Cynan ap Iago by an Irish Norse princess, Ragnhild of Dublin. The latter invaded from Dublin with Scandinavian help from his mother's people, a time-worn path for ambitious princes with small local resources, and briefly ruled the peninsula of Lleyn in 1075. But he was soon driven out due to local anger at his plundering Viking mercenaries. Trahaern then took over Lleyn to add to the rest of Gwynedd, but was killed at the Battle of Mynydd Carn in Pembrokeshire in 1081, when Gruffydd returned from Ireland for a second time and joined forces with a claimant to Deheubarth, Rhys ap Tewdr, at St. David's under the auspices of the bishopric. They challenged Trahaern's local ally Caradog ap Gruffydd ap Rhydderch, son of the late ruler killed by Gruffydd ap Llywelyn in 1055 and probably originally ruler of Gwent in the early 1060s. Caradog had then seized control of parts of Deheubarth and had daringly challenged Harold and his master King Edward in 1065 by raiding the king's new royal hunting lodge west of the lower Wye at Portskewett, near Chepstow. This would have brought English retaliation on him if the events of 1066 had not intervened. Instead, Caradog survived precariously as ruler of most of Deheubarth plus Gwent, in conflict with the brothers Maredudd and Rhys ap Owain ap Edwin – grandsons of King Edwin ap Cadell who had been overthrown in 1044 – but in alliance from 1075 with Trahaern. The new Norman lords imposed from *c*. 1070 on lower Gwent between Wye and Usk now entered the picture, aiding first one and then another rival, with no sense on the part of the feuding Welsh princes that the newcomers presented an existential threat to all of them and that they needed to unite. As with the rival claimants of Gwynedd and Deheubarth, calling in outside help from the Vikings of Dublin in the tenth and eleventh centuries, local ambitions and 'short-termism' were the order of the day – to the ultimate benefit of the outsiders. Maredudd was killed on the River Rhymney in 1072, and in 1078 Rhys was expelled and possibly killed by Trahaern in the latter's self-proclaimed revenge for Rhys' (1075) killing of Bleddyn of Gwynedd/Powys, as seen above. Trahaern now aided Caradog against Gruffydd ap Cynan and Rhys ap Tewdr, but was defeated and killed at the Battle of Mydydd Carn. The vacant throne of Gwynedd passed to Gruffydd ap Cynan while Rhys ap Tewdr took over all of Deheubarth, but Trahaern's family retained the rule of Arwystli.

The Norman barons of Cheshire under Robert of Rhuddlan (d. 1093), cousin and lieutenant of Hugh d'Avranches, were active in Gwynedd's coastal strip after around 1073, when Robert invaded as far as the Conwy, built Rhuddlan Castle on the coast, and secured rule of the lower Conwy Valley. By the late 1080s Robert was paying forty pounds a year rent to the king for rights as his tenant-in-chief in North Wales, which authorised both conquest and settlement of sub-vassals there. Gruffydd ap Cynan sought his support against Trahaern as he took over Lleyn in 1075, but they then fell out and Gruffydd attacked Rhudlan to no avail. As seen above, his losses there emboldened his restive subjects to expel him and his plundering Viking mercenaries, and he moved off to Ireland to muster troops for an invasion of Deheubarth. The Normans, led by Hugh and Robert, now invaded the main part of Gwynedd in force in 1081 – possibly coordinated with King William's Southern expedition to St David's that year, which meant that the lords of Deheubarth were preoccupied elsewhere. Gruffydd ap Cynan was defeated and captured at Corwen and was deported and imprisoned by Hugh at Chester Castle for up to a decade, and the Normans conquered most of the coastal territories as far west as Caernarfon. In the early 1080s coastal castles were erected on a strip of territory as far west as opposite Mon/Anglesey, and much of later Flintshire was incorporated in the earldom as two new English 'hundreds'. An English 'borough' was founded at Rhuddlan and a first castle at Caernarfon, and in 1092 an Anglo-Norman clerk, Hervey, became Bishop of Bangor. Much of the local Church's lands were taken for the abbey of St Werburgh, Chester. Imprisoned at Chester for years, Gruffydd eventually secured his release as client-ruler of Anglesey around 1091, possibly being regarded as able to keep the predatory Scandinavian fleets from Dublin that roamed the Irish Sea at bay better than a non-local Norman as he had a Dubliner mother and 'contacts'. A new Scandinavian warlord, Godred or Guthfrith 'Crovan' ('Crobh Ban' in Gaelic, 'White Hands', due to his distinctive gauntlets worn in battle), had arisen as ruler of the Isle of Man (1075) and had vassals as far away as the Hebrides – a potential threat to both Welsh and Normans. Using his rule of Mon to build up his warband and fleet again, the shrewd Gruffydd waited his chance for revenge for his long imprisonment and was able to kill Robert of Rhuddlan in a sudden 'strike' with three warships against his castle in July 1093. He landed on the beach nearby at the base of the Great Orme headland and proceeded to loot the castle's adjoining village and farms. Seeing the unexpected raiders carrying loot back to their ships from his battlements, Robert furiously charged down onto the beach with a couple of men to recapture it and was overpowered and killed; his men had to watch as the raiders then cut his head off and stuck it on the prow of their warship.

Gruffydd joined in a revolt on the mainland in 1094, but the Normans could intervene swiftly with their cavalry reinforcements and defeated it; he had to flee to his mother's homeland, Ireland. He retuned to Mon a couple of years later once Earl Hugh was distracted elsewhere. A second exile followed his return in 1098 as King William II's 'Marcher' vassals, earls Hugh of Chester and Hugh of Shrewsbury, invaded Mon, but the Normans now clashed with King Magnus 'Bareleg' of Norway (ruled 1093–1103), who had recently secured control of both the Orkneys and Man, dispossessed Godred's sons from the latter, and was now heading for Dublin. The Norse warlord regarded himself as lord of the Irish Sea, and his large and well-experienced fleet now headed for Mon/Anglesey to try to secure it too. The Normans mustered on the shore as it was sighted, and the Earl of Shrewsbury was killed by an arrow fired from a longship into the Norman ranks on the beach. Magnus' propagandists claimed their king had done this personally, hitting the earl expertly in the face below his helmet. As the Norse headed on for Ireland, the discomfited Normans retreated to Cheshire; Gruffydd was able to return. In the 1100s he regained most of his ancestral lands on the mainland, as well, as his main foe, the new Earl of Shrewsbury, Robert de Belleme, fell foul of the new King Henry I for backing his brother Robert of Normandy in the 1101–2 civil war and was dispossessed. Gruffydd found it politic to submit to the invading Henry in 1114, as the massive attack that the English king launched – said by the impressed Welsh chronicles to be aimed at wiping out the kingdom – was joined by Henry's son-in-law and vassal King Alexander of Scots (ruled 1107–1124), but the latter preferred to persuade the king that he would not win a guerrilla war in the mountains as the Welsh evaded battle, and Alexander arranged a treaty. Gruffydd was reaffirmed as a royal vassal on the same lines as the Marcher lords but remained practically independent. The earldom of Chester had passed from Hugh (d. 1101) to his underage son Richard, still under ten and as such a royal ward, whose estates were thus administered by Henry's officials.

Richard was to be drowned with Henry's son William in the 'White Ship disaster' in November 1120, as a foolish captain and his drunk crew tried to impress their passengers by overtaking the king's vessel on the return voyage from Normandy to England after Henry's 'summit' with the King of France. Instead the vessel struck a rock outside Barfleur harbour, and almost everybody onboard was drowned. The king had lost his wife Matilda of Scotland (Alexander's sister) in 1118 so he hastily remarried to Adeliza of Louvain, but he had no more children. The Welsh then attempted to regain the lands lost to the leaderless earldom, but were driven back in 1121 by the new earl, Hugh's sister's son Ranulf 'le Meschin' (d. 1129), who had plenty of experience of border wars in the hills as a leading lord in Cumberland. Under the latter's son and successor Ranulf 'le Gernon' the earldom became enmeshed in the civil war of 1138–53 between King Stephen and the Empress Matilda. Gwynedd consequently had a respite from attack, but its Church remained under threat of the legal supremacy claimed by the Archbishopric of Canterbury over all Wales. Gruffydd meanwhile lent support to the major Welsh rebellion against the Anglo-Norman settlers in Deheubarth in 1136 after Henry I died, his daughter Gwenllian having eloped with their leader Gruffydd ap Rhys (who Gruffydd had earlier given sanctuary in Gwynedd but tried to hand over to Henry I) some time around 1113–15; the latter was seeking his father-in-law's aid in 1136 when Gwenllian was killed attacking the settlers at Kidwelly/Cydweli Castle. Also killed in action against the Anglo-Normans, in 1132, was Gruffydd's eldest son and heir, Cadwallon.

The central Marches, 1066–1135

The kingdom of Powys had been ruled in a union with Gwynedd since its last previous king Cyngen ap Cadell fled to Rome under the pressure of Mercian attack in 854. But it was restored by Gwynedd's invader Earl (later King) Harold in summer 1063 following his defeat of Gruffydd ap Llewelyn ap Seissyl, under the latter's half-brothers, Bleddyn and Rhiwallon ap Cynfyn. They were installed by Harold as his vassals, breaking up

Gruffydd's unified Welsh state, but from 1066 faced the new threat of heavily armoured and land-hungry Norman lords on their eastern borders. The new king's close companion William FitzOsbern became the Earl of Hereford, ruling Herefordshire and either taking over or building Hereford Castle; he also took over the area of eastern Gwent at the mouth of the Wye, which had been attacked by local king Caradoc ap Gruffydd ap Rhydderch in 1065, and built Chepstow Castle. But FitzOsbern was killed in battle in Flanders fighting for King William's allies in 1071 (see below); he was succeeded by his son Roger de Breteuil, first lord of Wigmore Castle near Ludlow. The new (or extended 1050s?) castle at Hereford went to King Edward's Norman follower Richard FitzScrob, lord of 'Richard's Castle', and the new central Shropshire lordship of Clun, north-west of Ludlow, to a minor Norman baron called Picot. He died without male heirs and was succeeded by his daughter and heiress Adeliza FitzPicot, who married Robert or Picot de Say (*c.* 1015–1098), son of another Picot de Say (d. 1030), who was lord of the estate from which the family name came – Saye in the Orme region of Normandy. Robert/Picot, lord of Clun after his father-in-law, established the de Says at Clun: he and Adeliza had several sons including Sir William (probably the oldest), who predeceased his father in 1086 and married Agnes de Grantmesnil (the daughter of Hugh de Grantmesnil, Sheriff of Leicestershire), Henry (d. after 1130), who was to succeed to Clun, Robert, and Theodore. Shropshire was the centre of the Anglo-Saxon rebellion of Eadric 'the Wild', a minor landowner and possible connection (nephew according to chronicler Florence of Worcester) of King Aethelred's former Earl of Mercia, Eadric 'Streona' or 'the Acquisitive' (k. 1016/17). This senior Anglo-Saxon noble from western Mercia was the most notorious figure of the treachery- and disaster-laden reign of Aethelred 'Unraed' in 978–1016, a multiple defector who in turn betrayed Aethelred, his son and successor Edmund 'Ironside' and the Danish conqueror King Cnut, and was blamed by the unambiguously hostile Anglo-Saxon Chronicle editors for deserting Edmund at the vital Battle of Ashingdon in 1016 and so handing most of England over to the Danes. Having already betrayed Cnut to return to Edmund when the latter seemed to be winning, he now ensured Cnut's victory and preserved his grip on his earldom, but was soon executed by Cnut who could not trust him. His namesake the younger Eadric, son of an unknown Aelfric, was a far more honourable character who was prepared to risk his future by defying the might of the Norman war-machine in leading a guerrilla revolt, though this followed the new King William's sidelining of Earl Edwin of Mercia (son of the late Earl Aelfgar) and erection of a rash of resented castles across the province to ensure security for the incoming Norman landowners. The most important of these was Warwick Castle. There was clearly already a degree of confiscation of the Anglo-Saxon landed elite's estates underway across western Mercia by the time of Eadric's revolt, causing resentment into which he tapped successfully, and he may have lost his own lands and so been driven to gamble on revolt as he had no reason to stay loyal. He was known in Latin as 'Silvanus', i.e. 'of the Woods', as he probably lived in a camp in the forests after the confiscation of his lands by the Normans. He unsuccessfully attacked Hereford with the aid of King Bleddyn ap Cynfyn of Gwynedd and Powys in 1067, but Richard Fitz Scrob of 'Richard's Castle', who had been given the county sheriffdom and had probably occupied (or built if this was done post-1066) Hereford Castle, fought him off. He fled to Powys to seek refuge with Bleddyn, and in 1069 returned to lead a major rebellion in Shropshire and sacked Shrewsbury. This was probably coordinated with the risings elsewhere in Mercia, whose earl, Edwin, had submitted to William in autumn 1066 but was now allowing arriving Norman lords to set up castles at strategic points across his former territory and chose to join evicted junior landowners in revolt. The records suggest a coordinated appeal by Eadric and his allies for support elsewhere to overwhelm the enemy with a multitude of risings, and the more or less simultaneous revolt in Northumbria may have been timed to coincide with Eadric's; dangerously for the king, his rival King Swein of Denmark (cousin to the late King Harold) later arrived with a fleet in the Humber. But the Normans in the castle at Shrewsbury held out, and rescuers later arrived;

the Normans defeated the rebellion by having cavalry and being able to move swiftly between 'troublespots'. King William was able to march north across the region in autumn 1069 to defeat the main west Mercian rebel army at Stafford and take Chester, before heading east to tackle the other simultaneous rising in Northumbria. Now, or rather on his return from York to Chester, he set up Hugh d'Avranches as Earl of Chester, as seen above. Eadric was isolated, probably outnumbered by a better-armed arriving Norman force, and was driven out into the hills of western Herefordshire. He later submitted in exchange for the return of at least some of his property, as did his more famous fellow-rebel Hereward in the Fens, and may be the 'Eadric' who held lands at Much Wenlock from the local priory in the 'Domesday Book' in 1086. He served in William's invasion of Scotland in 1072 before disappearing from history, but remained a figure of local legend. He was still supposed to haunt the Long Mynd centuries later as leader of the 'Wild Hunt', a mythical ghostly cavalcade of huntsmen, horses and hounds allegedly heard in isolated locations in wild weather, and probably derived from the ancient Welsh legends of the demi-god Gwynn ap Nudd of the 'Otherworld'.

After marching across and subduing rebel western Mercia in the second half of 1069, King William established Hugh d'Avranches at his new castle in Chester as its first earl. To the south he established Roger of Montgomery (d. 1094), a close companion of his, as the first 'tenant-in-chief' of Shropshire (around seven-eighths of which were included in his estates) and lord of Shrewsbury, where he erected the first castle. The earldom of Shrewsbury followed; the royal grant of the lands around Shrewsbury that were the basis of the peerage's power was made in autumn 1069, but the peerage may have come a year or two later – probably autumn 1071. This duly made Roger the royal 'supremo' of the central Marches, the senior landowning peer to whom the smaller landowners owed allegiance and military service. Like most of the other new royal 'tenants-in-chief', the rank of senior landowners (often with peerages) directly below the king in the new 'feudal' (not a contemporary term) hierarchy imported from Normandy, Roger was from the landed nobility of Normandy – the men who had had the lands, horses, and militarily-trained tenants available to make a significant contribution to William's army in 1066. They duly scooped up the rewards. Given the turbulence of William's minority from 1035 to the mid-1040s and a number of subsequent rebellions – some with potential for success as backed by the King of France to 1060, William's overlord Henry I – by 1066 most of the more obstreperously autonomist or treacherous nobles in Normandy had shown their hands in acts of defiance to the duke's authority and been 'winnowed out' by William. Those who remained and had the resources to assist his campaign in England were almost all reliably loyal, and as such could be called upon to take on a similar role as the new king's local lieutenants across his new realm. Roger's father, another Roger (d. 1055), had been the landed 'Sieur de Montgommerie', lord of St Germain-de-Montgommerie and St Foy-de-Montgommerie near the major ducal castle of Falaise (after which the family was named), and had participated in the violent feuds of William's youth and ended up in exile at the court of his backer King Henry I in Paris, where he died; another son of his had murdered William's faithful steward Osbern – William FitzOsbern's father – in William's presence. The elder Roger also probably held the title and accompanying district legal authority of the 'Viscomte d'Hiemois', and his mother was probably the great-niece of Duke William's ancestress Duchess Gunnora, so he was one of the distant ducal kin like FitzOsbern. Like a modern mafia clan in a similarly turbulent state riven by feuding aristocrats, many of the great Norman nobles had a history of blood-vendettas against their neighbours, and the sons of old enemies (and sometimes the rivals themselves) were now uncomfortable allies in ruling England. But like Roger de Montgomery and FitzOsbern, memories of what their families had done in the past were temporarily put aside in the hard task of surviving as a new 'ruling class' in a hostile area – with the watchful king ready to crack down on defaulters. Unlike FitzOsbern, it is unclear if Roger fought at Hastings in 1066 or remained at home as one of William's regents with his Duchess Matilda, as one source indicates (another says that he led the right wing of cavalry in the battle), but he was soon his principal governor of both the central Marches and of the western half of Sussex, most of which he owned. In the latter he possessed the 'rape', or administrative district, of Arundel, a 'new town' and castle erected by him (believed to be so-called after the well-established local swallow, the 'Hirondelle') at the strategic gap in the South Downs made by the River Arun. He also owned the adjoining rape of Chichester to the west, and extensive lands in Wiltshire and the West Midlands, making him one of the richest and most powerful men in the kingdom.

Roger's equally formidable wife was Mabel de Belleme (d. 1079), through whom he and their sons inherited the 'honours' of Belleme (on the Norman/French frontier in southern Normandy, originally owing direct allegiance to the Kings of France not to the Duke) and Alencon and Seez within Normandy. This strong-willed and vindictive heiress was daughter of the equally strong-willed and violent William Talvas ('The Shield', a presumed reference to his toughness and imperviousness), hereditary lord of Belleme (d. 1052); her uncle was Bishop Yves of Seez (she inherited his lands around Seez too in 1070). Their local family had ruled the Belleme region since the late tenth century, and William's father, another William, had been allowed to fortify his two main strongholds of Alencon and Belleme by Duke Richard I by the 990s. They had links to local Francian nobility, and may well have regarded the distant dukes (whose lands had not originally encompassed this area of far southern Normandy) as interlopers who had no real claim on their loyalty. The aggressive and capable Mabel was regarded with distaste by the contemporary Anglo-Norman historian Orderic Vitalis as a murderous termagant; he described her as short in stature and jocular in manner, shrewd but vicious, and ruthless in pursuing grudges. Her official eulogy, which also referred to her small stature, paid tribute to her forcefulness, piety, and wisdom: she was 'Commanding, eloquent and wise/ Prompt to daring enterprise'. Possible exaggerations by her enemies aside ('unwomanly' women who commanded political power harshly like her and her sovereign's granddaughter, the Empress Matilda, were regarded with special indignation by male chroniclers), she was certainly one of the more ruthless and acquisitive operators of a turbulent border region, where the semi-autonomous lords played the Kings of France and Dukes of Normandy off against each other. A fearsome reputation and willingness to punish defiance with a bloodbath were qualities useful to keep order, and in that respect Mabel was an effective operator who would be equally at home intimidating potential rebels on another war-afflicted border region in Shropshire. Her father had made too many enemies by his vindictiveness, with a series of murders – reputedly including his first wife, Mabel's and her brother Arnulf's mother – and mutilations of his enemies that had led Arnulf to depose him around 1048; Mabel clearly took after him. It was this that led to Mabel marrying Roger de Montgomery, then the son of a leading lord in central Normandy, as she accompanied her father into exile. The latter married her off to Roger in return for his family promising to help restore him – which his death prevented. Now Mabel transferred her ruthless guardianship of her rights and lands to her husband's English lands, but her connection to the Marches was probably limited; she seems to have spent much of her time back in Normandy looking after her lands there. She was back in Normandy when the feuds she had stoked up by her callousness led to her downfall: on 2 December 1079 she was murdered in her bath at the castle of Bures on the River Dives in eastern

Normandy by Hugh Bunel, a former local landowner who she had unjustly dispossessed in 1077. He and his three brothers had sneaked onto the premises undetected, and after attacking Mabel and cutting off her head they escaped by destroying a bridge behind them. Mabel left at least ten children, of whom the eldest, Roger, died young; the next, the notorious 'brigand baron' Robert of Belleme, had been at Bures when his mother was killed but had been unable to catch the killers. He was clearly seen as the family heir to their Norman lands from his concentration on France not England, and now inherited Maud's Belleme estates where he followed the family tradition in playing off the Dukes of Normandy and Kings of France against each other and ignoring superior authority as much as possible. This was aided by the death of King William in September 1087 and succession to Normandy of his eldest son Robert Curthose, or 'Short Legs' (1052?–1134), a weaker if less violent character with tastes for drink and women, about whom the contemporary chroniclers complained that he allowed his barons to defy him and let them feud and pillage unchecked. Orderic Vitalis, Henry of Huntingdon, William of Malmesbury, and Robert of Torigny all report independently in their histories that despite Robert of Belleme's bravery, military capability, and skill in designing castles, he was a thug who enjoyed running what would nowadays be called 'extortion rackets' and torturing his prisoners. When the king died in 1087 Robert threw out all the royal castellans appointed to govern castles in his territory and replaced them with his own men, showng that he intended to resume practical autonomy, though he loyally backed the new Duke Robert in his subsequent struggle with his younger brother William Rufus, heir to England. Robert de Belleme also added to his lands and politico-military power by marrying the daughter and eventual heiress of Count Guy of Ponthieu, Normandy's neighbour to the east – technically King William's vassal but also potentially treacherous. (Guy appears on the

Bayeux Tapestry due to his piratical act of seizing and holding hostage the shipwrecked Earl Harold of Wessex on the latter's visit to Normandy in 1064/5 – his overlord William forced him to hand Harold over.) The third Montgomery son, Hugh, was to succeed his father to the earldom of Shrewsbury in 1094; next came the younger Roger, who married Almodis, heiress of La Marche in Aquitaine, but was more interested in his extensive lands in Lancashire where he was the main lord in the district *'inter Mersea et Ripam'* (i.e. the lands from the River Mersey to the River Ribble). After 1090 he also acquired most of the lands between Ribble and Lune to become the senior landowner and bulwark of royal power on the kingdom's north-west frontier, as of that date Cumbria was contested between England and Scotland and was usually held by the latter until King William II evicted its Earl Dolfin and occupied Carlisle, building a castle there in 1092. The fifth Montgomery son was Philip, and the youngest was Arnulf, who clearly had the same determination to make up for his poor political position as a landless younger son by force, cunning, and playing off his less-able elders against each other as the youngest of King William's sons, the later King Henry I. Arnulf would go on to take a leading role in the invasion of Deheubarth and become the Earl of Pembroke (see below). The four daughters included Sybil, who married Robert FitzHamon, the first Norman lord of Glamorgan (see below), and Maud, who married King William I's younger half-brother Robert, Count of Mortain and lord of Pevensey Castle in east Sussex.

The middle Marches opposite Powys became the base for adventurous lords moving west into Radnor and up the Severn Valley, building new motte-and-bailey castles as they went. Earl Roger of Shrewsbury duly established his western base at a site on the upper Severn called Montgomery, after his home in Normandy, the 'old castle' of the town, with a chain of eight nearby castles including the formidable 'Moat Lane' site near Llandinam that boasted a motte forty feet high and two baileys – clearly designed for a large garrison and a threat of major attack. These sites were now used to raid and later subdue the small adjoining Welsh 'commotes' of Ceri and Cedewain to the north/north-west and Arwystli to the west. As early as 1073–4 exploratory raids were crossing the mountains into Dyfed, a region whose divided state, aggravated by the constant drain of hit-and-run raids on the coast staged by the Dublin and Waterford Scandinavians, kept the indigenous princes weak. Other new lords on the central frontier included Roger's niece's husband Warin of Hesdin, 'the Bald', the new Flemish Sheriff of Shropshire, and Reginald de Bailleul (from the eponymous town in Normandy, and related to the new North Country barons De Balliol/Bailleul of County Durham, who were to acquire the Kingship of Scots thanks to Edward I in 1292), who built the new north Shropshire castle of L'Ooevre ('The Work'). Reginald was later to succeed Warin to both his sheriffdom and his wife; Warin's daughter married another incoming 'man on the make', the Breton Alan FitzFlaad (*c.* 1070–1114), who later succeeded to the sheriffdom in turn as a trusted supporter of the new King Henry I after 1100. Alan's father Flaald had been the seneschal of the Breton town and castle of Dol, and the dynasty were to have a distinguished future both in England as the 'Fitz Alans' (their descendants acquiring the castle and 'honour' of Arundel in Sussex that their superiors the Montgomery dynasty had held) and a royal future in Scotland as the Stewarts. Alan's elder son Sir William Fitz Alan succeeded him as lord of Oswestry in north-western Shropshire and as sheriff of the county; his younger son Walter emigrated to Scotland in the service of Norman-friendly King David I (ruled 1124–1153), formerly King Henry's governor of Cumbria in *c.* 1108–24, and became hereditary Steward of Scotland. (This was a normal procedure for the younger sons of the Anglo-Norman nobility across England; others involved included the North Country families of De Brus/Bruce and De Morville.) At another strategic point guarding the upper Severn Valley towards Welshpool, upriver of Shrewsbury, King William planted Roger Corbet in 1069; this middle-ranking baron of minor Norman origin named his castle Caus after his homeland, the Pays de Caux, and founded another long-lasting dynasty.

The marriage of Maud de Montgomery and the much older De Mortain, one of the greatest lords in England, was probably connected to the bridegroom's and his father-in-law's joint domination of Sussex. However in 1087–8 it came to assume a useful political purpose, too, after the surprise death of King William in September 1087, of injuries received while sacking the rebellious town of Mantes in the Vexin (the small county sandwiched between Normandy and the King of France's personal domains in the Seine valley, downriver from Paris). The dying king was currently at odds with his eldest son Robert Curthose, who had already launched one rebellion against his father in 1077, backed by King Philip of France, and was now in exile again. King William seems to have been dismissive of his eldest son's undersize and corpulent appearance as well as his potential ability, though it is not clear if it was this or the (not yet legally fixed) tradition in French inheritance law of a first son inheriting his father's hereditary lands and the second inheriting any he had acquired himself that caused King William to pass over Robert as the next King of England in favour of his third, but next surviving, son William Rufus. Robert was not at the king's bedside as he expired of a ruptured stomach in Rouen Castle, and the latter handed Rufus his crown and told him to go and take England (technically left to the custody of God, from whom the king had received it), which he duly did. Robert only inherited Normandy but considered England to be rightfully his, and he formed a conspiracy in spring 1088 to invade with hired shipping and seize it, aided by his allies in that country. The latter included both of his paternal uncles, Robert of

Mortain, the lord of Pevensey and Cornwall, and Bishop Odo, Earl of Kent (the latter imprisoned for supposed disloyalty in 1083–7 but released by the dying King's orders). As they held most of the coast of south-east England at the narrowest point of the Channel, plus Pevensey Bay where William I had landed in 1066, they were invaluable allies for an invader. The plot also drew in other senior nobles, such as Roger Bigod (the main lord in Norfolk since the disgrace of Ralph le Gael in 1075) and Suffolk, Hugh de Grantmesnil, lord of Leicestershire, and the Breton Count Alan, lord of Richmond in Yorkshire – and also Roger de Montgomery, who as lord of Arundel could either assist a Norman attack via his strip of coast or take his men to aid De Mortain and Odo further east. The number of plotters and their possession of vital strategic points gave them a massive advantage, and the invasion might have worked, but as on a later occasion (1101) Duke Robert was thwarted by a mixture of bad luck and his own sluggishness. A brave and skilful warrior in combat, as he was to show on the First Crusade in 1097–9, the new duke lacked the organizing ability and strategic ruthlessness of his father, and on this occasion he also lacked enough money to hire many ships and mercenary troops quickly – he had to sell off the Cotentin Pensinsula to his poorly resourced but ambitious younger brother Henry, and thus gave the latter a foothold in Normandy to his own future political detriment. Bad weather also impeded his sailing, and while he was held up, the quick-acting Rufus proceeded to rally his own supporters in England and put the main south-eastern military centres held by the rebels, Rochester and Pevensey Castles, under siege. As was usual for Anglo-Norman and later warfare in the centuries before cannon were developed, in a siege of a strongly defended walled castle the advantage lay with the defence, provided that they had enough men and supplies – all the attackers could do was sit it out and try to starve or intimidate the defenders. If enough castles were in revolt, a rebellion could thus survive for years by stretching the loyalists' resources, as the Empress Matilda and Earl Robert of Gloucester were to prove in the Marches and the south-west of England in the late 1130s and 1140s. Rufus was aware of this, and to add to his problems Pevensey Castle's design was based on a huge Roman fortress, with massive walls built as a 'Saxon Shore' fortress in the third century AD; Rochester was smaller but compact and had a massive keep. Taking either by storm was virtually impossible. Rufus resorted to psychological tactics, instead, and used his time while vainly besieging the two castles and awaiting Robert's fleet to make approaches to various of his opponents with offers of pardon and guarantees of all their current possessions if they surrendered. With no sign of Duke Robert arriving with a large force to assist his allies, the latter were outnumbered and unlikely to win a battle, and Roger of Montgomery – absent from the showdown in the south-east collecting his Marches troops – was one of those who decided that it was safer to preserve what he had than to gamble on Robert arriving in time to win the confrontation. Roger agreed to switch sides and was pardoned, and he was able to preserve his lands and power intact as the stalemate ended in victory for Rufus, with Duke Robert failing to land and De Mortain and Odo having to negotiate terms, too. The former was among those who the victor pardoned and allowed to keep his lands, probably as he was judged to have learnt his lesson and not to be a major threat, having been loyal to the late king all his life. But Rufus was more bitter against the defenders of Rochester Castle (a castle of Odo's), who included Roger de Montgomery's eldest surviving son Robert de Belleme – one of Duke Robert's vassals in Normandy and so with a reason to remain conspicuously loyal to the latter to avoid being accused and stripped of his lands later. The king, furious at how long Rochester had held him up, refused the Rochester rebels' offer to surrender in return for guarantees of their freedom and property, and preferred to hang them and seize their lands as a warning to put off other would-be defectors. But Earl Roger helped to negotiate a compromise whereby they would lose their English lands and go into exile. Odo, already imprisoned once for alleged treachery by the late king, was a more dangerous character to Rufus than the usually loyal De Mortain, but he may have held a grudge against Roger over the terms of settlement, as he lost his English earldom and lands and was banished to his see of Bayeux in Normandy. As the exiles, in company with Rufus' younger brother Henry, were sailing to Normandy Odo, who had arrived earlier, accused Robert de Belleme and Henry of plotting against Duke Robert, and the latter believed him. On arrival both Robert de Belleme and Henry were promptly arrested and imprisoned, Robert at Odo's own episcopal castle of Neuilly-l'Eveque, but Robert's wife Adeliza of Ponthieu (probably with his son William if the latter had been born by this date) and other kin refused to surrender his castles and the Duke duly attacked them. Ballon was taken, but at Saint Ceneri on the River Sarthe (where Robert's family were sheltering) commander Robert Quarell obeyed his employer's orders to hold out rather than negotiate quickly and held up the Duke for weeks until his provisions ran out. On surrender, he was blinded and his garrison mutilated by the frustrated duke, in a rare example of him emulating his father's terror tactics to overawe rebels. However the duke's resolve soon ended, and he abandoned the attempt to take the other defiant de Belleme castles, ended the campaign, and was later persuaded by Earl Roger's emissaries to pardon and release Robert. The troublemaking Odo ended up going on the First Crusade with his nephew the duke and dying en route to Jerusalem in 1097, while the mercurial duke forgave Robert de Belleme, who within a coiple of years was reckoned among his closest advisers. In 1090 Robert played a major role in defeating a civic revolt against the duke in Rouen; while the duke panicked and hid from the rioters, Robert and some of his allies rounded up and arrested rebellious citizens, while his ally Henry famously threw their leader off a tall tower to decapitate the rebellion. The barons then proceeded to hold their prisoners for ransom in squalid conditions to encourage swift payment by their relatives. As thanks for Robert's help, the duke then aided him in a private war to seize disputed castles from his neighbours the Grantsmesnils and de Courcys – which made enemies for Robert of their kin in England, too, to his detriment once he was made an earl there. Possibly the subsequent revolt by Robert's own apparently oppressed citizenry in the town of Domfront, who successfully requested of the duke that Henry take over as their lord, which he duly did in a surprise attack on Robert's garrison (1092), helped to alienate the two of them. Robert also came to distrust the duke enough to attempt to transfer his allegiance as lord of Belleme back to its earlier direct overlord, the conveniently more distant King of France. When William Rufus took over Normandy as regent for the crusading Duke Robert in 1097, however, Robert of Belleme hastened to assist his temporary overlord in his attack on the French-held Vexin, no doubt in mind of possible goodwill for future gains.

Roger of Montgomery survived as the main lord of the middle Marches and West Sussex until his death in 1094, when his English estates passed to his second surviving son, Hugh, as second Earl; his eldest surviving son Robert, who had expectations of his wife inheriting Ponthieu, took the Continental lands of his late mother Maud de Belleme. Hugh gambled on supporting another aristocratic conspiracy in favour of Duke Robert against William Rufus in 1095, this time led by Robert de Mowbray, Earl of Northumbria. Possibly Hugh hoped for more rewards and a greater royal leniency to act according to his own wishes (e.g. in attacking both Anglo-Norman and Welsh neighbours) under the notoriously 'slack' and easy-going Robert than under the energetic, financially predatory, harsh, and watchful Rufus. But this conspiracy was defeated too and its

leader was disgraced, stripped of his lands and titles, and exiled –
the earldom of Northumbria now followed those of Hereford
(1075), East Anglia (1075), and Kent (1083/1088) into oblivion
due to an untrustworthy holder. Hugh escaped with a fine of
three thousand pounds, a major sum in those days, and turned
his ambitions to expansion against Gwynedd in alliance with his
neighbour Hugh, Earl of Chester, and other ambitious nobles –
which the king was willing to support. The outcome was the
invasion of coastal Gwynedd in 1098 to strengthen the Norman
grip on the region from Rhuddlan West to Caernarfon and
occupy Mon/Anglesey, which was able to secure initial success
due to the resources of both the north and central Marches
(cavalry in particular) being thrown against the less-well-armed
Welsh, who were at a disadvantage fighting in lowlands country
and had to flee to the mountains. The invaders duly crossed the
Menai Straits to Mon. But, as mentioned above, this move led to
Hugh's unexpected death as the Normans confronted a passing
Norwegian fleet under King Magnus 'Bareleg' en route from
Man to Ireland. Around the end of July 1098, the Norman army
on the northern beaches of the island faced the Scandinavian
ships offshore: mutual insults were exchanged at a distance; the
Norse did not dare to land but fired arrows ashore, and one of
these (traditionally claimed to be shot by King Magnus himself)
hit Earl Hugh in the eye below the guard of his helmet and
killed him. The discomfited Normans abandoned their invasion
of Mon, though the Norse had more important targets in mind
in Dublin and sailed off again rather than trying to annex
the island. The Montgomery estates in England/Wales passed
to Hugh's elder brother Robert de Belleme, who was already
experienced at defying his sovereign and breaking the peace
whenever he wished from the vantage point of a large, compact
territory a safe distance away from the 'capital' in Normandy.
The acquisition of the Montgomery lands in England, plus the
'honour' of Tickhill in the north Midlands that Rufus gave him

(possibly as guardian of the late lord Roger de Builli's underage son), made Robert the wealthiest citizen in England after the king. He paid a massive feudal relief (inheritance tax) of three thousand pounds, and Orderic says that he now possessed fourteen English castles. There were also three family abbeys in Normandy to add to his financial income – Seez (once his great-uncle's bishopric), Troarn (where his mother was buried), and Almanesches (where his sister Emma was abbess). Notably none of Hugh's lands were diverted to other brothers, though Roger was well-provided-for already with his lands in the North-West, plus – apparently only for Rufus' reign – the 'honour' of Eye in Suffolk. Philip had departed on the First Crusade and was to die there, and the youngest brother, Arnulf, had joined in the Norman land-grabbing invasion of Dyfed in the mid-1090s (see below) and had acquired the comital title of and technical lordship of Pembroke by 1098. Arnulf was also granted the 'honour' of Holderness in eastern Yorkshire, forfeited by one of the 1095 plotters in the early 1090s.

Duke Robert was currently away on the First Crusade so William Rufus was administering Normandy in his absence, and the king allowed Robert de Belleme to succeed to the family's Marcher lands where he proceeded to act much as he pleased, as he did in Normandy. On 2 August 1100 Rufus was mysteriously killed in a hunting 'accident' in the New Forest, in the company of his younger brother Henry and assorted friends of the latter, including the current Marcher lord Robert FitzHamon of Glamorgan (see later) and the future Marcher lords the De Clares of Tonbridge, Kent. Whether any or all of these conspired to kill the king so that Henry could take the throne before Duke Robert (Rufus' named heir) returned home is uncertain and the incident may have been a genuine acccident, though the supposed killer – minor Norman nobleman Walter Tirel – was denying having been on the scene even when he was dying decades later. But Henry took the opportunity to ride for the 'capital' and the treasury at Winchester and seize the throne; when Robert returned to Normandy a few months later he refused to recognise the usurpation and proceeded to plan to invade England. The situation of 1088 looked as if it was being repeated, except that this time Robert arguably had legality on his side and was able to land his army in Hampshire in July 1101 with the aid of the late king's arrested treasurer Ranulf Flambard, Bishop of Durham (who had escaped from custody in the Tower of London). As before, the great lords had the choice of backing either brother, with a substantial faction favouring Robert – and as one of the latter's Norman vassals, Robert de Belleme, was at risk of having his overseas lands confiscated if he backed Henry, Duke Robert won. Luckily, neither brother had enough troops nor trusted supporters to risk a battle as they confronted each other in the Meon Valley, and a truce was negotiated. The later twelfth-century Jersey chronicler Wace says that Robert of Belleme, who had not openly backed either side, and his nephew William of Mortain were among the negotiators (presumably for Duke Robert), and that Robert FitzHamon of Glamorgan negotiated for Henry. The resultant Treaty of Alton left the status quo in place, with the duke accepting Henry as King of England but becoming his heir, as he had been to William Rufus. But neither trusted the other – their more hard-line supporters were still plotting – and the treaty was only a pause until the next round in the conflict. It was Robert of Belleme who took a leading role in the next plan to make Duke Robert the King of England, as his father had tried to do in 1088 and his brother in 1095, and to secure in his possession a compact 'bloc' of territory to raise revolt a long way from London and Winchester (the two main royal residences and de facto capitalsas of this date), with a 'bolt-hole' in Belleme on the Continent to flee to if needed. Having taken advantage of the chaos of the unexpected succession crisis in 1100 to build a new castle on the middle Severn below Shrewsbury, at

Bridgnorth, without royal permission, Robert could well revolt again once the duke requested this – quite apart from Henry having had experience of his unreliability in Normandy. Robert now faced a carefully planned royal offensive, more suitable to Henry's subtle character than to the duke's rashness; Orderic says that the cautious Henry spent the period from the July 1101 truce to spring 1102 building up evidence of his flouting the law and setting spies to watch his every move. Once the king was ready the usual assembly of leading nobles, at the royal court for a feast (probably Easter at Winchester), saw the king confront Robert with a list of forty-five charges of defying the law in England and Normandy. The king gave the accused time to prepare a reply, which Robert promptly used to collect his horse and followers and flee the court back to the Marches. Probably Henry had already been undermining him among the other senior nobles with accounts of his greed and arrogance, for nobody but his brothers Roger and Arnulf rallied to him as the royal army marched on his territory. The exact course of the resultant campaign is unclear as accounts differ, but one thing that is certain is that it was over before the king attended a Church Council with Archbishop Anselm in September. Florence of Worcester says that he first besieged Arundel Castle, head of the Montgomery holdings in Sussex and the most dangerous of their strongholds as the duke could sail from Normandy to relieve it, while Robert and his allies attacked eastwards from the Marches into Staffordshire. Then the king sent troops off to recover Tickhill in Derbyshire and left the Arundel siege to head for Bridgnorth; he also sent gifts to Robert's Welsh allies, who recognised that the rebel cause was hopeless and defected. The king then took both Bridgnorth and Shrewsbury within thirty days. The Anglo-Saxon Chronicle only refers to the royal sieges of firstly Arundel and then Bridgnorth; William of Malmesbury's account has Henry attack and take Bridgnorth first, Shrewsbury then surrendering, before tackling Robert himself at Arundel; Orderic says that Henry summoned the army of all England – that is, a feudal levy of all his vassals, great and small, plus the ancient Anglo-Saxon system of county levies, the 'fyrd' – for a first campaign, the three-month siege of Arundel, during which he left the latter for a period to take Tickhill. He then sent messages to Duke Robert to remind him of the treaty of Alton, viz. the assurance not to invade, and summoned the army again for a second, autumn campaign (i.e. after the harvest) to take Birdgnorth, which surrendered after three weeks. Meanwhile Robert's Staffordshire vassal William Pantulf defected and persuaded Robert's Welsh allies to do likewise and come to aid the king's army; they appear to have included Prince Iorweth ap Bleddyn of Powys, one of its contending dynasts, who entered Henry's service in 1102. As Henry attacked Shrewsbury and breached the walls, Robert, commanding the town's castle, hastened to negotiate his surrender. (Orderic came from Shropshire and is likeliest to have known the full story.) In all accounts, Henry then banished Robert from England for life and confiscated all his lands there; the same applied to his brothers Arnulf and Roger.

This failed rebellion thus brought down the second great dynasty of the Marches created by William I, that of Montgomery in the central Marches, after the fall of the southern Marches dynasty of FitzOsbern in 1075. In both cases, the more cautious and usually loyal founder, a personal 'trusty' of King William, had been succeeded by a rasher and over-ambitious son who brought the family down – though such were the complications and intrigues of Norman royal dynastic politics that a false move in backing the loser in a civil war, followed by confiscation, was probable at some point. The large scale of resources available to the great Marcher nobles – and to other lords such as Ralph le Guader – also gave them a greater sense of security in being able to defy the incumbent king or even to try to play 'kingmaker', with possession of substantial and easy-to-defend lands in

Normandy adding to the temptation to play off a separate King of England against a Duke of Normandy. On a more honourable or pragmatic level of conduct, it was genuinely unclear in 1087–8 and 1100–01 who was the rightful King of England (or, indeed, who would win a confrontation). Once Henry I had reunited England and Normandy, by invading the latter in 1106, this possibility ended for the moment, but strife over the English Crown between two evenly matched contenders with equal legal claims resumed after 1135 and duly caused another split among the Marchers, plus defiance of the sovereign in London. For the moment, the fall of the House of Montgomery left Henry determined to avoid building up any more over-mighty subjects in whom he could not trust in the Marches, and the earldom of Shrewsbury was kept vacant. The 'caput' (headquarters and chief comital residence) of the earldom at Old Montgomery Castle ('Hen Domen' in Welsh) went in 1105 to one of the king's ubiquitous 'new men', Baldwin de Boulers – actually from Boelare in Flanders, son of local baron Stephen de Boelare – who married secondly Sibyl, described in genealogical records as the king's niece, although it is not clear who her father was. On this lower social level other new lords established as Henry's vassals in the fomer Montgomery lands included Alan FitzFlaald (a Breton), ancestor of the Fitzalans, at Oswestry, and the L'Estrange dynasty (related to the L'Estranges of Hunstanton in Norfolk) at Knockin. The sheriffdom of Shropshire was also assimilated into the normal county structure of England with full legal powers, taking over the previous role of the earls of Montgomery as lords of Shrewsbury. The first holder of the enhanced office was the cleric Richard of Belmeis, later Bishop of London – as with Henry's favourite, Bishop Roger of Salisbury, in this pre-university world almost all fully literate men who could read and write Latin and reach a senior royal administrative position had been trained in Church institutions. Similarly, the disgrace and exile of Arnulf left a gap in the precarious new 'colony' in Pembrokeshire, and if the isolated new castle at Cardigan had not already been abandoned after its sacking in the 1094 local rebellion it was now; it had to be rebuilt by its next owner in 1110. However, Robert of Belleme and his brothers still held the family lands in Normandy plus Robert's wife's (1106) inheritance of Ponthieu, and in 1103 Robert went to war against the duke, who was for once attempting to restrain his local vendettas. His brother Arnulf, at odds with him over not being given any of their brother Hugh's inheritance in 1098, remained loyal to the duke and took the family castle of Almanesches from Robert, but the latter proceeded to storm it and torture or mutilate the new ducal garrison as a gesture of defiance.

In 1104 King Henry proceeded to dispossess Robert's nephew (and his own cousin) William, Count of Mortain and lord of Pevensey and of Cornwall, too; the arrogant and greedy young count had been demanding his late uncle Bishop Odo's earldom of Kent, and when this was refused he left England to unite with Duke Robert in a huff and was forfeited. William of Mortain and Robert of Belleme now allied to become Duke Robert's chief councillors. There is little doubt that they were planning their forcible restoration to power in England, but later in 1104 Henry forestalled this by invading Normandy in force – his army including the other major Marcher warlords, the new and underage Earl Richard of Chester and Robert FitzHamon of Glamorgan. Already Normandy was slipping into anarchy under the slack and careless rule of Duke Robert after his more capable new wife Sibyl of Conversano had died, and possibly the abrasiveness of Robert of Belleme (who Orderic says all England was glad to be rid of) added to the disaster as most of the Duke's vassals deserted him for Henry. Most of them did homage to Henry, and the duke was forced to accept this plus sit through a formal judicial commission investigating complaints of his misrule. He kept nominal control of his duchy for the moment, but he was now effectively neutralised, and the Belleme brothers and their allies were trapped on the losing side. In 1105 a dispute between the duke's men and Henry's new local governor around Bayeux, his loyalist Marcher henchman Robert FitzHamon (a local by origin), led to the latter being attacked and kidnapped by two of the duke's captains and imprisoned at Bayeux; the indignant Henry returned with an army to land at Barfleur in the Cotentin and overrun most of the duchy. He was joined by Bishop Serlo of Seez, a victim of local depredations by his unwanted neighbour Robert of Belleme, who helped to use these to play up the argument in his sermons that the duke's rule was descending into chaos and tyranny and marched on Bayeux demanding that FitzHamon be returned. Commander Gunter of Aunay, the latter's kidnapper, refused so Henry stormed the city and set it afire; the resultant carnage induced the equally obstreperous citizens of Caen to surrender their city, and Duke Robert had to flee. The fall of Falaise, reputed birthplace of Henry's and the duke's late father King William, was next to be achieved, but the struggles there saw the rescued FitzHamon struck on the head by a lance, knocked unconscious, and apparently rendered an invalid for the final two years of his life, leaving his lordship of Glamorgan leaderless. The attempt to take Falaise ultimately failed and Henry surprisingly withdrew to the coast and later returned to England, allegedly running short of money but more probably perturbed by the danger of his current disputes with Archbishop Anselm leading to his excommunication and possible desertion; but in 1106, after his settlement with the cleric, he returned to the attack. His siege of William of Mortain's castle of Tinchebrai in September 1106 brought the latter' s uncle Robert of Belleme, whose lands were in the area of southern Normandy still under Robert's control, with the duke to the rescue, and on 28 September the relief force was routed by Henry at the Battle of Tinchebrai. Most of the Norman barons and their neighbours, counts Alan of Brittany and Helias of Maine, fought for Henry, and a charge by the duke's knights failed to break the English line, composed mainly of infantry, after which a dismounted melee developed. After about an hour, counts Alan and Helias led a flank attack on the duke's army, and Robert of Belleme, commanding the rearguard, was the first to flee; Duke Robert was captured and agreed to hand over all his remaining territory to Henry and publicly abdicate in front of his leading magnates at Rouen, which he did. Duke Robert was then imprisoned for life and was later deported to Cardiff Castle, where he died in 1134 aged around eighty-two, the oldest of his dynasty but one of the unluckiest. Surprisingly for his record of treachery, Robert of Belleme was among those pardoned and he retained his vicountcies of Alencon, Seez, and the Hiemois, though he had to allow ducal castellans back into all castles that he had illegally taken from the duchy. According to Orderic he fled to Henry's neighbour Count Helias of Maine after the Battle of Tinchebrai and urged him to make war on Henry, but the sensible count refused and successfully offered to intercede with Henry on his behalf instead. But Robert had still not learned his lesson: he made another attempt to play Henry off against a powerful neighbour, this time the ruthless new King Louis VI of France in 1108–9 as the two men's relations broke down, and may also have taken up the cause of the ex-duke's infant son William Clito (a name meaning 'the Throne-Worthy'), as a French-backed candidate as replacement for Henry. Louis unsuccessfully demanded the return to his control of the French town of Gisors in the Vexin, seized by William Rufus in 1097, with its impressive new castle – built by Robert of Belleme for William to his own design. Henry refused and arrived in Normandy, and Robert fled to Louis and had his possessions seized. This finally secured Henry control of the Belleme border region, and when the fugitive Robert had the audacity to turn up at his court as an ambassador from Louis at Bonneville in November 1112, Henry arrested him for treason and threw him in a dungeon. Like William I he believed in keeping his most dangerous enemies prisoners for life, and Robert spent his remaining years in custody – first in Normandy and later at Wareham Castle in Dorset, England – despite attempts by Louis VI to have him released. He died some time around 1132, probably in his early-mid seventies, but his son William Talvas (*c.* 1093–1172), who had managed to keep control of Ponthieu (outside Henry's domains), was able to have his ancestral estates and abbeys in Belleme plus Alencon restored to him by request of Count Fulk of Anjou in 1119 – minus their citadels, which Henry still garrisoned. He then passed Ponthieu on to his son Guy by the 1130s, retaining his Belleme estates and castles, which Henry confiscated again shortly before the king's death in December 1135. The role of the Montgomery family in the Marches was, however, ended – and fortunately Robert's prominence as a classic 'robber baron' plundering his neighbours was not that common, though his opportunism was. Many of his contemporaries used their restless ambition, military talents and greed now to carve out lands for themselves in southern Italy, Sicily, and the Holy Land; Robert just used his talents for his own gain (and amusement) in his ancestral lands with no real sense of purpose, but still created some important castles, most notably Gisors in the Vexin, over which the kings of England and France were to fight for a century.

Bleddyn ap Cynfyn was murdered in 1075 in an act of treachery committed by his South Wales rival, Rhys of Deheubarth, but his eldest sons Madoc and Rhiryd managed to hang onto Powys as Gwynedd fell to other contenders. In 1093 Ranulf, Ralph de Tosni of Clifford, and Philip de Briouze/Braose (primarily a Sussex dynast as lord of Bramber Castle but with lands in the Marches too) led the successful invasion of Rhwng Gwy a Hafren, the land 'Between Wye and Severn', which became Radnorshire under Marcher rule. (This was probably the obscure Welsh district of Cynllibiwg, also known as 'Kenthlebac' according to the thirteenth-century Red

Book of the Exchequer, which lay between Wye and Severn). The main Norman fortress was built at Radnor and owned by de Braose and his heirs. Neighbouring Powys was subject to particularly bloody internal feuds under the sons and grandsons of Bleddyn ap Cynfyn in the 1090s–1110s, while weakened on its eastern borders by the establishment of new Norman 'Marcher' lordships based at castles such as Chirk, Oswestry, and Montgomery. Madoc and Rhiryd ap Bleddyn tried to annex Deheubarth in 1088 to recreate their uncle Gruffydd ap Llewelyn's united kingdom of the Cymry, but were killed when their victim returned from Ireland with Irish support; their brothers Cadwgan and Iorweth then took over the kingdom. Cadwgan assisted Gruffydd ap Cynan against the Normans in Gwynedd in 1098 but was driven into exile in Ireland with him. On his return the following year, he took over Ceredigion, and the Normans accepted him as their vassal in Powys and Ceredigion, but his son Llywelyn was killed in unclear circumstances, likely hinting at local resistance. Iorweth joined his Marcher neighbour Robert of Belleme, Earl of Montgomery, in revolt against King William's successor Henry I in 1102; he deserted him to join the invading royal army at the siege of Bridgnorth and win the king's favour, but Henry then arrested and imprisoned him in 1103–10, with the Welsh Brut y Tywysogion blaming the malice of unnamed royal councillors for framing him. His brother Maredudd was also imprisoned but escaped from royal custody; another contender, Hywel ap Goronwy ap Cadwgan, managed to secure the lordship of Ystrad Twyi and Cydweli by royal grant in 1102 but was brought down by his Anglo-Norman neighbours of Rhyd-y-gors Castle. They hired one of his vassals to lure him to his house and then attacked it at night, and Hywel was captured and beheaded; his lands were then seized (1106).

Iorweth's brother Cadwgan lost control of Ceredigion in 1109 amid rising chaos in Powys, spearheaded by his sons (the most dangerous being Owain) and the disinherited sons of his brother Rhiryd, led by Madoc. In 1109 Owain famously abducted the heiress Nest, daughter of Rhys ap Tewdr of Deheubarth and wife of Gerald, castellan of Pembroke Castle, after attacking her husband in an isolated inland castle, probably Cilgerran but possibly Carew. (They were the grandparents of the late twelfth- and early thirteenth-century historian Giraldus Cambrensis; see next section.) The accounts of the attack differ, and it is unlikely that Owain just happened to be visiting the region for a nearby eisteddfod and heard of his kinswoman's beauty and so either called in to see her or else decided on abduction on the spur of the moment. Whether or not he had planned the attack and whether he arrived as a guest of Gerald's and then seized the castle at night or attacked it by surprise from outside, he had enough men to gain control of it and made his way to Nest's bedchamber. Gerald was driven to hide or flee, through a sewer in the common accounts, and Owain seized and removed Nest to his hideout in the distant hills of Eglwysyg around Llangollen at the far end of Powys – the lurid story that he raped her in front of her children before kidnapping her may just be scandalous gossip. The promiscuous Nest may have been her kidnapper's accomplice: she was able to take along her children, who it is unlikely Owain would have bothered to take (except as hostages?) if the decision had been entirely his, as he needed swift movement to avoid pursuit. Nest may have given Owain at least one son, though her parentage of the boy in question, Owain's bastard, is unclear; her willing part in the abduction owes more to nineteenth-century writers than to any contemporary evidence. Owain was urged by his alarmed father, Cadwgan, to hand Nest back, as the Anglo-Norman authorities in nearby Shropshire, led by Richard de Belmeis, Bishop of London acting as royal steward of Shrewsbury, aided the outraged Gerald in making war on Powys and hired Owain's cousins and enemies, the sons of Rhiryd ap Bleddyn, to raise a

Welsh army and attack him. Nest's children were sent back to their father, and she was recovered by or went back to Gerald some time later. Owain had to flee to Ireland and seek help from his old friend 'High King' Muirchertach: the king sought to divide him from his father, Cadwgan, by insisting when the latter secured a royal grant of Ceredigion that he would have no dealings with his son. Owain eventually returned home to live as a virtual 'robber baron' outside the law or the control of his father or King Henry, temporarily in alliance with his cousin Madoc ap Rhiryd (as in a failed invasion of Meirionydd in 1110) but usually at odds with him as well.

Iorweth was released by the king to takeover a part of Powys as a royal vassal in 1110, Henry seeing him as more effective than Cadwgan, but ended up murdered by Madoc. Henry, evidently despairing of Cadwgan's usefulness as a vassal, removed him from his remaining lands in Ceredigion, but following Iorweth's murder he was restored – only to be murdered in his turn by Madoc, as well, at Welshpool a few months later in 1111. Henry now divided Powys between his son Owain and the murderous Madoc; Cadwgan's other sons were passed over. Owain now put paid to one major threat from within his family by deposing and blinding his equally ruthless cousin Madoc ap Rhiryd (1113/14), but his rise to full control of Powys only brought in the king to reduce this threat to royal authority. Henry then invaded Powys in 1114, and when Owain prudently surrendered the king deported him to Normandy to aserve in his army, but felt confident enough of his reformed character to restore him the following year. The king needed a local deputy who could appeal to and control the local Welsh and had not enough resources to impose an Anglo-Norman ruler and risk a major revolt. Owain played the role of loyal governor and agreed to help the king put down the revolt in Deheubarth by Gruffydd ap Rhys ap Tewdr in 1116, but was ambushed and killed by a force of Pembrokeshire Flemings led by Nest's vengeful husband Gerald in 1116. Thereafter the revival of an independent South Wales principality in Cantref Mawr by Gruffydd, later extending into the lowlands, ended Powys' hopes of controlling this region. Owain's surviving uncle Maredudd – handed over to Henry as a hostage by his brother Iorweth in 1103 but escaped in 1108 – had already ruled briefly as the English king's steward of Powys after Henry's arrest of Owain in 1114, and now succeeded as the senior among the remaining sons of Bleddyn. He ruled as senior to Madoc and Morgan, the surviving sons of Cadwgan. In 1121 he fled Henry's invasion of Powys and took refuge in Gwynedd, but his nephews led a successful guerrilla war in the forests, with one ambush seeing the king nearly killed as an arrow struck his mailcoat. Henry opened negotiations, and the rulers of Powys were permitted to retain their lands as his vassals. Maredudd succeeded in restoring stability to the turbulent kingdom over the next decade: he won a crucial clash with Gruffydd ap Cynan of Gwynedd in the Vale of Llangollen in 1132 and died later in the year, aged around sixty to sixty-five.

The southern Marches, 1066–1135

The Normans now took on the role of Earl Harold as the scourges of the Welsh, and the new King William appointed his old comrade William FitzOsbern (*c.* 1020–71) as the Earl of Hereford to control the southern part of the Marches. FitzOsbern, lord of Breteuil in Normandy, was the son of the new king's faithful steward Osbern, one of the leading officials in William's precarious regency years as a boy after Duke Robert died on pilgrimage to Jerusalem in 1035, the nephew of William's ancestress Duchess Gunnor (wife of Duke Richard I who died in 996), and married to Emma, daughter of Richard's maternal half-brother Count Rudolf of Ivry. Osbern was regent for a few years following Duke Richard's death. Osbern was killed in a hit by one of his enemies, probably William of Montgomery, at a ducal castle in the turbulent years of the regency after William's accession, in winter 1040/1, in William's presence – according to

Norman historian William of Jumieges in his bedchamber – while protecting him from the attackers. FitzOsbern, one of the 'inner circle' of senior nobles who were ducal relatives, was a close and loyal friend of William's from his boyhood and one of his most trusted commanders, and is said to have been one of those most confident in 1066 that the planned expedition to England would be a success and to have played a major role in convincing the doubters. Usefully, his brother Osbern was already working in England, as he had been one of King Edward's French chaplains and by 1066 held the important church of Bosham on Chichester Harbour, the family estate that Earl Godwin had passed on to his son Harold and from whence Harold sailed for Normandy on his mysterious visit of 1064/5, as seen in the Bayeux Tapestry. It is quite possible that Osbern passed on useful information to Duke William from his vantage point as the priest in charge of the church at the duke's foe's principal family home; after the Conquest he was to be made Bishop of Exeter, a vital strategic city in the south-west that had earlier revolted against William, in 1072. FitzOsbern was one of William's senior commanders at the Battle of Hastings, and unlike the claims of many of the new Anglo-Norman dynasties in England to be descended from an important veteran of the battle, this can be verified from contemporary accounts. The new king owed FitzOsbern a debt of gratitude for his unstinting and competent service, he was one of the few people William could totally trust; he was now given the crucial southern part of the Marches facing Morgannwg/ Glamorgan and beyond that Deheubarth, territory that had been part of the late King Harold's own lands pre-1066 and which had suffered partial Welsh reconquest in 1055–56. He also received extensive lands elsewhere in England, some of crucial military importance, such as the Isle of Wight, which formerly had been used as a base by naval-based enemies of the English crown, for instance King Swein of Denmark in his attacks in the late 990s and early 1000s. FitzOsbern's major construction there was the most important fortification on, and administrative centre of, the island, Carisbrooke Castle, home of its governors for centuries to come. Around 1070 in the earldom of Hereford he also now built a major new castle on the banks of the Wye, near its outlet into the Bristol Channel at Chepstow, to command the lower Wye and protect the Forest of Dean and Gloucester from attack. This fortification was only a few miles from the royal estate at Portskewett that Caradog ap Gruffydd of Deheubarth had notoriously raided in 1065, and was in a position to be used as the base for Norman expansion west over the lowlands of southern Gwent to the next major river to the west, the Usk, as was to occur in the mid-1070s. He also built a new castle at Gloucester, the next important town to the east commanding the lower Severn and the site of regular annual royal courts for crown-wearing ceremonies under King Edward, and was made earl of the eponymous county (probably in 1067). As of 1067–69 he also controlled the neighbouring county of Worcestershire to the north, and so was William's principal military commander of the south-west Midlands. His first wife, Adeliza (d. by 1070), was the daughter of the late Roger (I) de Tosni, lord of Tosni and Conches-sur-Ouche and castellan of Tillieres, by the daughter of Raymond Borrell, lord of Catalonia in northern Spain; her brother Ralph (II) de Tosni (*c.* 1036–1102), the current lord of those castles, also fought at Hastings in 1066 and was appointed by King William as lord of Flamstead in Essex.

In the usual manner of dividing up great lords' new holdings across several widely distant counties so as they could not control a compact bloc of land and use that as a base for rebellion, Ralph was also made one of the senior lords of the 'second rank' of Marcher barons below FitzOsbern in Herefordshire, as lord of the new Clifford Castle near Hay-on-Wye in western Herefordshire. This controlled the valley of the Wye as it narrowed west of Hereford at the entrance to the Black Mountains. Married to Isabel de Montfort, of the central French family that would later produce the two famous Simon de Montforts in the thirteenth century, Ralph had two sons, of whom the younger, Ralph (III), would survive to inherit the estates of Flamstead and Clifford; he also had a daughter, Godehildis, who would marry Baldwin of Bouillon (Flanders), the younger brother and heir of the childless First Crusade leader Godfrey of Bouillon, who would become the first ruler of Jerusalem after its reconquest from the Moslems in 1099. The modest and pious Godfrey refused the title of king as he maintained the only king in Jerusalem should be Jesus Christ, but Baldwin – who had also gone on the Crusade and acquired a new dominion as Count of Edessa on the upper Euphrates – was not so modest, and when he succeeded Godfrey in 1100 he then took the title of king, ruling to 1118. The lord of Clifford, who died in 1102, thus ended his life as father-in-law to the ruler of the Holy City itself – an unexpected achievement for a minor Norman lord.

FitzOsbern was involved in the king's reconquest of rebellious north-western Mercia in 1069, and later attended his court at York as the king moved in to crush the Northumbrian rebels. But he now became involved in furthering the king's overseas interests in northern France, which testifies to his restlessness and ambitions. King William's and the late Earl Tostig's father-in-law, Count Baldwin V of Flanders, had held the lands north-east of Normandy and was a vital link in William's chain of allies – the Flemish ports, especially Bruges, had been used by English exiles to plan or mount naval attacks on the coast for decades, most notably Queen Emma in 1037–39, Osgod Clapa in 1048, Earl Godwin in 1051–52 and Tostig in 1065–66. The death of Baldwin V in 1067 passed Flanders to William's wife Matilda's brother Baldwin VI, but he died in July 1070 leaving his dominions to his two underage sons by Countess Richildis of Hainault – Flanders to the elder, Arnulf, and Hainault (which Richildis had probably inherited from her father) to the younger, Baldwin. But this was challenged by Baldwin VI's ambitious younger brother Robert, who sought to depose his nephews despite his initial oath to recognise their rule and who was backed by the overlord of Flanders (and Normandy), King Philip I (ruled 1060–1108). Philip's father King Henry had been Duke/King William's early patron and had helped him to put down the most serious rebellion that he had faced as a young man at the Battle of Val-es-Dunes in 1047, but had then turned against Normandy and plotted with William's enemies to try to weaken him. His son Philip had inherited that distrust of the Norman ruler's potential as a threat to the French monarchy, and William's acquisition of the resources of England in 1066 had multiplied that threat many times. Now the French monarchy was out to weaken William by any means possible, and securing an ally in the ducal seat in Flanders in place of a Norman ally would be part of that strategy. Accordingly King Philip backed Robert's plans for rebellion, and in reply the Duchess-Regent Richildis offered her hand to the widowed William FitzOsbern if he would come and help defend her sons' rights from the rebels. FitzOsbern agreed, married her later in 1070, and brought in an expeditionary force of Anglo-Normans to assist her, with his sovereign King William at least backing him, even if he was not the originator of the scheme. But Robert won the resultant battle at Cassel on 22 February 1071 and FitzOsbern was killed, along with his new stepson Duke Arnulf; Robert then seized control of Flanders and retained it for his lifetime, but was forced to release the captured Duchess Richildis and allow her and her younger son Baldwin to retain Hainault.

FitzOsbern was succeeded in his lands, most crucially the earldom of Hereford/Gloucester and the Isle of Wight, by his second son by his first marriage, Roger. As was the usual practice by French legal custom, the eldest son, William, inherited his father's ancestral lands, i.e. the family's Norman estates headed by Breteuil, and the younger son inherited any lands gained by conquest. But Roger (born *c.* 1050) was a rash and ambitious young man, lacking his father's loyalty to their patron, and he became the first of the great lords of Norman England to use his resources to turn on his sovereign – a perennial problem for a king having to rely on over-mighty subjects. Granting vast resources of men and lands to leading nobles, plus easily defended castles (initially of wood, soon of stone) that could hold out for months against besieging royal armies, risked them using all this against the king – and William's usual tactic was to split up his grants of estates across the whole country to deprive one man of control of a whole region. But this was impractical on a threatened frontier such as Wales, where it was much safer to have one capable and militarily effective commander with adequate resources in charge of a whole region to coordinate its defence (or its expansion into 'enemy' territory if possible). This was the case on the Welsh frontier, and also in distant Northumbria on the Scots frontier (which had a long tradition of semi-autonomy so changing this would cause resentment) and on the crucial Channel/North Sea coasts of Kent and East Anglia, where Continental invaders could easily land. Now the reckless Roger, usually called 'de Breteuil', planned to turn on the king in alliance with another major royal 'tenant-in-chief' holding a compact regional bloc of land, the Breton Earl of East Anglia, Ralf 'le Guader' or 'de Gael', lord of Gael in Brittany, the son and successor of a deceased Breton senior official of King Edward (Ralph 'the Staller', i.e. royal constable).

The elder Ralph, one of the Frenchmen already resident in England before 1066 as an official of King Edward, and possibly born there too, had built up a bloc of lands in East Anglia and Hertfordshire and was made Earl of East Anglia – a crucial position to defend the vulnerable east coast from invasion by the late King Harold's cousin, King Swein Estrithson of Denmark – in 1067–69. The younger Ralph soon succeeded him, and probably gained royal confidence (and possibly the earldom) after defeating a rebel English attack on the principal town in the region, Norwich (the centre of his power) in 1069; he may have built the original Norwich Castle. The younger Ralph had the advantage and temptation as a Breton, long resident in England, of not being one of King William's hereditary subjects and so being less willing to obey him. Roger and Ralph now organised a plot to depose the king in 1075, apparently arranged at Ralph's wedding to Roger's sister Emma – a match that King William, possibly already suspicious of the two men, had banned but which went ahead anyway in an act of defiance. The wedding, at Exning in Cambridgeshire, and its accompanying feast were notorious in English historical memory for the treason to the king plotted there, and no doubt saw rash boasting by the two ambitious, drunken young magnates, and threats made against the king who the two families had blatantly defied in denial of their legal duties to obtain permission for the marriage from him as their overlord. Roger and Ralph may have made hasty promises to each other at the time as they were too scared to back out for fear of being reported and ruined anyway; their chances of success were dubious, with no likely backing from an exterior power. The predatory King Swein of Denmark, who had invaded the Humber Estuary in 1069 and had sheltered the fleeing mother and daughter of his late cousin King Harold, had died in 1074, and King Malcolm III of Scotland – married to the sister of the Anglo-Saxon claimant to England, King Edward's great-nephew Edgar Atheling – had faced invasion by William in 1072 and had had to do homage as his vassal and agree peace. But one of the guests at the wedding banquet, Earl Waltheof of Northumbria – the Anglo-Saxon son of the late Earl Siward (d. 1055) and already sacked once in 1069 for rebellion, and now married to King William's niece – backed out of his initial support for the rebels, and may have warned the king. (He was executed anyway early in 1076.) As Roger raised his tenants and marched from Herefordshire eastwards to assist the rebel Ralph, he was blocked at the Severn by a force of loyalists headed by one of his subordinate landowners, Walter de Lacy – the new lord of Weobley in Herefordshire and probably also by now Ludlow in southern Shropshire – aided by the famously austere and holy Bishop Wulfstan of Worcester, the one English bishop regarded with enough approval by King William and new (Italian) Archbishop Lanfranc to keep his see throughout William's reign. The rebellion fizzled out, and both Roger and Ralph were forced to surrender, and then arrested and tried for treason; Roger was imprisoned for the rest of William's reign and Ralph was banished to Brittany. Wigmore Castle on the northern borders of Herefordshire, built by FitzOsbern, passed from the earls of Hereford to the loyalist Ranulf or Ralph de Mortimer, son of the lord of Mortemer in Normandy and founder of a famous Marcher dynasty. lord of St Victor-en-Caux in Normandy, Ranulf (d. 1137) was the son of an obscure junior Norman baron called Roger, lord of Mortemer, who was known as 'son of the bishop' – apparently Hugh, Bishop of Coutances, who died around 1020. Roger's younger brother was another Ranulf or Ralph, father of Duke/King William's senior lieutenant William de Warenne (*c.* 1025–1088), first Earl of Surrey and lord of Reigate Castle, guarding one of the main passes in the North Downs from the Weald to London, and also of Lewes Castle, guarding the main pass in the eastern part of the South Downs and the lower Ouse Valley in Sussex. As lord of the 'rape' (district) of Lewes, de Warenne was the western neighbour of and principal lord in East Sussex with the king's half-brother Robert de Mortain, lord of Pevensey; he thus dominated Surrey and was one of the two or three leading men of East Sussex. As de Warenne's first cousin, Ranulf de Mortimer (or Mortemer) was close to the senior rank of royal trusties of the first Norman kings and, unlike Earl Roger of Hereford and de Warenne's neighbour de Mortain, he was unswervingly loyal to them. The other main second-ranking baron to benefit from Earl Roger's fall and now to assume military and socio-economic leadership in Herefordshire was Walter de Lacey, who had commanded the force that kept Roger back on the west side of the Severn in 1075 and so enabled King William to deal with Ranulf le Guader separately. De Lacey, who had allegedly fought at Hastings in 1066, now held not only Weobley Castle in northern Herefordshire and Ludlow Castle in southern Shropshire but Holme Lacey, east of Hereford. His brother Ilbert de Lacey was also a major lord in south-western

Yorkshire, a region ravaged and reduced to famine by the pitiless king in the punitive 'Harrying of the North' in 1070 after yet another rebellion, as the founder and first lord of Pontefract Castle. Walter de Lacey was to die around 1085, preceding his sovereign, and was succeeded at Weobley by one son, Hugh (d. before 1088), and at Ludlow and Holme Lacey by a second, Roger (d. after 1106), lord of an eponymous part of the lower Golden Valley as 'Ewias Lacey', who built the extant fortifications of Ludlow Castle and also built Castle Frome. A third son, Walter, was abbot of Gloucester Abbey. However, in 1088 Roger de Lacey took part in the major plot by his neighbours the de Montgomerys of Shrewsbury, Count Robert of Mortain, and Bishop Odo to replace King William II by his elder brother Robert Curthose, Duke of Normandy. He was assisted by Ralph de Mortimer of Wigmore and by Osbern FitzRichard, son and successor of Richard FitzScrob of Richard's Castle, who had a dangerous claim on the allegiance of local Welshmen and their rulers as husband to Nest, the daughter of Gruffydd ap Llywelyn (k. 1063) by Edith of Mercia. Richard and Nest's daughter's husband, Bernard of Neufmarche, an ambitious recent Norman incomer who from 1087/8 was lord of the 'Three Castles' on the Herefordshire/Monmouthshire border (Skenfrith, Grosmont and the White Castle) in succession to the late king's household knights Alfred of Marlborough and Gilbert FitzTurold, also aided the revolt, centred in Herefordshire; the rebels entered Hereford unchallenged and marched east to sack Gloucester before turning north up the Severn towards Worcester. However the aged Bishop Wulfstan, normally a man of peace, rallied his own household and the town's citizenry, armed them and led them out over the Severn to successfully ambush the overconfident rebels in their camp somewhere around Powick, reputedly killing around 500 of them. The revolt failed, and Roger de Lacey and the other leaders were pardoned, probably due to the number of senior lords involved in the plot; King William needed their expertise to defend the borders and could not spare the time to replace the entire local landowning leadership. But Roger had not learnt his lesson, and joined in Robert de Mowbray's Northumbrian revolt of 1095 too; this time he was among those participants who were disgraced and banished. His son Gilbert de Lacey had inherited some of his grandfather Walter's Normandy lands around 1085, and from this base unsuccessfully attempted to regain the English estates by appeal to King Henry I after the latter took over Normandy in 1106. (Roger was presumably dead by this point.) Some of the lands were duly returned, but not the strategically important Ludlow; other estates of Roger's had been allowed to pass to his brother Abbot Walter's daughter (Sybil?) and her husband, Henry's loyal supporter Payn FitzJohn, around 1106.

The earldoms of Hereford/Gloucester and East Anglia lapsed as a result of the 1075 rebellion. But restless and land-hungry Norman knights were moving forward to annex territory in South-East Wales independent of 'high politics': early settlers included Thurstan FitzRolf at Caerleon and the brothers Hamelin and Winebald of Ballen at Abergavenny in the mid-late 1070s; Winebald later took over Caerleon when Thurstan died. These castles controlled the Usk Valley and provided a Norman corridor from the group of castles in south-west Herefordshire held by Bernard of Neufmarche down the river to the sea beyond Caerleon – the latter a former Roman legionary fortress like Chester. By sea, William FitzBaldwin from Devon (son of the local 'strongman' and long-term county sheriff Baldwin of Meules, first lord of Okehampton) arrived in the Tywi Estuary near Carmarthen and built the castle of Rhydygors to protect a precarious first outpost in that region, to which Carmarthen and Llansteffan castles were later to be added. Caradog seemed oblivious to the danger, and neither he nor his rivals thought of uniting against the new arrivals; meanwhile, the Vikings were still a naval menace in the Irish Sea and in around 1073 sacked

St David's. Bishop Sulien (in office 1073–4?, 1079–86) was mostly resident safe inland at Llanbadarn Fawr. In 1067–8 a Norse/Irish fleet led by King Harold's refugee illegitimate sons Godwin and Magnus had operated in the Bristol Channel, but a Saxon revolt in Devon failed. Caradog preferred to ally with the new local Normans to attack his rivals, Rhys and Maredudd, the sons of Owain. He killed Maredudd on the River Rhymney in 1072; the latter's brother Rhys ap Owain was attacked by Norman raiders in 1073 and 1074, and his only success was in trapping and killing King Bleddyn of Gwynedd/Powys in a surprise attack in 1075. If he had hoped to expand inland into Powys and gain troops to take on his foes at home, his gamble failed: the murder of a popular and just ruler led to widespread outrage. He was expelled by Bleddyn's self-proclaimed avenger Trahaern of Gwynedd after defeat at the Battle of Godwick in 1078, and was killed a few months later by Caradog. Their cousin Rhys ap Tewdr ap Cadell, descended from Hywel Dda's grandson Einion (d. 984), took over Deheubarth. He had to pay homage to King William and pay rent for his lands (forty pounds a year, the same as the charge levied on Robert of Rhuddlan in Gwynedd) when the latter crossed his kingdom with an army en route to St David's in 1081. William II may have set up the first Norman base at Cardiff Castle, a motte within the walls of the old Roman fortress. If not, the castle was built – within a former Roman fortress in the manner of those at Pevensey and Chester – by King William II's trusty, Robert FitzHaimon, in 1088/9 as he moved into Glamorgan (see below).

Rhys retained his kingdom through the 1080s, but the pressure from Norman encroachment redoubled from 1087 under the new King William II, who had inherited lands around Gloucester from his mother Queen Matilda in 1083. Hamelin of Ballen at Abergavenny had no son, so his lands duly passed to his niece Emmeline's husband Brian FitzCount – the illegitimate son of the new King Henry I's ally, Count Alan of Brittany. Rhys was temporarily expelled from his kingdom by the elder sons of

Bleddyn ap Cynfyn, Madoc and Rhiryd, in 1088 but returned with a Viking fleet from Ireland – the usual resort of expelled Welsh princes – and killed them in battle. In 1091 a faction of nobles offered his crown to Gruffydd, son of Maredudd ap Owain, an exile in England; he invaded but was killed in battle at the mouth of the River Towy. But the victorious Rhys was himself killed in a skirmish with Norman settlers in Brycheiniog at Aberhonddhu, near Brecon, in April 1093, probably assisting rebels against the new local lord Bernard de Neufmarche. By this date one Norman baron, Richard FitzPons of Clifford Castle in the upper Wye Valley, had penetrated over the Brecon Beacons as far as Llandovery; their conquest of Brycheiniog seems to have followed the replacement of some West Herefordshire barons for rebelling against the new King William II in 1088.

The new regional strongman, Bernard de Neufmarche, had been granted the castles of Ewias Harold, Durstone and Snodhill and was thus the immediate neighbour of Brycheiniog, ruling the 'Golden Valley'. Married to the daughter of Princess Nest of Gwynedd (daughter of Gruffydd ap Llywelyn ap Seisyll and Edith of Mercia by Osbern FitzRichard of Richard's Castle in Herefordshire), he appears to have overrun Brycheiniog in summer–autumn 1088; castles were built at Brecon and (probably) Bronllys. This posed a serious threat to Rhys ap Tewdr: would the fertile lands of the Towy Valley be next? In July 1093 Rhys apparently assisted a Welsh rebellion in Brycheiniog, and was killed attacking Bernard at his new fortress at Brecon; a further local revolt was put down in 1094, as the Normans of Glamorgan came to Bernard's rescue and won a battle at Aber Llech. Castles were now built at Tretower and Crickhowell. But the execution of William FitzBaldwin, the founding lord of Rhydygors, by King William for treason in 1096 left that fortress abandoned to the Welsh by its discomfited garrison, and the king himself – who notably continued his father's practice of regular crown-wearing assemblies at Gloucester to overawe the local lords – 'showed the flag' with a prestigious expedition into Deheubarth in 1095, but was unable to bring the enemy to battle as the Welsh hid in the forests and hills. The same occurred to him on a subsequent expedition in 1097.

Dyfed was largely overrun by the Anglo-Norman barons after the death of Rhys ap Tewdr at the hands of the Norman settlers of Brycheiniog in spring 1093, with southern Pembrokeshire heavily settled and permanently lost. Earl Roger of Montgomery apparently led the initial expedition, which penetrated to Pembrokeshire in July 1093, and may have returned in 1094. He may have built the original Pembroke Castle – only a motte-and-bailey construction of timber with earthworks – on the peninsula between two rivers at the south end of Milford Haven as the centre of the new local lordship. Arnulf of Montgomery, youngest son of Earl Roger and probably in his mid-late twenties, took up this new lordship at Pembroke (which proved permanent), and either built himself or completed his father's new castle, and may have held the title of Earl of Pembroke, too, though no clear evidence has survived that King William Rufus granted this to him. He certainly coveted the local lands of the bishopric of St David's and is recorded by the Welsh annals as sending his castellan at Pembroke, Gerald of Windsor, to pillage them in 1097. The first Anglo-Norman Bishop of St Davids, Wilfrid (who took over authority some time around 1090–5, as subordinate to the Archbishop of Canterbury in contrast to his Welsh predecessors), duly complained to Archbishop Anselm. Normally Arnulf, a devout and canny grantee of gifts to churches – mostly with family connections of his, such as Seez in Belleme – in contrast to his impious elder brother Robert of Belleme, was on good terms with the Church, and was respected by the holy and moralistic Anselm. The records of his gifts being made in person show that he often journeyed to northern France, and much of 'his' rule at Pembroke may have been practically in the hands of the capable Gerald of Windsor, his constable there, who soon established a strong local presence and reputation. The latter was a typical ambitious 'new man', a younger son of the frst generation of Norman incomers to England in 1066 who carved out a career for himself in a new area; his father Walter FitzOtho was the first castellan of the new Windsor Castle (built *c*. 1080) for King William I, and Walter's elder son William inherited that role, with younger sons Robert inheriting Eton and Gerald inheriting the small Berkshire estate of Moulsham. Gerald famously fought off a Welsh attack on Pembroke Castle by local commanders Uchtred ap Edwin (an Anglo-Welsh name hinting at a mixed parentage) and Hywel ap Goronwy in 1096, and when some of his men despaired of holding out and deserted he quickly transferred their lands to their loyal juniors to give the latter an incentive to fight on. He then arranged for a fake letter to his absent Lord Arnulf to be captured by the Welsh, in which he boasted that he had enough provisions to hold out for four months and there was no need of a quick relief; the besiegers were duly demoralised and abandoned the siege. In early 1101 Arnulf aided the new King Henry I to arrange an alliance with Count Robert of Flanders against the threat of invasion of England by Henry's excluded elder brother, Duke Robert of Normandy. But he soon became involved in the war between Henry and Robert on the side of his brother Robert, putting family solidarity first, and in pursuit of this sent Gerald to arrange a pioneering alliance with his neighbour across the Irish Sea, King Muirchertach Ui Briain of Munster (ruled 1086–1119), great-grandson of 'High King' and national leader Brian Borumha (killed 1014) and son and successor of 'High King' Toirrdelbach Ui Briain (d. 1086). Succeeding his father in Munster in 1086, vigorous warlord Muirchertach had just seized the 'High Kingship' too in 1101 and was a powerful ally with experienced troops – though in the form of infantry not Norman-style cavalry – to lend, and needy Welsh princes (and in the 1050s also English magnates) had thus been allying with Irish rulers and hiring troops from them for centuries. The Vikings of Dublin and Waterford, Muirchertach's vassals, had also been raiding Dyfed/ Deheubarth as long, but Arnulf's move was the first Norman involvement across the Irish Sea, and was to lead his successors in Pembroke on to the invasion of Ireland in 1170 and a whole new field for Norman (and English) colonization. Arnulf went to Munster and married a daughter of Muirchertach who the Welsh records call 'Lothcota', and hired Munster troops for his brother Robert's campaign against Henry in 1102. As seen above, this was unsuccessful and the family were expropriated by Henry I as rebels; he lost his lands and apparently fled to Ireland, as local annals record that Muirchertach turned on and tried to arrest him to placate Henry but he fled overseas. He survived in exile, presumably on the Continent, for several more decades, while his wife was remarried to a more useful local ally by her father.

The castellanship and lordship (not earldom) of Pembroke was initially awarded by Henry I (*c.* 1102) to his own follower Saher, but this man proved unable to secure its safety – probably as lacking local connections in a fiercely clannish region – and by 1106 Henry restored Gerald of Windsor, whom he evidently decided to trust as a man with local experience. The latter went on to govern his precarious and isolated lordship successfully, balancing off Norman and Welsh lords against each other and importing Flemings to settle in Pembrokeshire in return for military service. The creation of what became known as 'Little England Beyond Wales', with English patterns of landholding and parishes, dates to this early part of the twelfth century. As arranged by Henry, Gerald also became the new husband of Rhys ap Tewdr's daughter Nest, who had fallen into Norman hands after her father's death and was probably deported to England as 'spoils of war' or a hostage for her family's cooperation after the 1094 campaign. She then became one of King Henry's many mistresses, probably before his accession in 1100, and bore him a son, Henry (d. 1158). After the king married the Anglo-Scottish princess Edith/Matilda (daughter of Malcolm III and St Margaret, the great-niece of Edmund 'Ironside') to secure English support as an insecure new king, she was married to Gerald by Henry and returned to Wales as lady of Pembroke Castle. They produced a large and famous family, from whom the Fitzgerald dynasties in Ireland (earls of Kildare and Desmond) descended. One son, Maurice FitzGerald, was to be among the leaders of the conquest of Ireland in the 1170s and before then owned Llansteffan Castle, protecting the western side of the Tywi Estuary; another son, William, owned the Pembrokeshire castle of Caer Yw and so gave his name to the eponymous family of Carew. These two married the daughters of the deposed and exiled Arnulf de Montgomery, previous lord of Pembroke, in a careful move by their father to acquire legality for their possession of Arnulf's old lands should this be challenged. A third son, David (d. 8 May 1176), succeeded Bernard as Bishop of St Davids in December 1148. Their daughter Angharad's third son by William de Barri was the historian Giraldus Cambrensis (1146–1223), who was born at Manorbier Castle. As referred to above, Gerald's wife was abducted, willingly or not, by their neighbour Owain ap Cadwgan of Powys in 1109, but Gerald soon recovered her and in 1116 had the satisfaction of leading his levies, mainly incoming Fleming settlers from Pembrokeshire, to ambush and kill Owain as the latter intervened in a local revolt in inland Deheubarth in 1116. Gerald held the lordship until his death around 1135; his widow was then persuaded by her sons to remarry to Gerald's constable of Cardigan Castle, Stephen, to help keep the isolated lordship linked to their Pembroke dominions, and had a further son, Robert FitzStephen (who in turn joined his half-brother Maurice in the invasion of Ireland).

One of the more secure new Norman lordships created in 1093 after the death of Rhys ap Tewdr was at Radnor and Builth (Wells) in the later Radnorshire, controlling the next region west of North-West Herefordshire as a compact new family domain. This was taken over by Philip de Briouze/Braose (*c.* 1075–1150), of a major West Sussex dynasty, who inherited his father William's lands in the rape of Bramber – between those of de Montgomery at Arundel and de Mortain at Pevensey – late in 1093. In 1094–95 he occupied Radnor and Builth and built a castle at the latter; the new lordship took over the Welsh cantref of Gwerthyrnion, a part of Powys reputedly once ruled by the family of the mythical fifth-century 'High King' Vortigern. He married Aenor, the daughter and heiress of the Breton incomer Judhael, lord of Totnes and Barnstaple in Devon; their son William (II) de Braose (d. 1190?) was to marry Bertha, the daughter of Miles FitzWalter of Gloucester/Hereford and Sibyl de Neufmarche, in a successful de Braose bid to acquire Sibyl's inheritance of Brecon to add to the adjoining Radnor. A more insecure lordship was set up on the north-west coast of Deheubarth at Cardigan, capital of the defunct Welsh principality of Ceredigion, where Arnulf de Montgomery and his father Roger built a castle at Dingereint on the 1093–94 expedition. The lordship, dependent on Arnulf's new lordship at Pembroke, was in danger after Arnulf was exiled as a rebel by Henry I in 1102/3 and was only secured by Henry I's new nominee, Gilbert Fitz Richard de Clare, after a royal grant of it in 1110. Gilbert had already occupied the abandoned castle of Rhyd-y-Gors on the lower Tywi Estuary in 1104, expelling the local Welsh lord Hywel ap Goronwy despite the latter having acquired a grant of it from King Henry. Gilbert, a typical ambitious and versatile 'new man' of Henry's 'service nobility', who the king trusted more than the arrogant and politically secure heirs of his father's great lords, was the son of Richard de Clare, of Tonbridge Castle in Kent, founder of the family's fortunes and nephew of Baldwin de Meules, lord of Okehampton and Sheriff of Devon – it may have been his cousin, Baldwin's son William's success in setting up a lordship in the Tywi Estuary on the south coast that lured him to Ceredigion. His family had been trusties of Henry's since before the new king's accession, and had been with him when Henry's brother King William Rufus was killed in the New Forest in August 1100 (leading to modern suspicions that they had been rewarded for their part in regicide). They were to play a leading role in Marcher and English politics for centuries as earls of Gloucester. Gilbert also founded castles in Ceredigion at Llanbadarn and Castell Gwallter *c.* 1110. Henry also gave other new frontier lordships to his own men. Gower went to Henry de Beaumont, now Earl of Warwick (1106), who with his twin brother Robert, Count of Meulan in Normandy and now Earl of Leicester (d. 1118), was one of the king's closest advisers and son of the Norman lord Roger of Beaumont (d. 1094) and heiress Adeline of Meulan. Cydweli/Kidwelly went to the king's chief minister, Bishop Roger of Salisbury (1106?), and later to Maurice de Londres (i.e. 'of London'), already lord of Ogwr in Morganwwg/Glamorgan as a trusted henchman of Robert FitzHamon; the district of Cemais went to Robert Fitz Martin, and Cantref Bychan to Richard Fitz Pons (d. 1138?), who was probably married to Maud de Tosni, the daughter of previous lord Ralph de Tosni of Clifford Castle in the middle Wye Valley and sister of current lord Ralph (II) de Tosni (d. 1126), also lord of Conches in Normandy. Richard's and Maud's son Walter 'de Clifford' (*c.* 1113–90) was to marry the heiress of Clifford, Ralph (II)'s daughter Margaret de Tosni, who was probably his cousin; from then on the family held both Clifford and Cantref Bychan. Bernard de Neufmarche kept the new lordship of Brecon until his death around 1125, and had a potential value as a conduit of local Welsh loyalty due to his marriage into the family of Gruffydd ap Lylwelyn – he had raised Welsh as well as English supporters for his part in the 1088 rebellion. The suspicious Henry needed his experstise as a commander and focus of loyalty, but required him to marry his daughter and heiress Sibyl to a royal trusty, Miles FitzWalter the hereditary Sheriff of Gloucester, in 1121. Bernard's son was supposed to have been disinherited for an attack on his mother's lover. Miles (d. 1143) duly succeeded Bernard as lord of Brecon, and in the English civil war from 1138 was to back the Empress Matilda against King Stephen; she confirmed him as Earl of Hereford in 1141. These years also saw the Anglicization of the kingdom of Deheubarth's see at St David's, under the king's nominee as bishop in 1115, Bernard (Queen Matilda's chaplain). He used the cult of St David and the claims in Rhigyfarch's 'Life' that David had become Archbishop of Wales to assert the primacy of his bishopric over that of Llandaff, and was fiercely resisted by the latter's new (1107) Norman Bishop Urban.

The fortunes of Deheubarth were restored from around 1116 by Rhys' son Gruffydd (born *c.* 1080?), who returned to overrun Dyfed in around 1113 and appears to have commenced his career as a guerrilla chief in the interior hills of Ystrad Tywi. He went to Gwynedd around 1115 to seek aid from Gruffydd ap Cynan, but was reported to Henry I who sought his extradition; the Welsh king agreed but his namesake was warned in time and fled to sanctuary at the church of Aberdaron. It was either now or later he married, as his second wife, Gruffydd ap Cynan's formidable daughter Gwenllian, mother of his younger sons Maredudd and Rhys. In spring 1116 he led what their opponents described as an unruly army of young troublemakers to burn Narbeth Castle, and thenceforward ruled inland Cantref Mawr (with the ancestral capital at the casle of Dinefwr). Henry I called in Owain ap Cadwgan of Powys to destroy him, but the invader was killed by his enemy Gerald of Windsor. Gruffydd held onto his inland territory, centred on the commote of Caeo, apart from a brief exile to Ireland following an English attack around 1127.

The south-east: the conquest of Morgannwg/ Glamorgan and Gwent

Caradog (the name derived from 'Caratacus', suggesting a claimed genealogical link to the old Silurian royal house), son of the late ruler Gruffydd ap Rhydderch (ruled 1044, 1047–55) took control of both Morgannwg and much of Deheubarth on the killing of Gruffydd ap Llywelyn by Earl Harold in 1063. His father may have come from a line of princes connected to the main dynasty of Glamorgan, the line of Mouric ap Tewdric (who had ruled since the fifth or sixth centuries), or else from the royal house of Dyfed – in either case, he was from a junior branch and was a 'new man' who had had to elbow his seniors aside to gain power, like his father's enemy. Caradog had to share Morgannwg with Cadwgan ap Meurig, who ruled the South-East (Gwent) until losing much of it to the Norman invader William FitzOsbern, Earl of Hereford, after 1070. Some time around 1070–75 the FitzOsbern dynasty founded Chepstow Castle, thus securing control of the lower Wye Valley and the lowlands west to the Usk. Caradog killed his rival Maredudd ap Owain of the main line of Deheubarth in 1072, lost out to the latter's brother Rhys in the subsequent succession struggle, but finally evicted his rival in 1078. He was at last defeated, and probably killed, at the Battle of Mynydd Carn by his rival Rhys ap Tewdr, cousin of Maredudd and Rhys ap Owain, in 1081. Morgannwg now went to Iestyn ap Gwrgan, of uncertain dynastic linkage, though Caradog's son Owain secured the lordship of Caerleon as a Norman vassal. By this stage it would appear that the Normans had at least reached the Rhymney Valley, and possibly held Cardiff permanently from King William I's expedition to St David's in 1081.

Glamorgan was acquired some time in the mid-late 1080s or early 1090s by the baron Robert FitzHamon, Iestyn's son-in-law, who legendarily started off as a mercenary knight called in by Iestyn to fight his rivals. Originating from Creully in Calvados, Normandy, and probably living in the Gloucester region as a tenant on the new King William II's lands there – he later refounded local Tewkesbury Abbey in 1092 – and in the king's military household, he was evidently an enterprising and land-hungry adventurer fond of taking risks. According to the same legend, he had eleven knights in his first warband as they entered Morgannwg to assist Iestyn, and the twelve divided up their employer's lands into twelve fiefs. The extant literary account of their adventures was written *c.* 1560 by the local landowner and antiquarian Sir Edward Stradling of St Donat's Castle, who had access to old records but probably invented a great deal. The legendary list of twelve knights, however, included some families who were not certainly active in the region this early and who may have been included due to their families pushing back their involvement as far as possible, without real evidence, to add to their reputation. More certainly involved were Sir William de Londres ('of London'), who acquired the lands of Ogwr (Uch Gwyr, i.e. 'Opposite/Below Gower') at the mouth of the eponymous river and built Ogmore Castle by its junction with the River Ewenny; Sir Payn de Turberville, who acquired the lands further up the Ogmore around the site of the new borough of Bridgend and built Coity Castle and probably the 'New Castle' on the west side of the river at Bridgend; Sir Gilbert Umfraville of Penmark Castle near the site of the present Cardiff Airport; Sir Reginald de Sully at Sully, east along the coast near Penarth; Sir Oliver St John at nearby Fonmon Castle (which in its present form dates from *c.* 1200); and Sir John Fleming at Wenvoe, inland nearer Cardiff. The Berkerolles duly appeared at St Athan, and a Sir Robert St Quintin (grandson of a supposed 1066 veteran) built the first Llanblethian Castle inland adjoining the new borough of Cowbridge, but it is not clear how early in the twelfth century this was; the current castle was not built until the later thirteenth century. Setting up his own followers in castles, FitzHamon proceeded to evict his father-in-law from power around 1091. Having parcelled up the kingdom, he married Sybil de Montgomery, daughter of Earl Roger of Shrewsbury and sister of the notorious Robert de Belleme, and ruled to March 1107 when he died after being seriously injured two years before in the capture of Bayeux (see above). He was succeeded by his daughter Mabel's husband Robert, Earl of Gloucester (born *c.* 1090), eldest illegitimate son of Henry I, as Henry cornered the lordship for his own proven loyalists.

Despite FitzHamon's crippling head injury in the war between King Henry and Duke Robert of Normandy at Bayeux in 1105, and his eventual death in 1107, the loss of the main progenitor of the Norman advance in Glamorgan did not lead to it stalling as it did in Deheubarth and Gwynedd in similar circumstances – the easier communications to the English border, by sea or by lowland roads, were to the benefit of the new settlers. This death indeed put Henry, as custodian of FitzHamon's daughter, in charge of the lordship of Glamorgan (and its accompanying lands to the east in Gwent and Gwynllwc or 'Gwentloog', the ancient cantref east of Cardiff) until such time as he chose to find a husband for his ward, FitzHamon's daughter Mabel. This added to his similar custody of the underage Earl of Chester from 1101, Richard d'Avranches – who was later married off to another of Henry's nieces, the daughter of his formidable sister Countess Adela of Blois by the late Crusader Count Stephen. Henry duly married of Mabel FitzHamon to his eldest illegitimate son Robert, born around 1090, and gave him the earldom of Gloucester and lordship of Glamorgan. Robert, who also held the lordship and castle of Bristol plus much of Somerset, was one of the largest landholders in the country, with around three hundred manors – only matched by his future foe Count Stephen of Mortain and Boulogne (the king's sister Adela of Blois' son) – and was apparently one of the few people who his father consulted about marrying his daughter and heiress, the widowed Empress Matilda, to Count Geoffrey of Anjou in 1127–28. He led the taking of an oath to Matilda as the king's heiress in 1126, and later escorted Matilda to Anjou for her wedding. In 1135 he was chief executor of the king's will. On a cultural level, he was important for future generations as patron and dedicatee of the author and 'historian' (of dubious accuracy and much imagination) Geoffrey of Monmouth when the latter, a minor church official in his employ, wrote his authoritative 'History of the Kings of Britain' around 1135, describing the alleged glorious past of a long dynasty of kings of Trojan origin in Britain and building up the myth of King Arthur. Robert's neighbours to the east included Brian FitzCount, lord of Abergavenny from 1119, who was an illegitimate son of Count Alan of Brittany (abdicated 1112, d. 1119), half-brother of the next Count Conan (d. 1148), and like Robert was brought up in Henry's household. Like Robert, Brian was duly provided with a rich heiress to marry by Henry – Matilda d'Oilly, heiress of Wallingford Castle in the middle Thames valley. He would join Robert on the embassy to Anjou in 1128 to escort Matilda to her marriage, and was apparently a close friend of Robert.

Such was Henry's political predominance and prestige across Wales that the Welsh 'Brut y Tywysogion' spoke of him as 'the man who had subdued under his authority all the island of Britain' (entry for 1116). This was however a matter of personal leadership as much as secure institutional success, and his death in December 1135 was to be followed by a backlash in Deheubarth (and to a lesser extent in Gwynedd) as local Welsh princes and lesser lords plucked up the courage to rebel once he was no longer there to punish such behaviour.

3

THE REIGN OF STEPHEN AND THE CIVIL WAR
1135–1154

The civil war between King Stephen and the Empress Matilda, and how Matilda's support was centred on the Welsh Marches under her half-brother, Earl Robert of Gloucester.

The northern Marches 1135–54

Gruffydd ap Cynan ended his long reign with a reasonably secure realm comprising most of his ancestors' lands, which would have been unexpected to any experienced spectator back in the 1080s or 1090s. The Anglo-Normans based in the earldom of Chester had a new, adult and experienced male commander in Earl Ranulf 'Le Meschin' (*c.* 1070–1129) after the death of his cousin the young Earl Richard in the 'White Ship' sinking disaster in 1120, along with Richard's wife Matilda of Blois, sister of the future King Stephen. Ralph, son of Ranulf de Briquessart (the viscount of the Bessin in France) by Richard's aunt Margaret of Avranches, was already established as a major lord in Cumberland and also had claims in Lincolnshire through his wife Lucy, heiress of the county sheriff Turold; Chester was never the centre of his interests. He was succeeded in turn by his son by Lucy, Ranulf de Gernon (1099–1153). Neither of these earls ever made an effort to regain the coastal strip west from the mouth of the Dee Estuary to Caernarfon or to refortify Rhuddlan; their interests lay in English politics and their lands spread across that country. The most they achieved was a cautious advance into inland Flintshire, west of the Dee Estuary where Basingwerk Abbey was founded in 1131 – but this area was to be lost to Gwynedd again in the late 1140s or early 1150s. When Henry I died in December 1135 Gruffydd was clearly on the alert to take advantage should any rebellions break out in the lands that the Anglo-Normans had taken to the south of Gwynedd, particularly Ceredigion, to which he had claims as his ancestors had ruled it – though his distant cousin and son-in-law Gruffydd ap Rhys ap Tewdr was a rival contender and their relations were uneasy. He duly intervened to help his son-in-law in the resulting 1136 rebellion that followed the death of Richard FitzGilbert, first Anglo-Norman lord of this region and owner of Cardigan Castle, in an ambush near Abergavenny in April. The allies won the Battle of Crug Mawr over Richard's men and secured most of Ceredigion, but were unable to take Cardigan Castle. Gruffydd died in 1137, aged over eighty, the longest-lived ruler in medieval Gwynedd after a reign of over forty years, plus an earlier career of partial rule over some of his lands that had commenced over sixty years before his death. He and his second son and successor Owain Gwynedd (born *c.* 1100) were the most powerful rulers of Welsh-governed Wales, and seemed to have restored Gwynedd to its ancestral power – provided that they avoided a direct clash with the more powerful Kingdom of England, aided by the English civil war in the 1140s. Owain now even managed to fully annex all the sub-principalities linked to fifth-century dynastic founder Cunedda's younger sons' families, Meirionydd and the eastern lands of Clywd, and during the 1140s took over parts of Powys. In 1150 he defeated Madoc ap Maredudd of Powys, his daughter Susanna's husband, at the Battle of Ewloe/Coleshill and took the cantref of Ial from him, holding it until King Henry II made him return it in 1157. He secured Ceredigion, in revolt against its Anglo-Norman lords in 1136, for his brother Cadwaladr, who gradually took over the kingdom from its northern frontier with Gwynedd.

The affairs of the northern Marches now became complicated by the struggle over the Crown in England. Henry I had lost his only son and heir William the 'Atheling' in the 'White Ship' disaster, and had sought to pass the crown on to his daughter Matilda, the widowed Empress of 'Holy Roman' Emperor Henry V (d. 1125) once it became clear that his second wife Adeliza of Louvain would not have a child. He compelled his nobles – headed by his illegitimate son Robert, Earl of Gloucester, the leading southern Marcher lord, and his cousin Countess Maud of Huntingdon's husband King David of Scotland – to swear allegiance to Matilda in 1126, but many seem to have been unhappy at the unprecedented diversion of the Crown to a female. Quite apart from her alleged faults of arrogance and a bad temper, which might only reflect criticism of her strong-willed determination to be as assertive as a man in a predominantly male world, Matilda was remarried to Henry's potentially dangerous neighbour in France, Count Geoffrey of Anjou, who the landed barons in Normandy hated as a predatory neighbour. Would the acquisitive Geoffrey demand a role in the government of England plus titles, lands, and jobs for his Angevin elite, depriving Anglo-Norman barons of these? The newlyweds then had three sons, commencing with the future Henry II of England in March 1133. But Henry I and Geoffrey – possibly intended as co-ruler with Matilda to the nobles' dismay – and Matilda and Geoffrey soon quarrelled, and Matilda was away in Anjou when her father died in Normandy (while fighting Geoffrey's vassals) in December 1135. Henry's sister Adela of Blois' younger son Stephen of Blois, Count of Mortain and (by marriage) Boulogne, quickly made for England before Matilda heard her father was dead, and seized the crown with the support of a faction of anti-Angevin nobles. But great men who had backed Matilda, such as Robert of Gloucester, did not initially attend his court, and the threat of revolt aided by Anjou undermined Stephen – not a new situation in England as the new kings in 1088 and 1101–02 had also faced revolt by dissidents in the baronial elite, but this time made worse by Stephen's tactics.

As we shall see, his hesitant and over-generous treatment of the first military challenge to him in 1136 encouraged other dissidents to revolt, and in 1139 this sporadic rash of minor rebellions coalesced into a coherent plot to put Matilda on the throne. This was spearheaded by Earl Robert of Gloucester, and in 1139 Matilda herself joined Robert and an invasion army to land in Sussex; Matilda made for her stepmother Adeliza of Louvain's castle at Arundel (formerly held by the middle Marches dynasty of de Montgomery) and Robert made for Bristol, which had the greatest port and most defensible castle in his Gloucester lordship. Stephen besieged Matilda and forced her into surrendering, but rather than arresting and imprisoning or deporting he chivalrously allowed her to join her half-brother at Bristol – avoiding thus outraging wavering elite opinion about ill-treating a woman, but showing that he could be defied and was not as dangerous and unrelenting a foe as his grandfather William I and uncles William II and Henry I. The revolt spread, centred on the southern Marches and South-West England and joined by nobles who were unlikely to have risked their lives and lands defying a more ruthless man. Indeed, the personally brave and admirable but politically hesitant and dithering Stephen seems to have inherited the poor judgement of his father, the late Count Stephen of Blois (d. 1101), who on the First Crusade had been sent by the Crusaders besieged in Antioch in Syria to obtain help from the Eastern Roman/Byzantine Emperor Alexius I but had given him such a bleak assessement of the Crusaders' chances that Alexius had not risked a dangerous march to relieve the city. Stephen had then gone home and left the doomed Crusaders to their fate, only to see them destroy the besiegers and take Jerusalem. His resultant reputation as a coward had so infuriated his wife Adela, William I's daughter, that she was said to have insisted he repair it by taking part in the next Crusading expedition to the Holy Land in 1101 – where he had got himself killed in the Battle of Ramallah/Ramleh and improved his reputation, no doubt to her satisfaction. Their son Stephen also hesitated in dealing ruthlessly with both Matilda at Arundel in 1139 and the rebels at Bristol in 1139–40, thus encouraging waverers to join in the revolt – including Earl Robert's close friend Brian FitzCount, lord of Brecon in the southern Marches but also by marriage lord of Wallingford Castle, which blocked the main route from Stephen's Thames Valley lands to rebel Bristol. The mechanics of self-preservation also encouraged lords with a prominent and ruthless local figure strong in his support for one side to join that faction, and so the Marches mostly followed the lead of Earl Robert and Brian FitzCount. As of 1139–40 Earl Ranulf of Chester was however loyal to Stephen – but the way that Stephen had granted away Cumbria to King David's son Earl Henry of Huntingdon, with the governorship of its main town Carlisle, ignored Ranulf's rights in that city as son of a prominent local landowner (a Cumbrian lord before he acquired the earldom of Chester) who had once been its governor. Such posts were normally hereditary, so it should have gone to his son – or so Ranulf appears to have believed, leading to a grudge against the new king. These supporters by the late 1130s were mostly in the Midlands and East of England; the most crucial senior magnates in this region were men like the Beaumont cousins (the earls of Warwick and Leicester, sons of the twins who Henry I had granted these titles), Earl Robert of Leicester's Warenne half-brother (William, d. 1148, the new third Earl of Surrey), the archetypal 'robber baron' Geoffrey de Mandeville (constable of the Tower of London and Earl of Essex), and Hugh Bigod (1100?–1177), first Earl of Norfolk. Bigod was also the maternal uncle of William d'Albini (or D'Aubigny), second hereditary royal 'butler' in succession to his father, who the trusting Stephen was to give the hand of his predecessor's stepmother Adeliza of Louvain and the control of her Arundel Castle after Matilda's surrender of it in 1139 – the D'Alibini dynasty were to become dynastically enmeshed with the Marcher lords Fitzalan of Oswestry and Clun who duly inherited Arundel in the thirteenth century. Stephen had to win these men over firmly in 1136–40 with a series of concessions; usually the landed magnate dominating a particular county received the earldom of that county, thus reversing the Conqueror's careful avoidance of making any one magnate powerful in a particular geographical area apart from the Marches, Northumbria, and the south-east coast. Indeed, the grants of blocs of territory to closely related allies – for instance, Worcester went to the Beaumonts, already dominating the Midlands – raised the danger of the emergence of substantial areas becoming dominated by one family to the detriment of the king. This creation of local principalities was the norm in feudal France, and was logical for the Blois noble Stephen to pursue, but it was not usual in most of England.

Stephen initially kept the ambitious William de Roumare, half-brother of Earl Ranulf of Chester, who needed a reward as his loyal governor in rebel-affected Normandy in 1137, out of the earldom of his own 'power-base' of Lincolnshire (close to his half-brother Ranulf's Cheshire lands) and placed him in Cambridge instead. But this was resisted, as he protested that such a role needed appropriately large estates in the county, and most of William's lands were in Lincolnshire not Cambridgeshire. It was more suitable from the recipients' points of view to give them control of a county where they had inherited estates and could support their administrative role adequately, and when Stephen finally gave William the earldom of Lincolnshire without the county town's castle (1140) the latter tried to seize it by force and called in Ranulf for help. Thus the earldom of Chester and its vassals became embroiled in the civil war, implicitly to Matilda's benefit though only if the king dared to challenge the audacious way in which (according to Orderic Vitalis' account) Ranulf and de Roumare proceeded to infiltrate their men into Lincoln undetected. Ralph paid a 'friendly' call on the castle's commander with his and William's wives, which would normally be a sign of pacific intent, and while they were lulling the castellan into a false sense of security some of their men strolled in through the castle gate to 'escourt' them as they left, who then snatched up crowbars and assaulted the guards, driving them out of the gate. The waiting William then ran into the castle with reinforcements, and it was seized and claimed on his behalf. The king chose to reply to this defiance with an armed expedition, causing Ranulf to retreat hastily to Chester and appeal to his fellow Marchers in Matilda's faction for aid. Robert of Gloucester, his closest military lieutenant sheriff, Miles of Gloucester, and their other allies responded quickly with an expedition in turn; the army was allegedly led by six earls, which testifies to the amount of resistance that Stephen now faced. The Lincoln incident thus precipitated the crucial Battle of Lincoln on 2 February, in which Stephen was captured, and the potential collapse of his cause in spring 1141 (see below, next section). The rebel army was also joined by Owain Gwynedd's younger brother Cadwaladr of Ceredigion, who took Gwynedd troops to aid the Marcher forces, and by more Welsh lords from Powys – all presumably hoping to be on the winning side and preferring to help, rather than aggrieve, the most powerful Marcher earls. But hopes of an end to the civil war as a result of the capture of Stephen was premature: he had to be released later after a revolt drove the Empress Matilda out of London, and Earl Robert was captured by Stephen's queen (also confusingly called Matilda) at the siege of Winchester to force an exchange. The war continued. But notably Earl Ranulf had not been an enthusiastic supporter of the empress, and when he and his troops joined her and Robert in the far south to besiege Stephen's brother Bishop Henry of Winchester in that city, he was criticised for hanging back from the fighting and entering into secret talks with the queen. He did not take part in the rebel retreat, where Robert was captured protecting the empress' rearguard at an action outside Stockbridge, and after the disaster he kept out of the main fighting in the South and continued to rule his Northern lands effectively as an autonomous principality. Stephen was too busy trying to gain important castles in the South to tackle him, and he remained unchallenged until 1146 when he came to an agreement with the king, which granted him the disputed town and castle of Lincoln, so preserving his gains of 1141 plus extensive lands in both the North-East and the North-West. The latter included the 'honour' of Lancaster from Mersey to Lune, previously held by Roger de Montgomery's son Roger of Poitou in the 1080s–90s. In effect Ranulf was said to be lord of a third of the kingdom, and the devolution of power to him in the northern Marches now extended to Lancashire, Lincoln, and his lands in the North-East, but in return he was required to reside at Court and accompany the king – who clearly did not trust him – on campaign, as his ex-ally Earl Robert of Gloucester had done in 1136–37. He aided the king at the siege of Brian FitzCount's crucial Thames Valley rebel base at Wallingford, and after the failure of this tried to gain permission to return home, as Owain Gwynedd of Gwynedd had taken advantage of his absence to take Mold in southern Flintshire, expelling his earldom's chief steward Robert de Montealto, and was encroaching on the Dee Valley. The earl was initially given permission to go, but instead the king changed his mind at the royal court at Northampton on 29 August and arrested him, charging him with crimes including illegally retaining royal property and probably alleging treason too. Ranulf protested his innocence and claimed he had not been given notice of any investigation when he was summoned to court so he could not present his defence properly, and Stephen seized back control of Lincoln and held his Christmas court and feast there later in 1146. This gain was presumably his main target, and Ranulf was later released; he remained of dubious loyalty to either faction, and when Empress Matilda's dynamic young son Henry FitzEmpress, later king, arrived in England with a large new army of Angevins (plus troops from Normandy, which his father Geoffrey had now conquered) in spring 1149, Ranulf prudently switched sides again. He let Henry's army cross his Lancashire lands to Carlisle to meet the future king's uncle King David of Scotland, who came there in April 1149 to knight and lend military support to his nephew, and not only attended David's court as a 'loyal' backer of Matilda, doing homage to both Henry and David, but agreed a treaty with David accepting his claims to Carlisle and Cumbria. He then joined the Scots/ Angevin army for an abortive attack on Stephen as the latter held his Whitsun court at York in May, but it is unclear how far the expedition went; one version has it that Ranulf soon went home to Chester. Thereafter the focus of the war shifted south again, and Ranulf remained undisturbed in his effectively autonomous principality until his death on 16 December 1153, aged fifty-four. His controversial reputation was such that there were rumours that he had been poisoned, and his removal probably anticipated a showdown between this aggressively independent warlord and his future sovereign, Henry FitzEmpress, who had by now reached agreement with Stephen on succeeding the latter to England, and was to show that he did not accept over-mighty subjects with equanimity. As of October 1154, instead of having to deal with a new and vigorous young king intent on restoring his rights and regaining disputed castles, Ranulf left his lands to his son by Earl Robert of Gloucester's daughter Maud (d. 1189), Hugh de Kevelioc (1147–81). The boy was a Royal ward, as normal for the underage son of a deceased royal tenant-in-chief, and so the Chester lands fell into the new king's hands – and in 1157 Henry required King David's underage grandson and successor, Malcolm IV, to hand back Cumbria and all the other lands that Stephen had given to David.

Cadwaladr also took the opportunities offered by the lack of any coherent royal policy for control of Wales. He murdered his neighbour Anarawd of Deheubarth, his brother's daughter Gwenllian's stepson, who was about to marry his sister in an alliance with Owin Gwynedd, in 1143. This was presumably intended to weaken the threat to him from Deheubarth to take over Ceredigion, to which both kingdoms had claims, and the probability that as Anaward was now Owain Gywnedd's ally the latter would let Cadwaladr be overthrown – which would also ease the chances of Owain's growing brood of sons to inherit Gwynedd free from Cadwaladr interfering. He faced revolt in Ceredigion, so Owain took the excuse to exile him. He fled to Ireland and fought his way back into Ceredigion with an army of Irish mercenaries, and Owain had to accept his return to prevent a costly civil war. Owain had recently lost his eldest illegitimate son and designated heir, Rhun – named after the great sixth-century ruler – in battle in 1142. He now sent his eldest surviving illegitimate son Hywel, whose mother was Irish, to assist the new ruler of Deheubarth, Cadwaladr's victim Anarawd's brother Cadell, to besiege Carmarthen and retake Llansteffan in 1146 and Wiston in 1147. These two joint campaigns served to reconcile the two kingdoms, implicitly at Cadwaladr's expense, with Owain as the senior partner in the alliance – foreshadowing the policy of Llywelyn ap Iorweth two generations later. In 1150–51 Owain's son Hywel drove Cadwaladr's son Cadfael out of his lands in Ceredigion and imprisoned him but was later expelled. After Cadwaladr's second exile by Owain in 1152, Cadwaladr took refuge with the future Henry II, now fighting Stephen and probably well-disposed to the Gwynedd prince for his help to Henry's mother Matilda. Succeeding to the English throne in 1154 and reviving royal power, Henry forced Cadwaladr's restoration on Owain in an expedition in 1157 and made him hand back Oswestry and Whittington castles, which he had taken from the English around 1146.

Meanwhile the Anglo-Normans were able to set up a new bishopric at St Asaph, held by nominees of the Archbishopric of Canterbury, which claimed religious suzerainty over all the Welsh bishoprics, in 1143, the first bishop being Gilbert. But Owain kept its holders – including the Marcher historian of Wales' legendary past, Geoffrey of Monmouth, in 1151–5 – from actually residing there into the 1160s.

The central and southern Marches and the Civil War, 1135 to 1154: Heartland of the challenge to King Stephen

To the south of Gwynedd, it was for a change an era of peace in formerly turbulent Powys, whose fratricidal princes had exhausted themselves in the 1100s–1120s and whose English royal overlords were otherwise preoccupied. A 'golden age' for Powys was achieved under Maredudd's son and successor Madoc from 1132–60, with Powys the most prosperous and peaceful kingdom in Wales – though militarily inferior to Owain of Gwynedd's realm in 1149–57 – and its ruler the much-praised patron of a bardic revival. The poetic Arthurian romance 'The Dream of Rhonabwy' was compiled in his reign, presenting it as an era of pride and prosperity not seen since Arthur's own time. Another major poet was Cynddelw, Byrdydd Fawr ('the Great Bard', died *c*. 1200), who composed Madoc's main eulogy in 1160. Madoc, married to Susanna, the sister of his predatory neighbour Owain Gwynedd, was a careful ally of the English Marcher earldoms of Chester and Gloucester, and as such assisted Earl Robert of Gloucester with his campaigns on behalf of the latter's sister Empress Matilda against 'usurper' King Stephen in 1138–47. Madoc had less success against Gwynedd, losing the Battle of Ewloe/Coleshill to Owain Gwynedd in 1150, after which Gwynedd confiscated the border cantref of Ial. Madoc had to wait until his ally Earl Robert's nephew Henry II, Matilda's son, came to the throne in 1154 and turned on Gwynedd; he assisted Henry's invasion of Gwynedd in 1157 and received Ial back as a reward. His younger brother Iorweth also participated in the invasion and received lands at Sutton in Shropshire as thanks for his services as an interpreter; Madoc would not give him any lands in Powys (to preserve its manpower resources intact for his own sons in the sucession) so he moved there permanently. The early-mid 1150s also saw the Welsh reconquest of the district of Maelienydd near Radnor, along with at least part of Rhwng Gwy a Hafren (Radnorshire), by Cadwallon ap Madoc, great-grandson of his dynasty's founder Elystan Glodrydd (fl. 1010). Cadwallon secured the recognition of his principality from Henry II at Gloucester in 1175 and inherited his brother Einion of Elfael's lands too in 1176, but was murdered three years later by his Marcher neighbours the Mortimers of Wigmore.

During Henry's reign Gruffydd ap Rhys ap Tewdr of Deheubarth only ruled the remote inland hills and forests, and was unable to penetrate the coastal plains. But from spring 1136 he led a large-scale Welsh revolt across Dyfed following Henry I's death. This was preceded by an outbreak in south-east Deheubarth on the news of the king's death, led not by Gruffydd but by the minor lord Hywel ap Maredudd, who brought in reinforcements from Brycheiniog/Brecon (lordship of Brian FitzCount) to aid the locals as they attacked the Anglicised lordship of Gower, ruled by the late king's intimates the Beaumonts (earls of Warwick). On New Year's Day 1136 the Welsh routed their enemies at the Battle of Lywchr/Loughor on Crug Mawr common, killing around 500 of them, and regained parts of Gower but could not tackle the strong-walled local castles at Oystermouth and Swansea. Despite the risk of revolt speading to his territory, the ambitious Richard FitzGilbert left his lands to journey to the new king's court before Easter 1136, acting there as one of his negotiators with the king's threatening neighbour King David of Scots (son of the Anglo-Saxon princess St Margaret and so with a remote claim on his throne, and brother to Henry I's deceased Queen Matilda), who had to be bought off with the grant of Cumbria and Northumberland to his son Earl Henry of Huntingdon. In this enmeshed world of a small and frequently inter-marrying circle of great nobles, David's late wife Queen Maud had been the daughter of the lord of Huntingdon and former (1069–70) Earl of Northumbria, Waltheof, the younger son of King Edward's Earl Siward of Northumbrria (d. 1055), and a niece of King

William I, and her and David's son Henry had inherited this 'honour' – which duly made his royal Scots descendants English peers who were obliged to do homage to the Kings of England for these lands. David, an Anglicised ruler brought up at the Anglo-Norman court and not only married to an Anglo-Norman semi-royal heiress but formerly governor of Cumbria for Henry I, had many Anglo-Norman barons – including relatives of Marcher lords – in his service, and unlike the Welsh princes was experienced and well-resourced in Anglo-Norman cavalry warfare. He wanted both Cumbria and part of his wife's father's earldom of Northumbria back, and Stephen had to oblige to keep him from backing the threat of revolt by King Henry's daughter the Empress Matilda – who Henry had made his heir and to whom he had forced his lords to take an oath of allegiance in 1126. On the king's death his nephew Stephen, now Count of Mortain (holding the remaining lands of the late Robert and William de Mortain) and through his wife Count of Boulogne, had pre-empted the absent empress and her unpopular second husband, Count Geoffrey of Anjou, and seized the English throne. The nobles had been caught by a *fait accompli* and had accepted this situation, some reluctantly as shown by their slowness in turning up at the new king's court to swear allegiance – among these Matilda's Marcher half-brother, Earl Robert of Gloucester (see below). Stephen had to buy their support, and in this way Richard FitzGilbert proceeded to ask for more Welsh lands but was turned down. Then one of the great lords of the south-west set up as a loyal 'new man' by his patron Henry I, Baldwin de Redvers (lord of Plympton in Devon, Christchurch in Dorset, and the Isle of Wight), proceeded to demand the hereditary sheriffdom of Devon and castellanship of the county town, Exeter, which would give him long-term control of this county. This was the sort of special role for controlling a county that had been more normal as a grant of favour to a much-needed regional commander on a dangerous frontier, such as that of Shrewsbury/

Shropshire to the Montgomerys, not a standard office for any county in England – and it would lead to one, not reliably loyal, noble dominating a region long-term, to the detriment of the king. This 'forcible devolution' and abrogation of royal powers to replace sheriffs and castellans at will was more normal in northern France, but the weak reign of Stephen was to see an effort by unscrupulous local lords to achieve it in England too – creating semi-autonomous lordships like those of the Marches all over England. In the special circumstances of the civil wars of 1136–54, if thwarted a claimant could auction off his services to the king's rival Empress Matilda (or vice versa if he was claiming these rights from her) and acquire the grants from them. On this occasion Stephen resisted and, as Baldwin of Redvers revolted, besieged his supporters in Exeter; Richard FitzGilbert (who was also hereditary lord of Tonbridge in Kent) and his Clare kin were among his army. This was not entirely disinterested, as the main rival to de Redvers for prominence in Devon was their cousin Richard FitzBaldwin, son of the late Baldwin of Meules, brother of the late lord William of Rhyd-y-Gors near Carmarthen, and lord of Okehampton. The rebels were blockaded in Exeter – which had previously risen against William I in 1068, led by King Harold's mother Gytha – and starved out, but Stephen granted them guarantees of their lives and property in return for a quick surrender. He was promptly blamed for this perceived blunder, as it was argued that if he had waited the defenders would soon have been desperate enough to surrender, accepting confiscation of their lands and exile or even a few exemplary executions. The effect was to encourage others to defy the weak king. In the meantime, Richard FitzGilbert set off back for Deheubarth with his men but was ambushed and killed en route near Abergavenny by Morgan and Iorweth ap Owain of Caerleon, current leaders of the diminished royal Welsh dynasty of Gwent, on 15 April. The latter had grievances towards all the Anglo-Norman lords for losing most of their ancestral lands to interlopers but may also have had links to plotters in Deheubarth and so decided to help them by killing the lord of Cardigan; creating an impetus for this revolt would also help their own chances of grabbing back local lands in the chaos. Richard was to be buried at his ancestral Tonbridge, not in Wales; his son Gilbert de Clare (d. 1151/3) inherited Tonbridge and the family lands in Hertfordshire (and was to be made Earl of Hertford by Stephen, concentrating his interests on controlling that county) while Richard's younger brother Gilbert clung on to what lands he could salvage in South-West Wales. These were mostly in Pembrokeshire, which had a stronger Anglo-Norman and Flemish settler presence and to which he relocated and duly acquired the revived earldom of Pembroke (*c.* 1139/40) at an unspecified date early in the civil war form the embattled king.

Revolt in Ceredigion and across Deheubarth now followed, while King Stephen sent Richard's younger brother Baldwin and Robert FitzHarold of Ewias Harold in south-west Herefordshire with troops to rescue the remote 'colony'. The inefficient Baldwin halted at Brecon and apparently gave himself up to gluttony, but Robert reached and rescued Carmarthen from attack. Gruffydd ap Cynan had left for Gwynedd to seek aid. While he was seeking aid from his father-in-law Gruffydd ap Cynan, his wife Gwenllian was killed (along with two sons, Morgan and Maelgwyn) as she attacked William de Londres, lord of Cydweli and Ogwr, at Cydweli/Kidwelly Castle. Her memorable leadership of her husband's army, a first for British/Welsh queens since Boudicca, and subsequent heroic death were remembered for centuries in local lore with the cry of 'Revenge for Gwenllian!' on battlefields, and the site of the clash was named Maes ('Field of') Gwenllian. Already a rebellion in Ceredigion in Henry's last months as king in 1135 had seen the rebels pay for a Scandinavian fleet from Ireland to come and help them in an unsuccessful siege of Cardigan Castle. In the far west a major Anglo-Norman-Fleming force under the local surviving strongman Robert FitzMartin of Cemaes and his Herefordshire reinforcements under Robert FitzHarold was routed by the two Gruffydds with a combined army of Deheubarth rebels and Gwynedd reinforcements at Crug Mawr near Cardigan in October 1136. The two leaders escaped alive, but most of their men were killed. Most of the principality of Ceredigion except Cardigan itself was now lost to the Welsh – only to be subsequently fought over by princes of Deheubarth and Gwynedd. Richard FitzGilbert's widow, Alice, sister of Ranulf de Gernon, the new Earl of Chester (1129), and her garrison managed to hold out at Cardigan Castle until Miles, Sheriff of Gloucester, brought a relief-force all the way from the Severn and forced the attackers to pull back. Although an administrator not a major landed peer, Miles, the third generation of hereditary sheriffs of Gloucester (preceded in that role by his father Walter, appointed sheriff by Henry I in 1106) and so the effective strongman of that county and his close ally Payn FitzJohn were now the leaders of the royal fight-back. Described subsequently as the rulers of the lands between the Severn and the sea under King Henry by the well-connected Marcher/Welsh historian Giraldus Cambrensis, they dominated the southern Marches as of 1135–6 along with the late king's two more noble lieutenants, Earl Robert of Gloucester (who was probably under suspicion already as half-brother of Empress Matilda and was currently being required to fight for the king against Matilda's invading husband Geoffrey in Normandy) and Brian FitzCount, lord of Abergavenny. Miles was also the patron of the local new monastery set up in a valley in the isolated Black Mountains wilderness by eagerly austere Augustinian canons at Llanthony Abbey *c.* 1100 (based on a small earlier cell founded by one of the de Laceys), which the rebellion in 1135–6 caused to relocate out of danger into Gloucestershire. Miles duly granted them a new site at Hempstead, where they built their priory of Llanthony Secunda – they then returned to the original site once it was safer from Welsh raids under Henry II's rule in *c.* 1170. Payn was a fomer trusty and personal intimate of Henry I who – with his Yorkshire magnate brother Eustace FitzJohn – had frequently attended the royal court and had also been among the magnates at Stephen's first Court in December 1135; he was the most powerful lord in Shropshire and Herefordshire as their sheriff. As mentioned earlier, he was probably married to the niece of the disgraced 1095 rebel Roger de Lacey, lord of Weobley, Ewias Lacey and Ludlow, and had been granted most of Roger's lands by his patron Henry I; Roger's son Gilbert had recovered some of them but not Ludlow, which was the basis of Payn's lordship and was indeed to become increasingly crucial in the role of principal administrative centre of the middle Marches through the coming three centuries. He was probably but not certainly linked by a marital alliance of his elder daughter to Miles' eldest son Roger in his lifetime.

The rebels managed to hold out in the remoter countryside by avoiding direct battle, unlike in the South-West of Wales where they were bolder and their enemies more exposed, and Payn FitzJohn was killed in an ambush in July 1137 while pursuing some of them. But the Anglo-Norman grip on South-East Wales was preserved. However, the rising arc of civil war in England intervened, as more discontented lords followed the example of the Devon rebels – according to written accounts, encouraged by the king's leniency at Exeter to risk rebelling. In 1138 one such revolt broke out in Shropshire. This was only a struggle for local power and influence, and an attempt to intimidate the new sovereign such as usually followed a succession (as in 1088 and 1101–2), but it was to be followed by a more concentrated and deadly attempt to replace Stephen as king by his cousin the Empress Matilda, daughter of King Henry. The Welsh made the most of this diversion of their foes' resources. In 1137 Carmarthen in the South was recaptured, and Anglo-Norman control of the districts of Emlyn and Cemaes to the North and North-West, south of the Teifi, was endangered. Meanwhile the death of Payn FitzJohn may well have seen some of his estates returned to the de Laceys, possibly including Weobley, now that Henry I, who distrusted them, was dead; but Ludlow and probably Ewias Lacey went to a minor Breton lord, Joce de Dinan (i.e. of Dinant), who had no local connections. The building of the extant castle was to be ascribed to Joce in the thirteenth-century 'Romance of Fulk FitzWarine', and the adjoining part of the town, the original centre of the borough, was to be named 'Dinham', so he may have established that too in Stephen's reign. Gilbert de Lacey (d. 1160s), son of the late rebel Roger, was not to recover Ludlow or Weobley until some time between 1145 and 1156, and we shall see that he now took the chance of defying the king who was denying him his inheritance.

Gruffydd ap Rhys and his sons Anarawd, Cadell, Maredudd, and Rhys had a limited degree of success in regaining territory, and made little impact on the coast except in the Carmarthen region. Returning from Gwynedd with the promised aid after his wife's death, Gruffydd fought a largely successful campaign in Pembrokeshire in 1137 but could not overrun the South, and later in the year he himself was killed in battle by the local Flemings. His eldest son Anarawd succeeded and killed the Fleming commander Letard in 1137, and had some success in regaining parts of Ceredigion with Scandinavian-Irish mercenary help, but was killed in 1143 by the followers of a rival claimant, Owain Gwynedd's younger brother Cadwaladr of Gwynedd. His brother Cadell succeeded as senior prince in Cantref Mawr, and in 1146 he and his brothers Maredudd and Rhys (the latter, born around 1132, in his first campaign) succeeded in taking Llansteffan Castle, on the west bank of the Towy Estuary downstream from Carmarthen. Wiston was taken in 1147 and Carmarthen itself in 1150, but Cadell abdicated in 1151 after being badly wounded in an ambush by the garrison of Tenby while out hunting. He left for Rome on pilgrimage in 1153, returned later to become a monk at Strata Florida Abbey, and died there in 1175. Maredudd now succeeded and in 1153 regained both Ceredigion and Tenby (the latter with Rhys' help).

The crucial event in the outbreak of a full dynastic civil war was Earl Robert of Gloucester's decision to renounce his fealty to Stephen and claim that his oath to Matilda in 1126 took precedence instead. This was announced by his messengers to Stephen in late spring 1138, during a minor though significant rebellion in the southern Marches that was not so much a dynastic challenge to the new king, as in 1088 or 1101–2 (there was no mention of transferring fealty to Matilda by the rebels), as an example of a 'trial of strength' for the king posed by disgruntled lords. The contemporary sources make it clear that Stephen's easy terms for the 1136 rebels at Exeter had encouraged just this sort of defiance. On this occasion, in spring 1138 the king faced invasion from King David of Scotland, who was now demanding control of Northumberland, part of his his late wife's father Waltheof's earldom of Northumbria, to add to Cumbria, and at the same time Stephen's rebel Welsh vassals in Deheubarth were holding out; the Shropshire/Herefordshire strongman Payn FitzJohn had been killed by them in July 1137. Stephen could not really trust Earl Robert as lord of Glamorgan and Gloucestershire, who he was compelling to stay in Normandy to fight the invading Geoffrey of Anjou under his henchmen's supervision, or Robert's ally the hereditary sheriff Miles of Gloucester (d. 1143), who had now inherited Brecon too through his marriage to Sibyl de Neufmarche, daughter of Bernard. At about this time Miles also started to call himself Earl of Hereford – it is likely that he forced Stephen to grant him this title to secure his loyalty (in vain), then made sure that when he revolted Matilda recognised it too; it put him on a social 'par' with Earl Robert, and as the latter had 'real' control of Gloucestershire plus the county title, Miles moved his ambitions next door to Herefordshire. The king now headed from his Easter Court at Northampton to Gloucester to supervise a counter-attack in Deheubarth himself, only to face a revolt in Herefordshire. Part of Stephen's initial 1135/6 offers of concessions to the potential rebel Miles of Gloucester – now in attendance on him at his town – had included arranging the marriage of Payn FitzJohn's elder daughter and heiress Sibyl to Miles' son and heir Roger, later second Earl of Hereford and lord of Brecon. The agreement was backed by the two families involved, but as it included all the lands taken by Henry I from the rebel de Laceys and given to Payn, including Weobley, this cut out Gilbert de Lacey's claims. Angered by this, Gilbert, holder of the family's Norman lands, and his cousin Geoffrey de Talbot revolted, and Geoffrey seized the town of Hereford. Stephen now besieged Geoffrey in Hereford Castle, set in the south-east corner of the town close to the cathedral, and celebrated Whitsun at the latter a few hundred yards away during the siege; after a few weeks, the castle surrendered in return for the rebels being allowed to leave unmolested, as at Exeter in 1136. Geoffrey fled to his other stronghold of Weobley, but was driven out of that too and fled – ending up at Earl Robert's Bristol Castle. The rebellion had seemingly collapsed, and Stephen headed back to Gloucester.

But now Earl Robert struck him a major blow by publicly renouncing fealty – a more definitive and legally framed action than merely staging a revolt by seizing royal lands or goods. By implying that Stephen's accession had been a fraud, he targeted the heart of his government's legitimacy through questioning his controversial coup. This was 'spun' as the act of an affronted man of honour who could not live with his conscience any longer, not the act of a greedy robber baron keen to cause chaos. Robert appears to have been in Normandy, where he had stayed on to force a truce on the duchy's threatening neighbour Geoffrey of Anjou (Matilda's husband) after Stephen ended his own campaign there in 1137. Robert had had qualms about swearing allegiance to Stephen after the latter's surprise coup, and had stayed away from his Court as long as he dared, until forced to come and swear allegiance on pain of war in 1136. It is unclear if he swore allegiance unconditionally or, according to one source, on condition that he would be maintained in his current status – presumably meaning the same honour and influence at Court that his father Henry I had granted him. If this is true, it indicates that he was anxious as to his security and power. His potential for revolt was thus already an issue, and his participation in the 1137 Norman campaign had seen him at odds with royal favourites such as the mercenary commander William of Ypres. Apparently the Archbishop of Rouen had to mediate between him and his enemies then, and it is possible that his semi-detached and aloof status at Court, as well as the threat of mischief-makers denouncing him to the king, pushed him over the brink into revolt. Quite independent of his conscience, he may have feared being sidelined from power or even deprived of his lands and decided to strike first. It was impossible for a ruler to please all contending factions at his Court indefinitely, and a grant of lands, office, a wife, or a Royal ward to one contender could cause defeated rivals to revolt in favour of a pretender. Keeping Earl Robert at Court in the king's entourage for a few years as a 'hostage' and/or offering him reassurance and riches would not have worked for Stephen long-term; a great lord was expected to be free to come and go as he pleased. Once he did revolt, he had the quantity of castles and men to make his rebellion dangerous and a bloc of territory a week's march from London. But most acts of armed defiance were usually containable if the king acted quickly. But the rebelling faction had command of the vital port of Bristol with its large castle, and the port's rebel garrison was further accessible by river, which enabled supplies to be brought in easier than the rebels had been able to do at Rochester in the parallel case of 1088. In both cases the strength of the castles' walls and the poor state of siege-artillery development meant that the rebel strongholds could not be stormed easily. The de Montgomery family, defying Henry I in 1102–3 in the northern Welsh Marches, had been further away from the king's centre of power but had not had such impregnable castles; it had taken Henry time to invade their remote estates, but once he did so he had less difficulty than Stephen did in 1138.

The failure of Stephen to press west and blockade Bristol quickly and successfully was excusable, and not just due to his alleged weakness of resolve. Instead, he merely chose to advance as far as Bath after the rebels at Bristol – now joined by the refugee Lacey and Talbot – had clashed with the local bishop's garrison at the latter; Geoffrey Talbot was captured raiding Bath by the bishop's men but the rebels proceeded to lure the bishop to a parley, kidnap him, and force an exchange, to Stephen's fury. Stephen secured Bath with his army, but did not press on to Bristol and instead moved off into Somerset to take Earl Robert's isolated castles of Castle Cary and Harptree. But the king faced a serious problem in retaking Robert's principal stronghold – though it can be argued that his main fault was allowing Robert to remain in Normandy in 1137–8 rather than keeping him at Court under surveillance. The views of contemporary chroniclers are vital evidence on how the crises that faced him were viewed at the time – and on why so many of his vassals felt it safe to take up arms consequent of his dangerous inability to make them fear him. On this issue, opinion is clear that he was seen as weak and ineffective after his failure to punish the rebels who had seized Exeter and been blockaded into surrender in 1136. He did, however, shortly remedy this by a second, more effective action in the Marches – the middle Marches this time, where William Fitzalan of Oswestry (1105–1160), who had succeeded his father Alan FitzFlaald in 1114, now joined the rebel cause. Brother of Walter FitzAlan, the High Steward of Scotland, and married to Christiana FitzRobert of Caen, who was possibly a niece of Earl Robert of Gloucester, he declared for the Earl and Empress Matilda and seized control of Shrewsbury; he was then Sheriff of Shropshire after Payn FitzJohn. At the time the king was busy retaking Dudley Castle a short distance away so he was able to intervene quickly; he marched on Shrewsbury and William fled with his family, leaving his uncle Arnulf de Hesdin in command of the castle. The town surrendered, but Arnulf refused to do so and allegedly sent insulting messages to the king; the account of local Orderic Vitalis has it that the enraged Stephen then had the ditch around the motte filled in and the main gate stormed. Arnulf and his garrison, around ninety-three men, were all hanged; the chronicler John of Worcester reported, with some shock, that five men of high social rank were executed, which was virtually unheard of in contemporary warfare. This duly quelled resistance and led to the surrender of rebel-held Dover Castle in Kent to the queen's (largely mercenary) army shortly afterwards. But in May or June 1139 Stephen faced a new Marcher challenge, some time between his Easter Court at Nottingham (where King David's son Henry, Earl of Huntingdon and now Northumberland, arrived to attend on his army and confirm the two sovereigns' reconciliation after their 1138 war) and the Midsummer council at Oxford. While Stephen was holding court at Worcester with his ultra-loyalist earls – including the town's own new earl – and attending a ceremony in the cathedral, he heard that Ludlow Castle was being held against him, possibly by Gilbert de Lacey, in which case the latter had seized it from the loyalist Joce de Dinan. Possibly at the instigation of the technically still loyal Miles of Gloucester, Stephen led his army there and succeeded in recovering the castle after a short siege. The episode was most notable for an incident where Stephen showed his bravery as a knight – and came close to being killed, which would have aborted the civil war. The defenders let down an iron grappling-hook from the west wall and entangled Earl Henry of Huntingdon, and the nearby Stephen leapt to his aid and succeeded in hacking through the iron before Henry could be hauled up into the castle and held hostage – exposing himself to fire from the walls for the duration. This episode is related by chronicler Henry of Huntingdon (no relation), and local chronicler John of Worcester hints that the earl was also at risk from the rival claimant to his earldom who was in Stephen's army, namely Henry's mother's son by her first husband, Simon de Senlis, Earl of Northampton. After the castle had fallen, the king moved on to Oxford, where he was to have a showdown with and arrest his late uncle's most powerful minister, the castle-hoarding cleric and treasurer Bishop Roger of Salisbury. The latter and his nephews, bishops Alexander of Lincoln and Nigel of Ely, all ended up arrested with their castles seized, which helped in the eclipse of Henry I's senior clerical trusties (more dependent on the king than secular lords as they could not pass on their lands to heirs) by secular nobles who could establish dynasties at the king's expense.

Stephen could have soon stopped the civil war in its infancy when he managed to corner the newly arrived Matilda at her stepmother's castle of Arundel as she landed from Normandy later in 1139; Earl Robert appears to have been with her, but had left for Bristol to join his garrison before the king arrived. The castle – a large double 'ward', one to either side of a central tower on a motte, as at Windsor – was blockaded into offering terms, but Stephen allowed Matilda safe passage to her half-brother Robert at Bristol rather than requiring Matilda to surrender – the logical outcome of a longer siege. This was a political disaster of the first order and showed his difference of temperament from his ruthlessly effective grandfather William I, uncles William II and Henry I and mother Adela. One interpretation of this apparent over-confidence has it that imprisoning a woman would have been to the the detriment of his chivalric instincts, though more plausibly he was unwilling to continue the siege for another few weeks with the current revolt spreading. Robert already held Bristol, and another revolt was now underway in the South-West as the exiled Baldwin de Redvers (of Wight and Christchurch as well as Plympton) returned to his Devon lands. Stephen needed to march against the rebels in person as he could not trust his leading loyalist magnates; he could therefore afford to let Matilda go free from Arundel to concentrate on military victory. The author of the *Gesta Stephani* subsequently claimed that Stephen's brother Bishop Henry of Winchester, a political cleric in his capacity as both a royal prince and papal legate and also very rich as abbot of Glastonbury, advised Stephen to let Matilda leave unharmed and said that it would be easier to tackle and capture Matilda and Earl Robert when they were together. The question must arise if the devious Henry was playing a double-game and was not as loyal to Stephen as he pretended – the longer the war went on, the higher price both claimants would pay for his support. Henry had intercepted Earl Robert, en route to Bristol, on his way to Arundel and let him travel on after a friendly discussion and kiss of peace – was this cousinly courtesy or double-dealing?

Stephen at Arundel in 1139 was not to know that this rebellion would spread too far for him to achieve the same successes that he had done against risings in 1136–8; his failure to follow up his success at Arundel by attacking Bristol was a serious tactical mistake. It had its military logic, as the town and castle of Bristol were strongly walled and had river-access down the Avon to the Bristol Channel, enabling supplies to be brought in; for a siege; it would have needed a large army and a lengthy blockade. If Stephen had attacked Bristol in later 1139 or spring 1140, it would have diverted his attention from nearer London and so enabled more potential defectors to risk abandoning him. But at least his military presence in the Bristol region would have shown that he was not to be defied – as he had shown in 1138 by an equally risky advance far into the turbulent Marches to attack rebel-held Hereford and Shrewsbury. He had at least some trustable foreign mercenaries already – men from his wife's county of Boulogne, brought in by her in 1138 to take Dover Castle. Psychologically, an offensive against Bristol was therefore likely to have impressed waverers between the factions. Instead, within weeks of the empress' arrival there two more major magnates, Miles of Gloucester, whose lands around that town could cut Bristol off from Earl Robert's lands in Glamorgan, and Brian FitzCount of Wallingford, who had defected. Stephen proceeded to besiege Wallingford instead, but soon moved off to attack Trowbridge, whereupon Earl Robert relieved Wallingford by driving off the remaining besiegers. From now on Matilda had major castles in the middle Thames and Wiltshire regions inhibiting any attack by Stephen on her base at Bristol.

The continuation of the civil war – now at a virtual equilibrium – depended on the failure of two rounds of peace talks that Bishop Henry took the lead in arranging in 1140. First he used his authority as papal legate to call a meeting near or at Bath around midsummer, with him Archbishop Theobald of Canterbury, and Queen Matilda represented by Stephen and Earl Robert – the only high-ranking representative of Matilda. This failed, and Bishop Henry proceeded on to France to consult the new King Louis VII, his adviser Abbot Suger of St Denis and other leading churchmen, and Stephen's brother Count Theobald of Blois. He brought back a set of proposals, to which the empress agreed but which Stephen refused. The details are unknown, but the participation of the King of France – overlord of Normandy, Blois, Boulogne and Anjou – and people such as Theobald and the Queen suggests that the family interests of both Stephen's and the Empress' families in the long-term were being considered. The Pope had backed Stephen's election, coronation, and right to the throne as all legal, and it is very unlikely that he would ever have abdicated his crown voluntarily; but the future of Normandy was another matter. It has been suggested that the eventual terms of settlement in 1153 give a clue to what was intended, with the empress' son Henry (II), aged seven in 1140, succeeding Stephen in England so that her claims of right were upheld via her son (who would probably be adult by the time that Stephen, now in his late forties, died). Normandy, however, might well have been assigned to Stephen's son Eustace, with the French king pleased to keep England and Normandy divided;

Boulogne would go to Eustace's younger brother and Anjou to the empress' second son. Stephen seems to have preferred to gamble that he could use his advantage of having a majority of the English magnates on his side to wear the enemy down. The war continued.

The capture of Stephen at Lincoln in February 1141 seemed a tipping point, as a quarrel with Earl Ranulf of Chester, occupier of the royal castle there (see above), led to Stephen dismissing him and Ranulf appealing to Earl Robert for aid. Stephen marched quickly up from London to besiege the castle, and Robert brought a large army to the rescue including both landowners forfeited by the king who had nothing to lose (such as Baldwin de Redvers) and Welsh mercenaries led by King Madoc of Powys and Cadwaladr, brother of Owain of Gwynedd. Numbers seem to have been around equal and the battle site is unclear, so any royal mistakes cannot be identified, but it is possible that Stephen was overconfident (fighting against the king in person was considered treason and so some rebels might have been hesitant) and the disinherited and the Welsh fought more ferociously than the royal knights were used to. For reasons of prestige, declining battle was not a viable option for Stephen, but his cavalry wing, led by six earls, proved deficient and was routed by Earl Robert's charge. The more professional mercenary army under William of Ypres drove the Welsh back but was unable to save the day, and once the royalists were in disarray they prudently withdrew, unmolested. Rather than entrusting himself to them, the valiant but naïve Stephen, who did not have a horse handy, carried on fighting on foot with a battleaxe until he was overwhelmed, and then refused to surrender to a 'commoner' who had overpowered him and insisted on doing so to Earl Robert personally instead; his prowess as a knight outmatched his strategic competence. Matilda managed to secure the temporary allegiance of Bishop Henry – now legate – and the Church, though her award of the Bishopric of Durham to King David's candidate in defiance of the legate's candidate (and thus the Pope) was a blunder. But her conduct on her arrival in London to negotiate the city's loyalty and to start preparations for her coronation apparently roused resentment. She had had experience of the need for flattery and caution in dealing with civic authorities with her first husband, Emperor Henry V, in Italy, but had clearly learnt nothing. On 24 June 1141 a sudden rising by the Londoners drove her out of Westminster back to her main bases of Oxford and Bristol. The East of England passed back into the hands of the queen's army, which otherwise could have hopefully been kept out of London until Matilda had enough troops to force a decisive battle. Matilda's position was still strong, as shown by new adherents like William de Beauchamp (claimant to the earldom of Worcester) that summer, and her husband's triumph in Normandy was a reason for lords like the Beaumonts with lands in both countries to come over to her to protect their position. Waleran de Beaumont, Stephen's choice as Earl of Worcester, had to accept his deposition in Beauchamp's favour and back Matilda once the family's Norman lands were under Angevin control.

When Matilda was unable to rely on Bishop Henry's allegiance, she advanced on Winchester in August with a substantial force, including King David's Scots and, according to the *Gesta Stephani*, the earls of Gloucester, Devon (de Redvers), Cornwall (her half-brother Reginald, an illegitimate son of Henry I), Hereford (Miles of Gloucester), Dorset (William de Mohun, lord of Dunster Castle in Somerset), and Warwick (Roger de Beaumont), plus Brian FitzCount and John the Marshal. Earl Ranulf of Chester was present but ineffective, and Geoffrey de Mandeville (Earl of Essex) defected to the queen. Miles of Gloucester had recently had his earldom of Hereford confirmed by grant from the new queen (or 'Lady of England' as some sources call her, with reference to the usual title borne by the wife of the Anglo-Saxon queens pre-1066); he was said to have boasted that he had hosted and paid all the expenses incurred by Matilda during her 1139–41 time in England. He had also acquired the abbacy of Gloucester Abbey for his young kinsman Gilbert Foliot, the future Bishop of London (1163) and 1160s foe of Archbishop Thomas Becket, and was clearly using the invaluable weight of his territory and manpower to become effective ruler of his district – which, due to his eldest son Roger's marriage to the heiress of the deceased Payn FitzJohn of Weobley and Ludlow, sheriff of Herefordshire and Shropshire, was extending into those counties. Reginald, lord of Tintagel Castle, was equally dominant in Cornwall (ethnically and linguistically distinct from England as a former stronghold of the pre-Saxon Britons), as was de Mohun in both Somerset and Dorset; in effect, Matilda was having to confirm a degree of decentralization to a few great nobles as last seen under Edward the Confessor. Given that Stephen was still captive and the initiative seemed to lie with Matilda, the size of her force was a sign of her widespread but not overwhelming support. Besieging Henry in his episcopal residence, Wolvesey Castle in Winchester, led to his retaliatory bombardment of her forces up the hill in the royal castle, which led to much of the town being set afire – and comments on the novelty of a cleric causing this sort of destruction. The queen's troops came to assist Bishop Henry, and cut off Matilda's supply route with the capture of Andover and Wherwell. Facing defeat or being starved out by William of Ypres' Fleming force, Empress Matilda and the rest of the leadership had to flee north-west towards Wiltshire. It is unclear how much the dramatic account of their escape in the biography of William Marshal, the son of John the Marshal and later Earl of Pembroke, is romanticised, but it portrays a desperate gallop across the downs to the Test Valley and then a straggling rearguard action around the river crossing at Stockbridge as the queen's troops caught up with the empress' men. Evidently the situation was desperate enough to require a speedy flight in preference to risking a battle. The empress' rearguard was caught up with and attacked at Stockbridge, though she escaped up the hill westwards across Danebury Down while Earl Robert held up the enemy; valuable members of her leadership, including Robert, were captured. The advantage now lay with the queen: she traded her hostages for Stephen. He was re-crowned and secured extra support from the people Matilda had alienated; the stalemate resumed.

No decisive success resulted for either candidate throughout the rest of the 1140s, though Stephen had the advantage across central and eastern England and Matilda's main supporters were isolated in the western and south-western regions – especially the crucial Marcher lordships held by Gloucester and his allies. They remained out of royal control until Matilda's son Henry (II) succeeded Stephen as king in October 1154, and was effectively autonomous as a patchwork of lordships owing allegiance to the shadow administration of Matilda and her half-brother Earl Robert. They were unable to advance their cause significantly until her son Henry arrived from Anjou in 1149 with the resources of conquered Normandy to assist his army, and Matilda seems to have usually resided at Devizes Castle in Wiltshire, not in the Marches. Robert commanded the latter from Bristol, apart from a campaign in Normandy to assist Geoffrey of Anjou in driving out the royalists there in 1142, and for some time from that autumn he was joined in Bristol by Matilda's son Henry, who appears to have been educated there. Robert also set up a new base in southern Oxfordshire at Faringdon Castle, but Stephen besieged and took it in 1145; Robert failed to relieve it. When Robert died in October 1147, probably aged around fifty-seven, he was succeeded by his much less effective son William as second earl; in effect, there was a vacuum in leadership once Matilda left for Normandy a few months later, and this did not end until Henry's return in 1149. The other south Marches strongman of the empress' regime, Miles of Gloucester, the new Earl of Hereford, also died in this period, having undergone a bruising trial of strength with the Bishop of Hereford, Robert de Bethune, in 1142–3 over his seizure of Church lands and goods to pay for his troops, which may testify to the strain of war even with his large-scale resources. He was excommunicated and shortly afterwards died in a hunting accident when he was shot by a stray arrow on Christmas Eve 1143; the monks of his 'capital', Gloucester's abbey, and of the second Llanthony priory at Hempstead then had a dispute over who was to have the honour of his burial on their property, which Llanthony won. The dispute with Bishop Bethune was sorted out by mediators, but Miles' eldest son, the new Earl Roger (d. 1155), held a grudge and forced the bishop's ally, the prior of Llanthony, to resign for preferring his ecclesiastical to his secular patron. Roger, evidently as keen to assert his rights as his father and even more uncompromising in his demands for loyalty, later quarrelled with ex-Abbot Foliot of Gloucester too, when the Pope made that man the new Bishop of Hereford and Foliot subsequently swore allegiance to Stephen. Politically and militarily the new Earl was not as dominant as his father – though the terms of his 1147 legal alliance with the new Earl of Gloucester, Robert's son William, gave him honorary recognition as leader of the empress' party in England. He attended on Matilda's son Henry when that young man returned to England in 1149 and joined him at Carlisle, but once Henry was king in 1154 he foolishly tried to hold onto his current position with all the lands and castles – some illegally gained – and rights his family had acquired from Stephen and Matilda. He refused to attend on the new king and was duly reduced to obedience by a personal expedition by Henry, probably in 1155, which a more realistic and less arrogant noble would have avoided by a graceful recognition of reality earlier.

4

THE REIGN OF HENRY II
1154–1189

Henry's struggles to dominate the Welsh Marcher lords; the role of Marcher lords in conquering lands in Ireland; the emergence of the earls of Pembroke as a major power.

The northern Marches

The reign began with a major invasion of Gwynedd in 1157 to bring Owain Gwynedd, son of Gruffydd ap Cynan, under English control and reconquer as much land as possible. On 17 July the major barons of England attended a royal summons to Northampton and agreed to bring troops to aid Henry for the war, and a march by a huge English army (a third of all the 'knight service' owed by Henry's English vassals) proceeded from Chester across the Dee and along the Flintshire coast, while a fleet moved offshore to lend assistance if needed. The intention was to overwhelm the Welsh by weight of numbers, and the fleet then moved on to seize Anglesey – probably to prevent Owain retreating there as the king reached the Menai Strait. But the landing was repulsed, and inland the invasion saw Henry's main army, joined by his vassal Madoc ap Maredudd of Powys, who prudently put his own realm's safety above 'ethnic solidarity', ambushed in the forests near Hawarden. The English could not see the numbers of attackers and panicked, and the royal standard-bearer threw down his banner and ran away, which would have signified to observers that this was an official signal for retreat. The threat of a disaster was only averted as the king arrived, after fighting his way out of a nearby ambush. He ordered his men to cut down the trees and create a secure road before advancing futher, and his weight of numbers told; Owain was forced to surrender hostages and the disputed eastern cantref of Tegeingl, i.e. most of Flintshire to the Clywd Valley. Henry constructed new castles at Basingwerk and Rhuddlan to protect his gains, and in July 1163 Owain had to journey to Woodstock, near Oxford, to do homage to his new overlord. This was a major assembly of the king's 'Celtic' vassals within the British mainland, as Rhys ap Gruffydd of Deheeubarth, five other unnamed Welsh lords, and King Malcolm IV of Scots were also summoned to do homage, and as such represented the king's tidy-minded formalization of his new system of rule whereby he was the overlord of a network of – hopefully obedient – vassals in Britain as he was in France.

Henry was still ambitious to extend his rule, but the result was, as the St David's Chronicle noted, that 'all the Welsh of Gwynedd, Deheubarth, and Powys with one accord cast off the Norman yoke' in summer 1164 – presumably coordinated to reduce the chances of Henry being able to take them one by one. He summoned a council to Northampton in October and there ordered his barons to provide infantry, not knights – more use in hill country – for his army, hiring overseas mercenaries and a Dublin Norse/Irish fleet, too. Gwynedd was the main target as the largest and most senior of the rebel states, if also the hardest to crack given its mountains. In July 1165 a massive overland march into Gwyned commenced from Shrewsbury, rather than Chester, aimed along the main trade route used by the hill-country farmers to the markets in Shropshire. The threatened rulers of Powys and Deheubarth rallied around Owain's leadership at the valley-junction of Corwen as Henry's huge army approached; even Rhys ap Gruffydd of Deheubarth, Owain's nephew, came to aid him despite the risk of attack by the de Clares in the rear. As in 1157, Henry's men had to cut down the trees and undergrowth en route to diminish the risk of ambush, this time along the Berwyn Mountains, and the troops floundered on the normally dry upland moors due to torrential rain. They could not reach Corwen, and Henry ran out of supplies and had to retreat; twenty-two Welsh hostages were hung in retaliation. After the English had retired, Owain regained Basingwerk and Rhuddlan. His leadership of the Welsh princes was even acknowledged by the English, whose legal documents referred to him as 'prince of the Welsh', senior to the other princes of Powys and Deheubarth; Henry was reduced to hoping that his prudence would make him an amenable junior 'partner' after his lucky escape in 1165 and he would control his fellow princes. Nor could the Archbishopric of Canterbury, held from 1162–70 by the aggressive ex-chancellor Thomas Becket – though the king's political demands over 'criminous clerics' accepting lay trials forced him into exile – make Owain accept its nominee as the Bishop of Bangor. Becket refused to consecrate Owain's own choice, Arthur, in the early 1160s – Owain had him consecrated in Ireland, instead, and kept the English candidate out of Gwynedd. Owain even cheekily offered military help to Henry's French overlord and sporadic foe, Louis VII (now sheltering the exiled Becket) in 1168, defying the king to do anything about it. Owain died on 28 April 1170, aged around seventy. His power and reputation were unparalleled for a post-1063 ruler of Wales, but his achievement, like that of Rhys of Deheubarth later, was hampered by his lack of a sole heir.

The division of Gwynedd between Owain's surviving sons and his ambitious yonger brother Cadwaldr, lord of Ceredigion, on his death in 1170 led to a further bout of inter-familial strife. Owain had at least two sons by his first wife, Gwladys, the eldest being Iorweth, who was married to the daughter of his ally Madoc ap Mareudd of Powys (d. 1160), and two more by his own cousin, Cristin, daughter of Goronwy ap Owain, plus assorted bastards who had rights to lands too under Welsh law. Owain's eldest, illegitimate son, the poet Hywel, was exiled by his half-brothers Dafydd and Rhodri (the sons of Cristin), who struck first and tried to seize the heartland of Arfon and Mon/ Anglesey. Like generations of exiled princely contenders before him, he collected an army from Ireland to invade, landed, and was killed in an ambush at Pentreath in Anglesey, allegedly at the instigation of their mother Cristin. His death, along with those of his seven foster brothers, the sons of Cynfor who accompanied him on the expedition, was lamented in a famous poem. Maelgwyn, one of Owain's illegitimate sons, received Anglesey, but was expelled in 1173 by his half-brothers Dafydd and Rhodri, by then controlling the east of the kingdom, and the oldest surviving brother, Iorweth 'Flatnose' of Arfon, did not last long. Some observers, for example Giraldus Cambrensis, call Iorweth Owain's only legitimate son, as the Church regarded Owain's marriage to Cristin illegal and Dafydd and Rhodri thus ineligible for the throne, as they were cousins. But either in 1170–1 or a couple of years thereafter these two secued Arfon, too, depriving Iorweth. Eventually the conflict stabilised with the rule of Dafydd in East and Rhodri in West Gwynedd, the River Conwy dividing their lands. Dafydd married Emma de Laval, half-sister of King Henry, and prudently sent him aid as he faced revolt by his sons Henry, the 'Young King' (crowned co-ruler in 1170), and Richard (Duke of Aquitaine from 1172) in 1173–4. In contrast to the careful Dafydd was his Anglo-Norman neighbour Earl Hugh of Chester, a former Royal ward from his father's death in 1153 until his coming-of-age, who slipped off to his lands on the Norman-Breton border where he held the hereditary viscountcy of Avranches. Henry's ally Duke Conan of Brittany had died in 1171, and though his daughter and heiress Constance was betrothed to Henry's younger son Geoffrey – intended as the next duke as an Angevin agent – the region was in practice as devolved and lawless as England's outer regions had been in the 1140s. Earl Hugh joined in rebel Breton attacks into western Normandy in an effort to cut the duchy in two and link up with the rebel 'Young King' and his French backers in the east, but the latter and their Flemish allies were driven back by Henry II, who relieved Louis' siege of Verneuil in August. He then speedily turned on Hugh and the Bretons, who fled in panic back to Dol across the frontier and as Henry approached surrendered. Hugh ended up as a royal captive, although the 'Young King's ally Earl Robert of Leicester (d. 1190) and his private army escaped King Henry to sail to East Anglia and there link up with the rebel Earl of Norfolk, Hugh Bigod. This combined force was then defeated by the royalists at Fornham in September 1173, and in 1174 an invasion by the rebels' ally King William of Scotland famously ended up with him being ambushed and captured in the fog as he attacked Alnwick Castle. The rebellion ended with the 'Young King' and most of his allies pardoned and restored to their lands and offices, some on payment of fines, though Queen Eleanor remained in confinement. Earl Hugh of Chester was among four senior rebels kept in custody to await the king's judgement after the Anglo-French Treaty of Montlouis formally ended the war; he was pardoned and released in 1177 and later joined the royal campaigns in Ireland. He died on 30 June 1181 at Leek in Staffordshire, aged thirty-four; he had married Beatrice de Montfort, daughter of Count Simon (d. by 1188) who owned the family's hereditary lordship at Montfort l'Amaury around thirty miles west of Paris near the Norman frontier, in 1169. Her mother was the daughter of the 1173–4 rebel Earl of Leicester and his formidable wife Petronilla, who rode into battle in the rebellion with her husband, and this connection may have helped to draw Hugh into rebellion. (This connection made Hugh brother-in-law of the future leader of the Albigensian Crusade, another Simon de Montfort, the father of the eponymous 1260s English reformer.) Hugh was succeeded by his only son, Ranulf de Blondeville, who was aged eleven in 1181 and so became a Royal ward; his other children were girls. Earl Ranulf was conspicuously loyal to his royal guardian and at the end of Henry's reign, in 1188/9, was chosen by him for the tricky role of second husband to the widowed Duchess Constance of Brittany, after her first husband, the king's disloyal son Geoffrey, was killed in a tournament in Paris. His local lands at Avranches made him a player in Breton politics and gave him troops to use to help enforce stability in the turbulent duchy, and he at times claimed to be its duke but was probably not recognised as such. He was thus stepfather to Geoffrey's and Constance's son Arthur, born after Geoffrey's death, who was genealogically next in line for the English throne after the new King Richard I in 1189–99, and spent most of his time in Richard's reign on the Continent; however he soon separated from Constance, probably at her wish, and in 1196 kidnapped her and took her back by force after she was summoned to Richard's court with Arthur and looked likely to reside there rather than in Brittany. She later managed to escape him again, and in 1199 had the marriage dissolved – probably on the grounds of her desertion. He then married the local heiress Clemence of Fougeres in south-west Normandy. Having opposed Geoffrey's next brother John's attempt to seize the throne, when Richard was captured and held to ransom by the Emperor Henry VI on his way back from the Third Crusade in 1193–4, Ranulf's position was bound to be difficult when John seized the throne from Arthur on Richard's death in April 1199 – and he appears to have opposed John's accession and fled to join his stepson at the court of John's erstwhile patron and now enemy, King Philip II Augustus of France. Arthur then launched an attempt to regain control of Brittany and seize Normandy and Anjou with Philips' help, but ended up captured by John as he besieged his grandmother Queen Eleanor at Mirabeau – and Earl Hugh's position became even more difficult when Arthur disappeared from John's custody in Rouen in spring 1203, believed to have been murdered by him. But with his English earldom as well as his Breton/Norman lands to protect, Ranulf was to prove more prudent than his father. In turn, John needed him as an ally and allowed him to retire to England as a loyal subject after the loss of Normandy to Philip's invasion in 1204; Ranulf then stayed out of major challenges to John even in 1215. His main historical significance would be his lack of a male heir, as this brought his earldom into the hands of his next sister Matilda, or Maud (1171–1233)'s, heirs and eventually into the hands of the English Crown, where it stayed. Maud also had a part to play in Scots history as the ancestress of the most serious rival claimants to the throne after the death of the child Queen Margaret of Scots, 'the Maid of Norway', in 1290. In August 1190 King Richard married her off to Earl David of Huntingdon (1145–1219), the younger brother and male heir of the sonless King William of Scots, and although she did not become Queen of Scots as William later had a son (Alexander II), she did provide the progenitors of the later dynasties of Balliol and Bruce who in turn wore that crown. Her eldest daughter Margaret (d. 1233?) married Alan, lord of Galloway, and was the grandmother of John Balliol, Edward I's choice as vassal-king of Scots in 1292–6; her third daughter, Ada, married Henry de Hastings and was ancestress of the Hastings' claims to Scotland; and her fourth daughter, Isabella (d. 1251), was mother of the Bruce claimant to Scotland in 1292 and great-grandmother of King Robert Bruce (ruled 1306–1329). Margaret was thus a crucial figure in medieval English and Scots history. Her son John 'the Scot' (1207–1237) succeeded David as Earl of Huntingdon in 1219 and succeeded the childless Ranulf as Earl of Chester in 1232, but died without children – handing the earldoms back to the Crown. Among Ranulf's and Maud's younger sisters, Hawise (1180–1243?) married Robert de Quincy and inherited the earldom of Lincoln by gift of her brother Ranulf (becoming countess when her brother died in 1232) and the major Lincolnshire castle of Bolingbroke, later birthplace of King Henry IV, built by Ranulf; Agnes was heiress of Powis Castle in North Wales, Chartley in the Peak District with its large honour, and Bugbrooke in Northamptonshire, and married William de Ferrers; and Mabel married William d'Albini (d. 1221), third Earl of Arundel and descendant of Henry I's Queen Adeliza of Louvain by her second marriage to William d'Albini. By their marriages and their children's marriages Ranulf and his sisters were thus widely active in the senior ranks of the Anglo-Scots-Norman elite, and the Marches were only a useful provider of revenue and (in times of war) troops for their families, rather than the centre of their political ambition as under the early earls of Chester. If Gwynedd finally fell to the English it would be to the king, not as a private fief of the earldom as Earl Hugh had intended in the 1080s – and it was duly made the centrepiece of the new principality given to the king's heir from 1301.

The central Marches and Powys, 1154 to 1189
Division into North and South Powys

Powys was divided on the death of Madoc ap Maredudd at Lent 1160, His eldest son and probable heir Llywelyn was killed within weeks. His other sons Gruffydd Maelor (d. 1191), Owain Fychan, and the illegitimate Owain Brogyntyn (so-called from his English estate at Pockington) took the North: Ial, Maelor Cymraeg, Maelor Sysneag, Mochnant Is Rhaeder, and Cynllaith, centred at Dinas Bran. His nephew Owain Cyfeiliog (abdicated 1195) took the South, centred on the cantrefs of Mochnant Uwch Rhaeder, Ceirinion, and Cyfeiliog, with annexed Arwystli. He had been granted Cyfeiliog by Madoc in 1149 and founded the abbey of Strata Marcella on his lands; upon his abdication he became a monk there. The cantrefs of Penllyn and Edeirnion were detached from the North by their more powerful neighbours of Gwynedd, while the South ('Powys Wenwynwyn') lost Mechain to a cadet branch. The River Rhaeadr served as the border between North and South. The weaker South was fought over between England and Gwynedd from 1240–77, but the latter was unlikely to prevail due to the greater resources available to the English Crown. Nor were its practical-minded rulers, hereditary foes of the line of Gwynedd and mindful of their earlier dispossession by Llywelyn Fawr in 1208, likely to be loyal to the latter's heirs unless through fear and calculation.

The southern Marches, 1154 to 1189. The added Irish dimension from 1169; a Marcher kingmaker turns himself into a king

The deaths of powerful local pro-Matilda dynasts such as Earl Robert of Gloucester (1147) and Earl Miles of Hereford (1143) had left their less dominant or forceful sons in charge of their lands, and the new King Henry II was able to face down those that challenged his demands for full restoration of any disputed castles or lands to himself and to attain recognition by all of his authority. Necessarily dependent on the goodwill of those magnates who backed him and his mother in his first years in England after 1149 as the disgruntled could defect to his rival Stephen, he was put in a stronger position as first his father Count Geoffrey of Anjou, who also now ruled Normandy by conquest, died in 1151 leaving his lands to Henry (who marginalised his two younger brothers whatever Count Geoffrey had intended to leave them) and then Stephen, his adult son Eustace unexpectedly dying, came to terms with Henry and accepted him as his heir in a Thames valley campaign in 1153. To add to the weight of resources in Henry's favour, he had succeeded in persuading his unreliable French overlord King Louis VII's ex-wife Duchess Eleanor of Aquitaine to marry him in May 1152 so he was now lord *de iure uxoris* of all Aquitaine and Poitou, ruling from the north-east border of Normandy at the Somme across wide swathes of northern and western France as far south as the Pyrenees. He could throw the resources of all these lands into the balance in a war against any defiant baron, and had the energy and determination to do this besides an iron will and no tolerance for defiance – from October 1154 he was master of England, too, with no likely challenger, as Stephen's prudent younger son William had been bought off with his mother's lands of Boulogne. The new king, aged twenty-one, expected to be obeyed and was likely to war on any defaulters with the same energy and ruthlessness of his grandfather Henry I, and the wiser nobles who had built up lands and fortunes at the expense of Stephen and Matilda by playing one off against the other submitted and handed over anything that the king demanded, usually including dubiously acquired castles and titles. In 1157 Henry was to insist that the new, young King Malcolm IV of Scotland handed back Cumbria and Northumberland to restore the border to the pre-1136 Solway-Cheviots line, and his reassertion of royal rights would also extend to the Marches as he sought to control Anglo-Norman barons and Welsh princes alike. Earl Roger of Hereford, son of Miles of Gloucester, was among the few nobles who were daring enough to refuse a summons to Court and object to handing over disputed lands, but was reduced to submission by a royal campaign, probably in 1155. He then conveniently died later in 1155, probably aged in his mid-thirties, and Henry proceeded to cancel the grant of the earldom made to Miles by his mother in 1141 – just when Matilda had been in no position to refuse due to her need of the lordship's troops and money. Roger's younger brother Miles was not allowed to inherit the earldom, but as he was loyal he kept the hereditary sheriffdoms of Gloucester and Herefordshire – though it is not certain that he retained them both beyond 1157/8 (Gloucs) and 1158/9 (Herefordshire). He then died on Crusade to the Holy Land in 1159 or 1160, usefully for the king without children (like Roger). He had a younger brother, Maher, who now inherited the lordship of Abergavenny and Brecon, but the latter was not allowed either of the sheriffdoms, as the king was determined to reverse the alienation of these crucial senior county administrative offices to great nobles in 1135–54 and kept them for his own men. From now on, the Marcher counties nearer England would form part of the normal shire administrative system for collecting taxes and raising troops, though the grant of legal powers to judge cases and punish offenders still remained with local lords within their own estates. Maher died within a year or so of his attendance at the royal Council of Clarendon (a major royal hunting estate near Salisbury) in 1164, and his lordships then passed on to the last of the brothers, William, who like him appears to have been unmarried. Once William also died, in a fire at the castle of Bronllys in 1166, the vast estates of the Gloucester/Hereford/Brecon family were divided up among the brothers' sisters as co-heiresses; the eldest sister, Margaret (1122/3–1197), had married Humphrey (II) de Bohun (d. 1164/5), son and successor of Humphrey (I) de Bohun, the hereditary lord of Trowbridge, in Wiltshire. Founder of Monkton Farleigh priory near Bath, Humphrey (II) had recently died, so Margaret's part of the inheritance was to pass on to their son, Humphrey (III), who was born around 1144; around 1173 the latter was to marry Earl Henry of Huntingdon's daughter Margaret of Huntingdon (1145–1201), widow of Count Conan of Brittany, who died in 1171. This brought the de Bohuns into the prestigious inner circle of royalty: Margaret of Huntingdon was sister to Earl Henry's sons, the successive Kings of Scotland Malcolm IV (ruled 1153–1165) and William the Lion (ruled 1165–1214), and to the current Earl David of Huntingdon (d. 1219). Margaret of Huntingdon's mother was a de Warenne, of the family of the earls of Surrey, so the marriage also brought the de Bohuns (a branch of whom had lands in Surrey and West Sussex, centred on Midhurst) into their orbit. Humphrey (III) de Bohun, in attendance as Constable (i.e. head of the armed forces) on Henry II and lord of Caldicot Castle (inherited from his mother's brothers) and of Trowbridge, would be one of the king's close advisers until his death in 1181; the office of constable had previously been held under Henry I, Stephen, and Matilda by Miles of Hereford, so in effect it passed hereditarily to him via his mother. He would then be succeeded in his lands and as constable by his son by Margaret of Huntingdon, Henry de Bohun (1177–1220), who finally succeeded in the famly quest of regaining the earldom of Hereford from King John in another auction of titles and offices by an insecure new king needing support in 1199. For his efforts he also acquired the heiress (Maud de Mandeville) of the earls of Essex plus her rights to that title; her father, John's Justiciar and trusted senior administrator Geoffrey FitzPeter (d. 1213), had acquired the heiress of the de Mandeville family, whose greatness as lords of parts of East

Anglia dated back to the unsavoury reign of terror launched by King Stephen's brigand-like local henchman Earl Geoffrey de Mandeville of Essex in the early 1140s.

Margaret had two younger sisters: Bertha, born around 1130, and Lucy. who married a Fitzherbert of Winchester and did not pass on any major Marcher lands. The former had married in 1150 William de Braose/Briouze (1112–1192), son of Philip de Braose, third lord of Bramber in West Sussex, and of the heiress Aenor of Totnes and Barnstaple in Devon. Her portion of the family estates – including the lordships of Radnor and Builth – duly passed to the de Braoses, who now entered Marcher politics and wars as among the first rank of its lords. Her mother Sibyl de Neufmarche's death in 1165 had already passed Sibyl's Hay Castle on the border of Herefordshire and Brecon, guarding the main road up the Wye Valley to Brecon and Builth and on to Deheubarth, to Bertha and William, and in 1174 the king finally confirmed that the lordships of Brecon/'Brecknock' (an Anglicisation of the Welsh name Brycheiniog) and Abergavenny would now pass to them, too. William became Sheriff of Herefordshire in 1174, confirming his local prominence – though only as a personal and revocable royal grant, not a hereditary right. Their elder son, William de Braose (*c.* 1152–1211), was married in the mid-late 1160s to Maud de St Valery, heiress of her father Bernard de St Valery of Hinton Waldrist in Berkshire; their ambitions and arrogance would land the de Braoses in a fatal clash with King John.

Beyond the secure part of the southern Marches, the reconstituted kingdom of Deheubarth that had been forged by Gruffydd ap Rhys and his elder sons during the distractions of the 1136–43 civil wars was at risk of reconquest, but survived Angevin and local Marcher ambitions for the moment. The youngest son of Gruffydd ap Rhys (d. 1137) and his second wife Gwenllian of Gwynedd, Rhys, was born around 1132 and started his career as commander of his brother's forces at the successful siege of Llansteffan in 1146. He took St Clears, the next castle west of Carmarthen, as his first independent command in 1153 and succeeded his brother Maredudd in 1155. Rhys ruled a kingdom of Deheubarth that held most of its old inland territories, with southern Pembrokeshire and the Loughor-Gower region the main areas remaining to the English, but was easily outmatched by the manpower available to the new king of England as of 1154, Henry II. In 1156 Rhys built Aberdyfi/Aberdovey Castle to secure his control of Ceredigion from Gwynedd, using Anglo-Norman fortification technology to his own benefit. But in 1157 he was forced to submit, as Henry followed up his semi-successful invasion of Gwynedd with a threat to sue his large and now experienced army to invade his lands, too. Like the prudent King Malcolm IV of Scots earlier that year, he obeyed a summons to the royal Court, and accepted his reduction to being prince of inland Cantref Mawr. Ceredigion was restored to its de Clare lords to confirm the legality of William II's and Henry I's grants – Earl Gilbert of Pembroke, who had had to make do with ruling that adjacent lordship from the 1136 revolt, had died in 1148, so his son by Elizabeth de Beaumont, Richard FitzGilbert (the famous 'Strongbow', later conqueror of Ireland), inherited Ceredigion/Cardigan to add to his estates and also to his troops available for his future adventures. Cantref Bychan to the south-east went to Walter Clifford (*c.* 1113–1190), lord of Clifford Castle on the Wye near Hay and son and heir to Henry I's grantee of the cantref, Richard FitzPons. Married to Margaret de Tosni, the heiress of Clifford, he was in due course to achieve the extra useful bonus of his daughter, the legendary 'Fair Rosamund' (d. 1176), as mistress to Henry II, as that ruler's relationship with his wife Eleanor of Aquitaine soured in the late 1160s. It is unclear if this affair formed a part of Eleanor's reasons for turning on her husband and aiding her elder sons Henry and Richard in their rebellion in 1173–4, but she ended up captured and imprisoned for the rest of her husband's life; Henry reputedly built a special maze and other garden works for Rosamund at his principal rural retreat of Woodstock Palace outside Oxford, and Rosamund was buried at nearby Godstow Nunnery when she died. It is unclear how much of her story is fiction and if she ever fled from Henry's advances to become a nun there, but it is virtually impossible that the legend that Eleanor had her poisoned – or did this in person, given the dates – is true.

Rhys ap Gruffydd had to abandon his royal title too in 1157, as Henry maintained his claim there was only one sovereign in Wales – himself, as overlord of English and Welsh dynasts alike. Walter Clifford now invaded Cantref Mawr too, and Rhys drove him out and proceeded to retake Llandovery and Ceredigion; Henry invaded again in 1158 to force him to return them. In 1159 he attacked Carmarthen while Henry was overseas campaigning in southern France against the duchy of Toulouse, but the king's half-uncle Earl Reginald of Cornwall, bastard of Henry I, landed with an army from Devon to relieve it and then unsuccessfully invaded Cantref Mawr with the earls of Gloucester and Pembroke and the ever-hopeful claimant Cadwaladr of Gwynedd. A further clash with the English and Rhys' capture of Llandovery during Henry's absence abroad in 1162 led to a third royal campaign early the following year, and Henry pursued Rhys into the hilly fastnesses of Pencader in Ceredigion. The king stormed his rebellious vassals' defences, and Rhys surrendered and was deported to England. He was released after doing homage to Henry at Woodstock that summer, at a special council where Henry summoned all his major mainland Celtic vassals – Rhys, Owain of Gwynedd, five of the other leading men of Wales (unnamed), and King Malcolm of Scots – to do homage and so secure his rights as their overlord. Forced to abandon his pretensions to a princely title and accept vassalage – hence his usual title, 'the Lord Rhys' – Rhys nevertheless managed to retake most of Ceredigion in 1164 in an invasion, after the local English authorities refused to do justice for the killing of his nephew and captain of the *teulu* (household) troops, his late elder brother's son Einion ap Anarawd, by the de Clares. Only Cardigan Castle held out. He regained most of the rest of inland Deheubarth when Henry was unable to suppress his next revolt in 1165 due to the priority of the king's campaign in Gwynedd, and this time retook Cardigan Castle, which he then rebuilt as his principal residence. He also took over patronage of local Strata Florida Abbey, founded earlier that century by settler Robert FitzStephen, and it became the burial-place for his dynasty. He then joined Owain of Gwynedd in his stand against the invading Henry at Corwen – the bad weather frustrated the English army's attempts to penetrate the thick forests. Henry had to retreat and Rhys remained unchallenged, but the king blinded his hostage son Maredudd in revenge. In 1167 he aided Owain Gwynedd to take Rhuddlan in a second Northern campaign, and in 1168 he marched into the upper Wye Valley to demolish Builth Castle and so discomfit the de Braoses.

The complicated affairs of Ireland now impinged on southern Marcher affairs and on the relationship between the English king and his power-hungry leading subjects there. The weak Irish 'High Kingship' had had pretensions to national leadership across the island in the manner of the English kingship in Britain for centuries, and indeed was far older than the latter. But unlike in England there was neither one emergent and dominant power among the constituent kingdoms of the island, as England was in Britain from the 910s, nor a coherent and long-lasting dynasty in permanent control of the kingship – though possibly Brian Borumha ('of the Tributes'), King of Munster, could have achieved this for his Ua Briain dynasty had he not been killed and his military power badly weakened at his great victory over his Leinster and Viking foes at Clontarf in 1014. Rather, the Irish High Kingship had used to be held exclusively by the two rival lines of the Ua Niall dynasty in the eastern Irish kingdom of Midhe, alternating rule between them, and the other four provincial kingdoms of Ireland – Munster in the south-west, Leinster in the south-east, Ulster in the north, and Connacht in the west – and their competing dynasties had traditionally been subordinate to this kingship, though often militarily its equals. Beneath them in rank were a multiplicity of minor local tribal kingdoms in each province, with no tradition of bureaucratic centralization and effective devolution to the local level, plus extreme levels of feuding and the rise and fall of rival dynasties. Though the Ua Niall had proved unable to defeat the Scandinavian Viking settlers in the ninth and tenth centuries, with Biran doing this instead, his seizure of the High Kingship for his Munster outsiders in 1002 had lapsed with his death. From then on the resurgent Ua Niall had faced claims to the kingship from Munster and in due course from a newly powerful Connacht, too, and the three kingdoms of Midhe, Munster and Connacht subsequently had waged war over the High Kingship. There was a desire in some quarters for greater stability and centralization under a more secure central kingship, as in England, and the more far-sighted high kings used the national hierarchy of the Irish Church to assist attempts at this, the Church having a nationwide hierarchy then missing in secular life or military organization, but the weight of tradition – particularly in Irish law as guarded jealously by a corps of experts, the *brehons* – in favour of keeping up the old practices was aided by the jealousy of sidelined rulers against any man who attempted to secure a new order of centralised kingship. The sheer weight of inertia, tradition, plus local resistance – backed by experienced armies – against any centraliser was too great for such attempts to succeed, until a new factor from outside with no local loyalties or concern for traditional law was to be introduced. This was now provided by an Anglo-Norman Marcher mercenary force. The expedition followed the unremarkable overthrow of the latest able and militarily successful provincial king to be considered a threat by his overlord, as King Diarmait mac Murchada of Leinster, in his mid-fifties and provincial king since he had succeeded his brother Enna in 1126, was tackled by the new 'High King', Ruadhri Ua Conchobair (Anglicised as 'Rory O'Connor'), King of Connacht in the far west since 1156. Ruadhri had recently benefited from ancient local resistance to the pretensions of the Ua Niall dynasties, whose power was centred in Midhe, to dominate Ulster as Muirchertach Mac Lochlainn, head of one of the two rival Ua Niall lines (the Cenel nEoghain who had moved from Midhe into Tir Eoghain, i.e. 'Tyrone', in western Ulster) and was 'High King', too, in 1156–66, was overthrown and killed by his mutinous vassals. This feud put the king of Connacht in charge of the 'High Kingship', but his power base was in western Ireland and his rule in the east was precarious. He then targeted his most dangerous local foe, Diarmait as king of Leinster, and in 1166 backed an invasion of Leinster by a coalition of local kings jealous of the latter – led by Tighernain Ua Ruairc (aka 'O'Rourke'), king of the Midhe sub-province of Breifne and apparently still smarting at the humiliation of Diarmait, having abducted his wife Debforguill fourteen years before. (This relationship had not lasted and he had long since had her returned; Diarmait had two current legal wives, as allowed by Irish law.) Tighernain's army expelled Diarmiat from Leinster in 1166 and he fled overseas to seek help from Henry II, who he eventually tracked down in distant Aquitaine. The English king took the opportunity to make Diarmait do homage to him, thus extending his overlordship of an ever-expanding coalition of sub-rulers from Britain to Ireland, and allowed him to recruit an army of mercenaries to get his kingdom back. The involvement of an English ruler in Ireland was virtually unprecedented, though previously assorted Scandinavian warlords ruling in the Orkneys, Hebrides and Man, plus their sporadic overlords the Kings of Norway, had intervened in Dublin and north-eastern Ireland from time to time. Jarl Sigurd, 'The Stout', of Orkney had led an army to Dublin to help the Vikings there and the then king of

Leinster revolt against Brian Borumha in 1014, and King Magnus of Norway had landed in Dublin as its new overlord with his fleet and and then invaded Ulster in 1098 and 1102–3 – on the first occasion killing the Earl of Shrewsbury in a beach-side clash in Anglesey en route. The Irish rulers of Viking Dublin had aided Earl, later King, Harold to invade England with his father Earl Godwin and secure the return of his estates and rank in 1052, and had aided Harold's illegitimate sons in an unsuccessful attack on Norman-held Devon in 1068. Now it was England's turn to intervene in Ireland, a process that would lead to seven hundred and fifty years of English rule – largely due to the ambitions and skills of the Marchers.

The de Clare earls of Pembroke were the logical choice to be approached to help Diarmait, with their estates just across the Irish Sea from Leinster and a history of trade between the ports of the two regions – and of raiding and occasionally settlement in Dyfed/Deheubarth by Vikings from Waterford and Dublin from the late ninth century right through to the 1070s. Moreover, the reconquest of Ceredigion by Owain Gwynedd's younger brother Cadwaladr and his men, and further their unsuccessful rivals the sons of Rhys ap Tewdr of Deheubarth, in the 1140s had blocked expansion by the earldom in that direction on the mainland. The restless Cadwaladr had become involved in Gwynedd politics again to try to evict his elder brother and the latter's sons, and was to die in 1172; but that had only brought Rhys ap Gruffydd of Deheubarth, a currently acceptable vassal of King Henry's, back to control Cardigan. Trying to expel him could arouse Henry's wrath; the logic of expansion for land-hungry knights and a probably bored elite in Henry's carefully controlled Wales lay towards Ireland. The current Earl *de iure* as of 1166–7 was William (born *c.* 1130), nicknamed 'Strongbow' like his father Gilbert, who had succeeded the latter in 1148 – but his title does not seem to have been accepted by the king, as it is not used in official documents and he was usually known as 'the lord of Striguil', that is, Chepstow Castle in Gwent. His family's relationships with both King Stephen and Henry II had been fraught for some years and had involved mutual mistrust since the mid-1140s, probably arising from the quarrel between Stephen and Ranulf de Gernons, Earl of Chester (brother to the wife of Earl Gilbert's elder brother, Richard de Clare) in 1146. (See previous chapter.) This had led to the deceased Richard de Clare's son Gilbert de Clare (d. 1151), Earl of Hertford and head of the English branch of the family, being offered as a hostage for Ranulf's good behaviour on the latter's release from custody; Ranulf defaulted and Stephen took his revenge by seizing Gilbert's Kent and Sussex castles, including Pevensey and probably Leeds Castle, to give to his own son Eustace in 1146–7, despite the claims to them of Gilbert's uncle the Earl of Pembroke. After Pembroke's death in 1148 his son Richard had appeared loyally at Stephen's court in the early 1150s in an attempt to mend his dynasty's reputation, but this had duly led to suspicion by Stephen's enemy and successor Henry II, who had not given Richard his father's earldom. Possibly Richard now sought to improve his reputation with the king by heading the expediton to restore Diarmait, and the extent of his demands of his new ally show that he intended to gain enough resources in a subdued Leinster to make himself so powerful that he was indispensable to the king and would have to be treated with more respect. When Diarmait visited Pembroke, probably in winter 1167–8, Richard secured an invitation to help regain his throne but insisted on receiving his daughter Aoife (born 1145) in marriage. This also explicitly made Richard the heir to and next king *de iure uxoris* of Leinster – thus disinheriting Diarmait's sons, of whom, even if only Diarmait's marriage to Aoife's mother was counted as legal, she still had a full brother, Conchobar, alive, and so was the rightful heir under both Anglo-Norman and Irish law. (He was currently a hostage of the 'High King's at Tara and was soon to be executed in revenge for the invasion, but was alive at this point.) By Irish law and tradition, Conchobar's half-brother Domnhall also had a legal claim to be heir, and after him the succession of brothers and then cousins was preferred if a king had no sons; Richard's claim to the throne was thus a bold and totally unlawful move and showed his willingness to gamble. Richard carefully waited to secure King Henry's agreement to him going before he sailed to Ireland himself in 1170, though the Pope had already permitted and encouraged Henry to invade Ireland to bring back the recalcitrant Irish Church into full obedience to Rome and its canion law via supervision of Church reform by the see of Canterbury (1155). Henry's permission for the distrusted Richard to lead the expedition had to wait until early 1170 due to the pressure of the peripatetic king's business. But it would appear unlikely that Richard had told Henry that he intended to be named as Diarmait's heir, or so leading modern historians such as W. L. Warren believe. It flew in the face of all that Henry had achieved since 1154 to have one of his barons – and one whose main lands were not easy to attack in the event of a revolt – install himself as a king in Ireland, giving the de Clares massive resources to use against him if they so minded and putting Richard on an eminence above all his other Marcher barons. In this light it would appear that Richard probably double-crossed the king by turning himself from a kingmaker into a king (if only a provincial, not 'the' King of Ireland). Henry's great-uncle William II had allowed Norman lords plus the ex-pretender to England, Edgar Atheling (briefly king in 1066 after the death of Harold Godwinson at Hastings), to install a new pro-Norman king, Edgar, in Scotland by a similar design, to use Norman arms to defeat an old-fashioned Brittonic army in 1097; but this was different. The resulting personal expedition by Henry to Ireland in 1171 was his reponse to the threat that Richard would become too powerful. Contemporary historian William of Newburgh says that Henry felt compelled to go due to the effrontery of Richard in being so successful despite the former's disapproval.

In spring 1169 Richard prepared an expedition to assist Diarmait, and on 1 May an advance force of thirty knights, sixty infantrymen and a hundred archers landed at Bannow Bay near Wexford, commanded by Richard's vassal Robert FitzStephen, the son of Princess Nest by her second marriage, to Stephen the 1130s constable of Cardigan Castle. Robert was castellan there in succession to his father, and had also had experience of the king's invasion of Gwynedd in 1157, where he commanded the unsuccessful landing on Anglesey and his half-brother Henry, Nests' son by King Henry I, was killed. He was accompanied by his half-sister Angharad's son by Gerald de Barri, William de Barri, the brother of Giraldus Cambrensis. The following day a smaller second force landed nearby, and they joined up with around five hundred men led by Diarmait to march on Wexford; the town's Scandinavian citizens repulsed the first attack and killed eighteen attackers but surrendered the next day (possibly at the intercession of two visiting bishops). Wexford was then occupied and swore allegiance to Diarmait as king of Leinster, and the town and the nearby land around Barrow Bay was given as a fief to FitzStephen and his half-brother Maurice FitzGerald, the lord of Llansteffan Castle on the lower Tywi below Carmarthen. Based at Ferns, FitzStephen then assisted Diarmait in an attack on the western Leinster border kingdom of Osraige (Ossory) around three weeks later, followed by a series of border campaigns against the northern Leinster sub-kingdoms who still backed the 'High King' Ruadhri; he also marched on Tara in an apparent attempt to depose and evict Ruadhri but the latter held out and was persuaded by Diarmait's enemy Tighernain Ua Ruairc to execute his hostages, including the attacker's son Conchobar. Probably Diarmait was hoping that his advance would cause the sub-kings he attacked to abandon the politically weak Connacht 'High King' as the latter had managed to win his throne back in 1166 by a similar rash of defections from his Ua Niall predecessor Muirchertach; if so, he failed. Irish kings had frequently used outside – that is, Viking – mercenaries to seize power before, and the latter at Dublin, Waterford and Limerick had thus survived and played off one king against another. This time, the mercenaries had an even better military weapon in the form of cavalry but got the better of their employer. Ruadhri invaded Leinster, but could not prevail against the better-armed, mailcoated Anglo-Normans with their discipline, flexible tactics, archers, and cavalry, and an indecisive war ended with the Church mediating negotiations at Ferns. The subsequent treaty saw Ruadhri accepting Diarmait's restoration as king of Leinster and the latter resuming homage to him; this would normally have ended the war but it left the main Anglo-Norman expedition still in preparation out of the equation, and Richard de Clare was determined to press on with this.

Having secured his king's evidently reluctant agreement to him going, in spring 1170 he sent Maurice FitzGerald with the next wave of invaders to Leinster to back up the small force with which FitzStephen was holding his new fiefdom around Wexford. An advance force of around a hundred men (mostly Welsh archers and with only ten knights according to Giraldus Cambrensis) landed at and fortified a peninsula at Baginbun Head, on the south-east Irish coast near the formerly Viking (and still largely ethnically Scandinavian) port town of Waterford in early May. They were led by Raymond le Gros ('The Fat') FitzGerald, son of William FitzGerald, the lord of Carew in Pembrokeshire (son of Gerald of Windsor and Princess Nest of Dehaubarth), and thus cousin of Giraldus Cambrensis. A much larger force of Leinster and Waterford Scandinavian troops attacked them, but could not storm the defences and was routed – as tradition holds by the Normans/Welsh rounding up a nearby local herd of cattle and driving them into the attackers to cause confusions. The invaders then moved on quickly to take Waterford, and Maurice arrived to join them with his troops. The emboldened Diarmait took them on to attack the currently independent port of Dublin further up the east coast, the main base of Viking settlement in Ireland since the mid-ninth century, formerly centre of the powerful Norse kingdom of the family of Ivarr 'the Boneless' (d. 873) into the mid-eleventh century and at times a subordinate vassal of Leinster. Dublin surrendered and was occupied by the Anglo-Normans, and Diarmait sent Robert FitzStephen to aid his own son-in-law the Ua Briain King of Thomond (in north-west Munster), which was on the frontier with Connacht and could thus threaten the 'High King' Ruadhri in his own home kingdom. In August 1170 Richard de Clare arrived in person in Leinster, and was married to Diarmait's daughter Aoife as promised on 29 August. On Diarmait's death at Ferns at the beginning of May 1171 he duly claimed the succession to Leinster, and sought to enforce it with his troops; the late king's younger son Domnhall was sidelined and the Anglo-Normans secured control. Richard and his Anglo-Norman allies now started taking over Irish lands as they had done in Wales – and they appeared as much of a threat to King Henry as did the Welsh lords. The king was already in political difficulties, as his failed attempt to reconcile with the fulminating exiled Archbishop Becket that year ended with the latter back in England but ignoring his promises and excommunicating his foes. The king is famously supposed to have exclaimed at the news, 'Who will rid me of this turbulent priest?', though the exact words may have been different; these differ in various versions, and the less sensationalist clerical bureaucrat John of Salisbury says that he fulminated that his men were traitors if they could not rid him of one insolent troublemaker. The result was the murder of the archbishop in his own cathedral on 28 December 1170, and with Christendom horrified and the threat of a papal excommunication, Henry needed both to buy time and to distance himself from any papal mission arriving to investigate or punish him. An expedition to Wales and Ireland in spring 1171 was thus a godsend, putting him out of the reach of the arrival of angry Church officials. He raised an army and marched into Pembrokeshire to confront his own lords, and went on to campaign in Ireland to remind his over-mighty vassals of his watchfulness and supremacy. Evicting the adventurers might have brought revolt from the disappointed men in retaliation, especially as Henry had allowed the expedition to go ahead, and it was a general and unofficial 'rule' of contemporary society that gains of land made by the sword should be kept even if the conqueror's overlord had not specifically allowed the expedition. But the king needed to reassert his supremacy and make sure that all conquests in Ireland were to be made with his authority – which would mean that as Richard de Clare was now a king, Henry should be his superior, the 'High King'.

Rhys of Deheubarth met the king en route to Pembrokeshire at Newnham on the Severn to offer his submission and support, and was guaranteed his lands in return for a rent of 300 horses and 4,000 cattle. He met Henry again en route home in 1172 at Laugharne and was excused the horses still due. Under the eventual accommodation that Rhys reached with Henry during these meetings, he ruled his lands formally as an English 'justiciar' or legal representative. He was practically independent and claimed the title of Prince of South Wales, though he never regained most of the coast. Securing control of Ceredigion from the de Clares, he managed to remove virtually all the inland English lords, such as the Cliffords of Cantref Bychan and the FitzGeralds of Emlyn. Rebuilding Cardigan Castle as his principal residence in the English style (a practice of adapting the enemy's defensive strengths copied by the Gwynedd princes at Dolwyddelan) and funding Strata Florida Abbey, he also held a prestigious eisteddfod at Cardigan Castle at Christmas 1176 to reinforce his role as the Welsh leader in the South, and used literary propaganda, viz. by his bard Gwynfardd Brycheiniog, to promote the cult of his kingdom's most famous religious figure, Dewi Sant, as the patron saint of Wales, boosting Deheubarth's prestige in the process. Arguably he, rather than any princes of the divided Gwynedd or Powys, was the pre-eminent figure in 'native' Wales from *c.* 1170 to his death in 1197.

Richard de Clare had faced a mass-scale local Irish revolt as he assumed the kingship of Leinster, with an attack launched from

Desmond in southern Munster on Waterford to the south while a Scandinavian/Irish fleet under Ascall attacked Dublin by sea. Both were driven off and Ascall was killed in a sortie from the city by the Anglo-Norman commander at Dublin, Miles de Cogan. High King Ruadhri then launched a larger attack by land at the head of a coalition of kings from across southern Ireland, including his ferocious subordinate Toirrdelbach of Breifne, Murchadh Ua Cerbhall, the King of Ossory/Osraige in eastern Munster, and Domnhall Ua Briain, the King of Munster; the danger of the Anglo-Normans dominating the Irish Sea on both coasts also brought King Rognvald mac Godfrey of the Isle of Man, who had his own ambitions to rule in Dublin as his ancestors had once done, to assist them with a fleet. Dublin was blockaded for two months or so, though the attackers kept out of reach of the superior Anglo-Norman weaponry and avoided battle in an attempt to starve them out. Richard reportedly offered to do homage to Ruadhri as his overlord if the invaders could keep all that they had gained, which would have put him in the normal position of a King of Leinster regarding the High King; but this infuriated Henry II and he was told instead that he would only be given the ports of Dublin, Waterford and Wexford – the fomer independent Viking kingdoms on the periphery of the state. He refused, and the siege went on until the lack of Irish military discipline compared to the expert Anglo-Normans proved their undoing, as the latter attacked the Irish camp up the Liffey at Castleknock by surprise and caught the enemy, short of guards, bathing in the river or eating. Hundreds were allegedly killed and the attackers secured enough supplies to hold out for much longer, and after this the disheartened Irish withdrew. Meanwhile, a similar blockade of the smaller Anglo-Norman force in less defensible Wexford under Robert FitzStephen had caused them to pull out to a stronger position at Carrick, but they were surrounded there too and starved out, unable to bring the enemy to a winnable battle, and were forced to negotiate. FitzStephen was taken as a hostage for the invaders leaving the area, and after the news of the defeat at Dublin reached the Irish they burnt Wexford and withdrew inland, taking FitzStephen as a hostage. The town was then reoccupied by the invaders. But with King Henry in Pembroke with around 500 mounted knights and several thousand infantry prepared to embark, Richard de Clare had hastened back to Pembrokeshire and made a correct gamble that the king would not go to the trouble of deposing him if he could be sure that the new King of Leinster and his lords were under his control. He offered Henry his submission and homage and formally surrendered his gains to him on the understanding that they would be granted back to him as a fief, and Henry accepted this compromise.

Henry then crossed to Ireland, his expedition taking along a large siege-train, which indicates his intention to take major towns and castles in person and 'show the flag' to both Anglo-Norman and native landholders. He landed at Waterford in October and marched in to Dublin. He met with no overt resistance, but he proceded to occupy Dublin, the major trading-port and centre of the former independent Scandinavian kingdom, and turn it into an autonomous city free from the control of Leinster or any other lordships, with its own administration subject to him. Dublin would be the administrative and military headquarters of English royal power in Ireland for the next 750 years, and Henry acquired control of the other major ports of Waterford and Wexford, too, with their own royal officials and garrisons. As 'Strongbow' now had control of Leinster, Henry proceeded to set up a new Anglo Norman ruler – only nominally a lord, not king – to rule the adjoining kingdom of Midhe and keep him in check. This policy of divide and rule saw a rival, central Marches baron, Hugh de Lacey (*c.* 1130–1186) from Herefordshire, appointed as lord of Midhe/'Meath' to keep an eye on the de Clares in Leinster. Hugh was the son and successor of Gilbert de Lacey of Ewias Lacey, the rightful lord of Ludlow Castle, who had recovered this from Stephen's nominee Joce de Dinan some time around 1150; Hugh took over his father's lands when the latter became a Templar knight around 1158 and his elder brother Robert died. First married to Rohaise of Monmouth, he had two sons, Walter (1172?–1241), who would inherit Ludlow and also Hugh's new main castle in Midhe at Trim, and Hugh (c. 1175–1242), who would later become earl of Ulster. Walter was married off to one of the daughters of the controversial William de Braose (d. 1211), lord of Brecon, and his equally formidable wife Maud of St Valery (murdered by King John in 1210). As a widower, Hugh would marry High King Raudhri's daughter Rose as his second wife in their uneasy accommodation of the mid-1170s.

Most of the junior Irish sub-kings who ruled the mini-states of central and eastern Ireland, on the next political rung down from the provincial kingdoms, prudently gave in on Henry's 1171–2 expedition rather than have their lands ravaged – reportedly fifteen of them submitted to Henry on his expedition and were confirmed in their lands as his vassals, creating a similar structure – of sub-vassals owing fealty to senior lords and them in turn owing fealty to the king – as in England. High King Ruadhri ua Conchobair held aloof, but he did not dare challenge Henry in battle after his mauling by Richard de Clare in 1170, and in 1172 he submitted to Henry's envoy Hugh de Lacey, now or soon to be made the new lord of Midhe. In the Treaty of Windsor in 1175, made by his representative the Archbishop of Tuam, he finally submitted to become Henry's loyal vassal – without abdicating his title or making it subordinate to the King of England, more as a matter of personal obligation to a more senior colleague. Ruadhri owed him fealty and paid a sum – cow-hides rather than money as they were easier to acquire in the rural Irish economy – for his kingdom as a vassal would, but in return could call on the king's men in Dublin for help if he needed it. The implication was that Henry was following a pattern set in the Marches with

the greater Welsh lords, who were allowed to keep the peace and
maintain their existing authority in their extant lands over their
own vassals provided that they paid homage to Henry – who
did not have the time or resources to occupy their lands himself.
Like Rhys ap Gruffydd of Deheubarth, Ruadhri was to survive
on a parallel plane of junior semi-autonomy to the great Anglo-
Norman lords, and could even be used against the latter should
they prove traitors. But Ruadhri (or the political and military
structure that sustained him) was too weak for this sort of role,
as minor wars and feuds among the local kings of non-occupied
Ireland continued; in particular he proved unable to secure the
peace within and obedience of the warring sub-kings of Munster.
In 1177 Henry resorted to dividing the latter up among his own
nominees, implicitly juggling one against the other to prevent
the emergence of one over-mighty Anglo-Norman lord such as
'Strongbow'. Meanwhile the king's departure from Waterford
back to England in April 1172 – to finally come to terms with
the Church over the killing of Becket –saw Hugh de Lacey put in
charge of Dublin as its commander and probably also justiciar,
i.e. supreme legal official, of Ireland. Hugh rather than the
distrusted Richard de Clare was the king's representative in and
effective 'first viceroy' of Ireland, and as such he built Trim Castle
as his headquarters and led an expedition west across Midhe to
deal with the claims of his rival as its lord, Tigerhnain Ua Ruairc,
who was resisting by force of arms. A truce saw them meeting for
discussions on the Hill of Ward, but the peace talks went wrong
and ended up with someone throwing a lance at Hugh, killing
an interpreter, and the Anglo-Normans attacking and beheading
Tighernain. His head was then taken off as a trophy and put up
on the gate of Dublin, the normal such fate for traitors – and it
is possible that the alleged 'unprovoked attack' on the Anglo-
Normans was the 'cover-up' for a targeted killing of their most
dangerous local foe. Midhe was now subdued, but the priorities
of the revolt by Henry's sons saw Hugh halt the attack while he

took troops off to Normandy to aid his king in 1173, and he was in command at Verneuil near the French frontier later that year as the king's treacherous eldest son, Henry the Young King, and Louis VII invaded. He later returned to Midhe as governor of Ireland again, but only in 1177, and then supervised the attack on Munster that year which Henry decided on – presumably under pressure by land-hungry barons backed by Hugh to let them off the leash, but also in apparent irritation at the continuing clashes between Anglo-Normans and Irish which High King Ruadhri was unable or unwilling to control. Already John de Courcy, a minor Somerset lord intent on building up his own principality to rival Richard de Clare and Hugh Lacey, had invaded southern Ulster without royal permission and taken Downpatrick earlier in 1177, but he had been repulsed by the local kings. Now Henry granted the 1169 commander Robert FitzStephen, ransomed from his 1172 captors the McCarthys in Munster and with useful local knowledge of the region from his time as a hostage, and his half-sister Gwladys de Barri's son Miles Cogan (1171–2 commander in Dublin) to take over Munster from Lismore to the sea, with the exception of the lucrative port-town of Cork, which was reserved to the king. The invasion of Munster followed and the land was divided up among various feudal fiefs; but the western and north-western areas in particular held out, with the rugged terrain helping guerrillas, and the new regime was precarious and often ended up with its isolated castles under siege. A major revolt in Desmond, southern Munster, in 1182 led to de Cogan being killed and the demoralised FitzStephen having to call in new warriors with a promise of fiefs, among whom was his half-sister Angharad's eldest son by William de Barri, Philip (*c.* 1140–1200), who was to found the extensive Barry dynasty in Ireland. Philip's brother Robert was already in the invading army as of 1169–70; now he and his recruits came to help FitzStephen, and Philip and his cousin Raymond 'le Gros' FitzGerald made sure to secure their claim as the childless FitzStephen's heir to to the three cantreds of Olethan (i.e. the Irish tribal kingdom of 'Ui Liathain'), Muschiri-on-Durnegan ('Musk Donegan', later known as Orrery and Kilmore), and Killyde (Killede) from their current lord, his cousin Ralph FitzStephen. Philip set up a new and long-lasting lordship there, and was temporarily accompanied by his brother Giraldus Cambrensis, the cleric and chronicler. The attempt by Philip de Braose, uncle of the current family head and lord of Brecon, William de Braose (d. 1211), to secure control of the north-west Munster sub-kingdom of Thomond, homeland of the Ui Briains, after a royal grant of it in 1172 was however a disaster, and he appears to have lost his nerve in the face of major local resistance and fled back east, never cementing control there. The new Anglo-Norman lords in Munster eventually had to make do with seven of the twenty-one lordships of the kingdom, bunched together near Cork, and allowed the native dynasts to continue to hold the others in a precarious documented division of the kingdom. Robert FitzStephen appears to have left his Munster domain after the 1182 rebellion and his handover of his lands to his nephews and returned east; he probably died in 1183. The new strongman of Munster, with his initial lands centred on the seized sub-kingdom of Thomond in the north, was to be Theobald Butler, hereditary Chief Butler of England after his father and brother of the royal administrator (and later Archbishop of Canterbury) Hubert Walter, who not coincidentally was the nephew of the king's justiciar Ranulf de Glanville. He secured a post on the expedition that accompanied Prince John to Ireland in April 1185 and there acquired the lands of Thomond, founding the Butler dynasties, later earls of Desmond and Kildare.

The new lord of Ireland was now technically the king's youngest son John (born December 1166), unprovided-for in the division of his father's lands and so nicknamed 'Lackland', but he did not arrive in Ireland until 1185 and so Hugh continued in command until he was recalled in the early 1180s for his unlicensed second marriage to High King Ruadhri's daughter Rose. He was able to return to Ireland later as just lord of Midhe, and in that capacity was assassinated in July 1186 while supervising the building of a new castle at Durrow; he was buried at the nearby abbey. Richard de Clare died naturally, on 20 April 1176, and was succeeded by his underage son Gilbert as earl of Pembroke but not as king of Leinster; the King of England was to be the only ruler of the Anglo-Normans with royal rank. Henry now took command of the earldom and its Irish lands as feudal overlord to Gilbert, who became a Royal ward, and continued this role when Gilbert died young in 1185 and was succeeded by his sister Isabel de Clare, Countess of Pembroke.

Back in South Wales, the main threat to the peace in the final years of King Henry's reign arose from the break-up of the dynastic unity of Deheubarth. Rhys of Dehaubarth had a large and turbulent family, and faced feuding among his numerous sons in his later years. Married to Gwenllian, daughter of Madoc ap Maredudd (d. 1160) of Powys, the promiscuous warlord had at least four legitimate sons plus up to thirteen other children by at least five mistresses – and Welsh law favoured an equal claim for all, not the Norman system of male primogeniture. One daughter, Gwenllian, married Ednyfed Vychan (d. 1246), the famous steward and senior counsellor of Llywelyn ap Iorweth in Gwynedd from 1215–46; their descendants were the Tudor dynasty, and via this link Henry VII claimed the inheritance of Deheubarth (and used its heraldic arms) in his invasion of 1485. As a patron of international developments in monasticism, the outward-looking Rhys patronised not only the Cistercians (at Whitland) but the new Premonstratensian Order from France, giving them their first monastery in Wales at Tallylychau; but his confiscations of the endowments of older local Welsh houses (*clasau*) to fund these ventures damaged them and emulated the actions of rapacious Marcher barons. Rhys' shrewd judgement and determination to keep the peace with Henry, who had other preoccupations with his treacherous sons and with kings Louis VII (to 1180) and Philip Augustus of France, delivered stability and peace for most of the 1170s and 1180s. He had assessed that his best chances of fending off conquest by the Marchers lay in being a loyal vassal of the king, who had more reason to mistrust his over-mighty baronial rivals provided that he stayed loyal, and he kept to this policy without chancing his arm by meddling with the feuding in Henry's turbulent family. His good relationship with the English monarchy continued, with Henry returning his hostage son Hywel (known as Sais, 'the Englishman', from his adoption of English manners) after long captivity. He aided Henry against the king's rebel sons in 1173–4 and took his army to Tutbury Castle, in Derbyshire, to besiege rebels, helping to contain that Peak District rebel base so its lords could not aid the Earl of Huntingdon's (King William of Scotland's brother David) and Earl Robert of Leicester's men to the south-east to link up with the Bigods in East Anglia, and he sent a further thousand men to aid the king in Normandy. In 1175 he led a group of his South Welsh vassals (of Senghenydd, Breichiniog, upland Gwent, Elfael, Gwerthynion/ Builth, and Afan) to the royal court at Gloucester to do homage (29 June) after Henry had suppressed the rebellion, thus acting as the royal lynchpin for the restored hierarchical order of feudal vassalship in South Wales and guaranteeing his junior allies' loyalty. In 1177 he attended Court at Oxford and was granted part of Meirionydd as a counter-weight to the currently loyal but implicitly revanchist dynasty of Gwynedd to his north. Gwynedd was currently distracted by wars among Owain Gwynedd's sons, with the more pro-English Dafydd further away from this region in the North-East; the local princes of that dynasty, the sons of Cynan ap Owain, were still defying the king, so bringing him into the region to put them under pressure. They attacked his lands in reprisal, and Rhys proceeded to marry a daughter to their uncle and rival Rhodri, lord of Arfon and Lleyn, to ally wth the latter against them. But he still hankered after his dynasty's pre-1090s lands in the far east of Deheubarth, which now lay under Anglo-Norman baronial control with the de Braoses ruling the Builth region with the upper Wye; he rebuilt Rhayader Castle in the upper Wye Valley to boost his power there and threaten them (1177). In 1184 he journeyed to Worcester to sort out Anglo-Welsh tension on the border, after the local Welsh lords in Gwent had murdered Ranulf le Poer, Sheriff of Herefordshire, in a long-running feud that Henry's justiciar Ranulf de Glanville had to deal with. Glanville made a reciprocal visit to Deheubarth to deal with disputes between Rhys and the people of Herefordshire and Cheshire (a sign of the extent of Rhys' reach) in 1186. In 1188 he acted as an enthusiastic host as Archbishop Baldwin of Canterbury toured South, then West, and finally North Wales to raise recruits for the Third Crusade, meeting him at Radnor. Baldwin's assistant was the ubiquitous clerical historian Giraldus Cambrensis, who accompanied and wrote up the tour and so gives us a window into the Welsh world of 1188.

The 'Lordship of Glamorgan' had descended from Earl Robert (d. 1147) to his son William (d. 23 November 1183), who married Hawise de Beaumont but had only daughters and their husbands. The lordship's vassals included some technically dependent Welsh principalities in the northern Welsh part of Glamorgan through the twelfth century into the thirteenth – most notably Afan, ruled by Iestyn ap Gwrgan's descendants, and Senghenydd. Ifor Bach, lord of Senghenydd in the 1150s and 1160s, was most famous for kidnapping Earl William of Gloucester and his wife and children from Cardiff Castle in 1158 after the earl seized some land and refused to return it. Scaling the walls at night with a party of his men, he kidnapped the earl and his family from their beds and carried them off into the remote forests inland around Machen. He then kept them until the lands had been restored. His son Gruffydd had succeeded to Senghenydd by June 1175, when he accompanied Rhys ap Gruffydd of Deheubarth to Gloucester to do homage to

Henry II. He died in 1210 and was succeeded by his son Rhys (d. 1156); a younger son, Gruffydd Bychan, lived at Leckwith, west of Cardiff, presumably inheriting the family's lands in the Vale of Glamorgan, and married the heiress of Roger de Sturmi, the Norman lord of Stormy (i.e. de Sturmi) Down near Bridgend. The de Sturmis, one of the lower ranks of Marcher lords, had originally come from Somerset; a junior branch of their family duly went on in the thirteenth century to settle in northern Munster in Ireland, acquiring lands in Eile Ua Cearbhall ('Ely O'Carroll'), east of Limerick.

Iestyn's sons Caradog and Gruffydd were princes of Afan in the mid-twelth century, ruling the Llynfi Valley inland from Bridgend and the Afan Valley inland of what is now Port Talbot. They were succeeded by the former's son Morgan, known as Arglwydd ('the Lord'), who died around 1208; Morgan was succeeded by his sons Lleision and Morgan Gam. The latter was also lord of the borough and estate of Newcastle at Bridgend (encompassing the valley south-east of Afan), and died in 1241. He passed Afan to his son Morgan Fychan (d. 1288), and left the castle and lordship of Newcastle at Bridgend (on the west bank of the Ogwr below its confluence with the Llynfi), which extended west to the border with the estates of the new Margam Abbey, to his daughter Matilda, who married into the local Marcher dynasty of Turberville. They were the lords of Coity Castle (the next lordship to the east of the River Ogwr) from the time that the first Payn de Turberville, nicknamed 'the Devious', is said to have arrived in Glamogman *c.* 1120 and married Sara, daughter and heiress of the Welsh lord Morgan of Coety. He is referred to in charters of 1126 and 1127. His elder son Simon de Turberville was lord of the new town of Bridgend on the east bank of the River Ogwr where it carves its way through a ridge of hills several miles inland of the sea, the lordship of Afan owning the land on the west bank; he is said to have fouded the Old Castle of Bridgend (since disappeared) on this bank by the extant church of Oldcastle. He was succeeded by his younger brother Gilbert Turberville (d. 1140s) who made grants to the nearby new priory at Ewenny; his son was Payn (II), who died in 1207. Payn's son Gilbert (II) joined in the Welsh revolt of 1216, and married Morgan Gam's daughter Matilda, heiress of Newcastle on the west bank of the Ogwr and of Landymor in Gower. Their son was Gilbert (III) de Turberville, who died around 1277, and their grandson was Sir Richard (d. 1283/5). Morgan Fychan's son was Lleision, lord of Afan, who died in 1308; his son John d'Avene sold up the Afan estate around 1350. The dynastic descent from Iestyn also continued via the family of John's uncle Rhys, owner of Baglan east of Swansea where Archbishop Baldwin and his entourage had memorably had a perilous crossing of the tidal estuary of the River Neath on the Crusade recruiting tour of 1188.

The final remnant of the pre-Conquest kingdom of Glamorgan in the lowlands was the lordship of Caerleon, held in the mid-twelfth century by Morgan son of Owain (d. 1158), son of the 1060s South Wales dynast Caradog ap Gruuffydd. His brother Iorweth had killed Richard de Clare, lord of Ceredigion, in an ambush at Grwyne Fawr near Abergavenny during the great revolt of 1136. Morgan reconquered upper Gwent from the Anglo-Norman settlers in the late 1130s, and succeeded Morgan as lord of the Usk Valley. In 1171 his foe Rhys ap Gruffydd persuaded Henry II, en route for Ireland, to join him in besieging Caerleon and evicting Iorweth, who had to retreat to Machen but returned in July 1173 to besiege and retake his principal fortress. He was deprived of Caerleon again by the king in 1175 after his ruthless son Hywel blinded and castrated his uncle Owain Pen-Carn in a presumed fight over the succession, but regained it later by coming to terms with Rhys – probably due to his daughter Nest's affair with that ruler. He died before 1184 and Hywel succeeded him; in that year Hywel was castellan of Newcastle, Bridgend. The other major Welsh ruler of the district was Seissyl ap Dyfnwal, lord of Gwent Uwch Coed ('above the wood', i.e.

north of the Wentwood forested ridge that stretched across mid-Gwent) and resident at Castell Arnallt ('Castle Arnold' to the English) at modern Llanover near Abergavenny. The lordship of the latter had been held early that century by Hamelin de Ballen, and Seissyl may have been the son of Hamelin's daughter Joyce and so had a claim on the lands – at least by Welsh law – that had been circumvented when the husband of Hamelin's niece, the Norman/Breton lord Brian FitzCount, inherited Abergavenny instead. Whether this fuelled a grudge by Seissyl and his Welsh neighbours or whether this threat was believed by the new lords of Abergavenny, Seissyl was supposed to have been involved in the death of a subsequent owner of the castle and lordship, Henry FitzMiles, the third son of Earl Miles of Hereford (d. 1143), around 1160 to 1165. Henry's sister Bertha of Hereford then brought the Abergavenny lands and castle to her son by William de Braose (d. 1179), lord of Brecon and Radnor, who together with their son William (c. 1150–1211) was a mortal foe of Seissyl. A subsequent notorious incident saw the younger William invite his uncle's presumed murderer Seissyl and his elder son Geoffrey, along with a number of neighbouring Welsh landowners, to a supposedly peaceful banquet at Abergavenny Castle at Christmas 1177 to discuss better relations and resolving disputes – and then slaughter them. Some of the murderers then rode swiftly to Seissyl's home at Castell Arallt to kill his younger son Cadwaladr, too, wiping out the dynasty, and confiscated its lands and those of its murdered neighbours. The episode left a stain on the family reputation of de Braose and was long remembered by the Welsh, but despite evident concern at the royal court at this blatant and potentially rebellion-causing episode, the elder de Braose merely lost some official positions and grants of estates. The younger de Braose was usually assumed to be the main culprit. No compensation was offered to the victims' families, though the adjacent Welsh dynasts of Caerleon did carry out a degree of vigilante justice by burning Abergavenny and wrecking de

Braose-held Dingestow Castle in 1182. The normally moralist and half-Welsh clerical historian Giraldus Cambrensis, who did not hesitate to criticise even Angevin princes, indeed defended the reputation of the younger de Braose, who had personally killed Seissyl's younger son even if he had not personally taken the lead in the banquet massacre, and praised his and his wife's piety and gifts to the Church. The younger de Braose went on to become a trusty of King Richard, was his sheriff of Herefordshire in 1192–9, avoided any involvement in Prince John's plots, and was with Richard when the king was mortally wounded besieging Chalus Castle in Poitou in 1199. The tactic of clearing inconvenient Welsh claimants to lands out of the way by murder was to be repeated later on by the Mortimers against the royal house of Powys, and although it was rare was notably mostly used by members of the the more successful (i.e. ruthless) Marcher dynasties.

5

THE GREATEST KNIGHT AND HIS SONS, 1189–1235

The greatest Marcher dynasts threaten to overshadow the king; William Marshal's rise from landless junior knight to Earl of Pembroke and right-hand man to Richard I; the reign of King John and his most notorious crimes; the Marcher barons go to war with John; Marshal saves the throne, but overshadows young Henry III; the rise of Llywelyn 'Fawr'.

The rise of William Marshal

Richard de Clare, Earl of Pembroke and now lord/King of Leinster as of 1171, died in July 1176; his and his Leinster wife Princess Aoife's son Gilbert succeeded to the earldom and other lordships but was not recognised as King of Leinster by Henry II. A Royal ward with his lands administered by the king's men, he died in 1185; his sister Isabella (*c.* 1172–1220) succeeded but was also under royal control as a female heiress and underage Royal ward. On 6 July 1189 the king's death brought Richard the Lionheart, currently Duke of Aquitaine but at war with his father, to the throne in the unpropitious circumstances of Richard having joined Henry's foe King Philip of France in rebellion. The two were endeavouring to coerce Henry into handing over more territory to Richard by an attack on his homeland, Anjou, and Maine, and abandon potential plans to divide up the Angevin empire with Richard's surviving younger brother John. Henry died shortly after the two rebels had defeated him, driving him out of Le Mans in Maine, and had forced him to accept Richard as his sole heir – indeed Henry had been threatening Richard with his revenge and hinting at disinheritance when he died suddenly. Richard secured the throne and all of the Angevin dominions, and the earldom of Pembroke was granted to his choice of husband for Isabella, William Marshal (*c.* 1146–1219), paragon of contemporary chivalry and reputedly a model for Chretien de Troyes' Arthurian creation Sir Lancelot. Marshal, indeed, had come within an ace of killing his new sovereign only a few days before his accession, as he was in Henry's army in the civil war in Maine, and while fighting a rearguard action to protect the king's retreat from burning Le Mans clashed with Richard and chivalrously avoided injuring or killing him as he had the better of the single combat. Richard did not bear grudges, in contrast to John, and as of July 1189 he added a valiant and clear-headed warrior to protect both the earldom of Pembroke and its Irish lands from attack as he headed off on the imminent Third Crusade. Marshal – so-called because he was the son and heir of the hereditary royal 'marshal' at the court – had had a turbulent career and was very much a self-made man as one of the knightly elite. His reputation and acheivements were indeed such that he was to have the distinction of a very rare non-royal or clerical contemporary biography, in the form of a verse 'Life' compiled soon after his death, the 'Historie de Guillaume le Marechal', which was based on a docmentary account by his squire. He had commenced his colourful career in English politics and warfare as a boy in the 1136–54 civil war, when his father John FitzGilbert, the 'Marshal', an adherent of Empress Matilda, held the castles of Ludgershall, Devizes and Newbury in northern Wiltshire for her as a lynchpin of her cause, and lost an eye in the rearguard action protecting her as she fled from the siege of Winchester in 1141. John was besieged in his Newbury castle by King Stephen in 1152, and William had by this point fallen into the king's hands as a hostage. As the castle held out, the king had William paraded in front of the walls and threatened to throw him over them from a trebuchet, but John was not intimidated: the 'Histoire' recounts that he jeered at the King that he was still virile enough to produce more sons and did not care what happened to this one. Rather than carrying out his threat, Stephen honourably backed down and ended up playing with William instead – but held onto him as a hostage until his peace treaty with his challenger Henry (II) late in 1153. As a teenager William, a younger son with his elder brother due to become marshal and inherit the family lands, was trained as a squire and future knight in Normandy, but lacked land or money. He made his name instead as a participant and increasingly a victor in chivalric tournaments, where the ability to hold your nerve on horseback in a one-to-one charge against an opponent and knock them off their horses with a lance was vital. A favourite of Queen Eleanor of Aquitaine (hereditary ruler of Aquitaine and Poitou from 1137–1204) and later with her eldest son the 'Young King' Henry, his first memorable appearance at a serious clash as a combatant was when his uncle and patron, Earl Patrick of Salisbury, was escourting Eleanor across her southern French dominions in 1168 and an attempt was made to attack, and probably to kidnap, her by one of her restless feudal vassals, Guy of Lusignan. This hot-headed and rash younger son of the lord of Lusignan in Poitou was later to go out to the Kingdom of Jerusalem to marry its heiress Sibylla, sister of the 'Leper King' Baldwin IV, succeed her son by her first husband as king *de iure uxoris* in 1186, and thanks to his strategic ineptitude lose the Battle of Hattin, most of his army, and the True Cross to Saladin. The fall of Jerusalem and the Third Crusade followed as a result of his spectacular incompetence, and even King Richard of England could not get more than half his lands back; recognising him as a potential disaster as king and unwanted by most of his nobles, Richard successfully offered him the rule of Cyprus instead (1192). Now Guy started his disastrous career by a bungled attack on Eleanor, and although he failed to capture her, William Marshal and others of her bodyguard were injured and captured protecting her as she escaped, and Earl Patrick was killed (probably by mistake as he would have been worth far more as a hostage). After the incident the attacker claimed that they had been the ones ambushed, but William helped to disprove this with his testimony and said his uncle the earl had been stabbed in the back while unarmed; he himself was reputedly dragged away through the woods in too great haste for anyone to bother to treat his injuries, and regarded the Poitevins as thuggish brigands ever afterwards. After his ransoming William was increasingly prominent as a favourite of Eleanor and her eldest son, though still landless and poor, and it is possible that his close relationship with the queen and the incident of his capture whilst protecting her contributed to the story of the adulterous Queen Guinevere and her rescuer and lover Sir Lancelot in the contemporary story of 'Le Chevalier de la Charette' ('The Knight of the Cart') by the great Arthurian poet Chretien de Troyes. He was regarded highly enough by Henry II to be appointed as tutor in knightly pursuits and chivalric values to the king's eldest son and heir, Henry the 'Young King', around 1180, but was sent packing by the latter in 1182 after rumours of his relationship with the boorish, reckless, and spoilt, if charming, prince's wife Margaret, sister of King Philip of France. He denied the claim, but the prince was too weak to stand up to his cronies despite the rumour being seen as unlikely. When the 'Young King' was in the throes of a failing revolt against his father over the latter's supposed partiality for his next brother Richard, Duke of Aquitaine, in 1183, their younger brother Geoffrey vainly advised him to summon William back as the one man who could save his cause, which testifies to the still-junior knight's reputation.

William Marshal was summoned to attend on Henry II in the 1188–9 wars with King Philip of France, in which the distrustful presumed heir to the English throne plus Normandy and Anjou/ Maine, Duke Richard of Aquitaine (who had succeeded the original planned heir, the 'Young King', when the latter died during his revolt in June 1183), backed the invader. Philip and Richard were suspected of trying to drive the king out of some or all of his Continental lands, and William was sent to fight for the king in Chateauroux (in south-west Anjou) and promised its heiress, Dionysia, as bait. This match did not take place, and William was apparently later offered the hand of Countess Isabel of Pembroke, a Royal ward whose hand was in the king's gift, by the king. The latter died before this could be arranged; William was in attendance at the king's deathbed at Chinon on 6 July 1189 during an embarrassing revolt by Richard and was the man who sent a messenger to the latter to tell him he was now king. As executor of the royal will, William was at Fontevrault Abbey (the Angevin dynastic mausoleum) to organise the funeral when Richard arrived. The 'Histoire de Guillaume le Marechal' says that William was alarmed at Richard's arrival lest he be arrested for nearly killing Richard in their recent battlefield encounter, but the new king assured him, 'You are pardoned, I bear you no malice', and they were reconciled. Richard now took over the Royal wards on his accession, and immediately confirmed the arrangement to marry William to Isabel de Clare. They were married in August 1189, with the 'Histoire' saying that as soon as he had permission William rushed from the king's side to Dieppe to take a boat to London and hurry to the Tower of London, where Isabel and other high-status wards and hostages were kept by Henry II. William was around twenty-five years older than his wife; they had five sons (who all succeeded to the Pembroke title and died without children in turn) and two daughters. The other major royal marital arrangements concerning Royal wards as heiresses that involved the Marches saw Prince John married off at Marlborough Castle on 28 August 1189 to the bride his father had promised him in 1176, Isabella of Gloucester, daughter and successor of the late Earl William (d. November 1183), son of Earl Robert, who was her bridgeroom's cousin, which could be used later to claim that the marriage broke Church canon law. As well as holding the earldom and its lordship of Glamorgan plus Newport Castle, Isabella was the owner of Bristol with its strategically important castle on the River Avon, the former stronghold of Earl Robert in the 1136–54 civil war. To this domain Richard added extra lands and castles for John – the counties of Derby and Nottingham and later on Devon, Cornwall, Somerset, and Dorset, and the castles of Tickhill and

Peverel in Derbyshire, Wallingford, Ludgershall in Wiltshire, and Lancaster. All this was unfortunately to be the launch pad for John's revolts in 1191 and 1193–4, but a less generous gift would have been likely to arouse even earlier plots, and John was required to reside in France while Richard was on Crusade. But John and Isabella had no children, and though John was able to retain her lands for the duration of the marriage, this ended when he came to the throne and divorced her – thus preventing the Crown swallowing up the earldom of Gloucester and lordship of Glamorgan. This marriage of cousins proceeded without waiting to gain official papal dispensation for its breach of canon law, a cumbersome and probably expensive process for which the impatient Richard had no time as he prepared for the Crusade and sorted out his arrangements for the governance of his kingdom in his absence, and due to this oversight the infuriated Church, led by Archbishop Baldwin of Canterbury, duly put an interdict on John's and Isabella's lands (i.e. requiring all Church services to cease, which meant no legal baptisms, marriages, or funerals, and the serious implication of unblessed sinners going to Hell). This was later lifted by negotiations with Pope Clement III when Baldwin had left on Crusade and John's political goodwill was needed by the majority of the nation's senior clerics in combating the aggressive and unpopular regent Bishop Longchamp of Ely, but the couple were banned from having sexual relations so some uncertainty over its legality remained.

William Marshal's new lands in July 1189 included not only the earldom of Pembroke, including the eponymous castle plus others such as Narbeth and Haverfordwest, and the 'honour' of Chepstow/'Striguil' and substantial parts of Leinster in Ireland but possessions in Normandy too – possessions for defending which he showed more concern for than Ireland in the turbulent early years of King John's reign after 1199. William rebuilt Pembroke Castle in its current form and also did extensive work at Chepstow Castle, but was not granted the title of Earl of Pembroke or all of its lands by Richard, and he had to wait until the accession of King John. Early in his marriage he and his wife went to Ireland, where they set up their base at Ross (formerly a Leinster royal estate of Isabel's grandfather) and bult the new castle, plus founding the adjoining town borough of New Ross. He later built Carlow Castle, too, around 1210. He was left behind in England as Richard went on Crusade in 1190 and was one of the nobles who resented the greed and arrogance of the regent, Bishop William Longchamp of Ely, so much that they joined in a revolt to depose him led by the ambitious and unscrupulous Prince John (now a Marcher lord as Earl of Glamorgan *de iure uxoris*) in 1191. However, when John went further and used the opportunity offered by Richard's illegal capture and imprisonment by the Duke of Austria en route home from the Crusade to revolt, claiming the Crown, William backed the loyalists led by Queen Eleanor, though his brother John the Marshal was fighting for John. He duly helped to besiege Prince John's castles and raise Richard's ransom, and when Richard returned in summer 1194 joined him to firstly reduce the surviving rebel castles, principally Nottingham, and then to reconquer lands in Normandy that King Philip of France had seized. His elder brother the 'Marshal' had been killed (without a son to inherit) in John's service during the 1193–4 rebellion, which helped his relations with the latter, and both Richard and John confirmed his resultant inheritance of the title and duties of marshal plus the Marlborough Castle estates.

King John: An increasingly fractured elite and a distrusted, vengeful king

On John's accession when Richard was fatally wounded during a minor siege in Poitou in April 1199 William backed him to be King rather than John's late elder brother Geoffrey's under-age son Duke Arthur of Brittany, in contrast to the other major Marcher magnate Earl Ranulf of Chester, and he was a stalwart of John's occasionally brilliant and frequently erratic defence of Normandy in 1199–1204. The disappearance and probable murder of Arthur at John's hands shifted local opinion against him and aided Philip of France's conquest in 1203–4, and barons like William who had extensive lands in Normandy faced a dilemma: if they were to hold onto these lands they would have to do homage to their new lord, King Philip, but he was at war with John so that might easily be interpreted as treason by the latter. Some shrewd and large families duly made arrangements for one branch to hold their English lands and another branch to hold their French lands so that nobody had to hold lands simultaneously from two hostile kings and thus face confiscation by one of them; but William did not have that luxury. Instead John initially allowed him to do homage to King Philip but retain his English/Welsh/Irish lands too as a rare sign of royal trust. However Philip subsequently insisted that oaths to him had to be exclusive and could not be hedged around by other oaths to his rival sovereign and William duly swore fealty to him on those terms and faced royal suspicion. His power and effective autonomy as a lord in Ireland also involved him in a dispute with the increasingly assertive new royal justiciar there, Meiler FitzHenry – the son of Henry I's son by Princess Nest of Deheubarth, Henry, who had been killed in 1158, and so both a royal relative and a cousin of the FitzGeralds and the de Barrys. Meiler was also a Marcher lord himself, as lord of Narbeth and the cantref of Pebidiog in Pembrokeshire. Meiler was seeking to rein in semi-autonomous lords in the English-ruled areas of Ireland at the centralising John's request, and had already clashed with John de Courcy the conqueror of Ulster – who was evicted and replaced as Earl and governor of Ulster in 1205 by another major Marcher lord, Hugh (II) de Lacey (*c.* 1175–1242). Younger son of Hugh de Lacey, the lord of Ludlow in Shropshire and of Midhe/Meath in Ireland (1172), Hugh (II) was the younger brother of Walter de Lacey (1172?–1241), who currently held those combined lordships and was thus the second largest ruler of combined lands in the Marches and Ireland after William. Another subject of distrust and attempted dispossession by King John was Richard de Burgh, the new Anglo-Norman lord of

Thomond in north-west Munster and of adjacent Limerick, who was now seeking to takeover Connacht to his north and could thus become as powerful as 'Strongbow' had in Leinster and de Courcy had in Ulster. But the great lords in Ireland had the advantage of distance from potential royal attack, or even from an expedition sent from Dublin, where Meiler was building the first Dublin Castle from 1204, provided that their sub-vassals remained loyal – and both de Burgh and William Marshal now stood up to Meiler and resisted his attempts to curb their power. William's nephew John was currently marshal in Ireland, and backed the king and FitzHenry against his uncle in their disputes in 1207–8 – perhaps hoping for some of his lands? In 1207 William left the king's court for his lands in Leinster as his relations with the wary John deteriorated, his retention of Norman lands now posing the possibility in the king's mind that he would back King Philip in case of war to keep these, and William and his vassals subsequently resisted orders from Meiler to hand over the north-western border territory of future County Offaly to new royal appointees. The local Anglo-Norman vassals there sent in a protest to the Dublin authorities, which was ignored as insolence, and a confrontation ensued that William had to sort out by returning to England to negotiate a compromise with the king. FitzHenry was also summoned to court but left his subordinates with orders to attack William's lands while the latter was in England so the facts on the ground would be altered to his benefit. New Ross was burnt by the justiciar's troops, but Countess Isabel and her vassals fought off the attackers. A settlement was duly reached, with the king needing William's goodwill and eventually returning Offaly to him, and FitzHenry was soon replaced as justiciar; but the Marshals were under suspicion again in 1210–11 as John fought their Marcher and Irish neighbours the de Braoses.

In Gwynedd stability was soon to break down again, and after a brief period of chaos was to lead to the re-emergence of a state stronger than it had been since before the Norman Conquest. With the majority of the rulers of Middle and South Wales forced to accept Gwynedd's ovelordship or accepting it voluntarily to win aid against the Marchers, this posed a new threat to the latter. The English Crown was preoccupied with Richard I's Crusade, captivity and ransom, and campaigns to defend Normandy in 1189–99, and then his disputed successor John faced the threat of his nephew Arthur plus the latter's supporter King Philip Augustus of France in 1199–1202, then Philip's conquest of Normandy, Maine and Anjou in 1202–4, and then John's attempt to reconquer the lost lands and dispute with the papacy after 1204. (This also involved the Earl of Chester Ranulf de Blondeville, principal Northern Marches dynast, in the Normandy crisis as he was Arthur's stepfather and backer, so he was mostly absent from Chester.) The Crown could not help the Marchers resist Gwynedd until John had restored a degree of stability and turned to Welsh affairs in 1210, and after John's temporary success in reducing Gwynedd to vassal status again in 1210, John was to be disracted again by an invasion threat in 1213, an attempt to use his Continental allies to retrieve Normandy by invading France in 1215, and the Magna Carta crisis and rebellion in 1215–16. Would both the Marchers and the mid- and southern Welsh princes be forced to realign themselves to a – temporary – accommodation with and loss of lands to Gwynedd?

The main victor of the 1170s civil wars in Gwynedd, Dafydd ap Owain (ruled 1170–1194), had married Henry II's half-sister Emma de Laval, which also gave him a link to her full brother Hamelin Plantagenet (*c.* 1140–1203), bastard son of Henry's father Geoffrey of Anjou and husband of the heiress of the de Warenne family (earls of Surrey), Isabella, Countess of Surrey (*c.* 1142–1203). Widow of King Stephen's younger son Count William of Boulogne (d. 1158), Isabella was the daughter of the Norman baron William 'Talvas', son of the disgraced ex-Marcher lord Robert de Belleme, Earl of Shrewsbury. The link placed David within the extended royal family of the Plantagenets and helped to bring him in the circle of trusty senior royal vassals, and as a royal ally he had a grant of lands in England, too. He even temporarily deposed his brother and co-ruler Rhodri, ruler of Arfon, Lleyn, and Anglesey (i.e. West Gwynedd) until the latter escaped from prison and managed to regain Anglesey and Arfon. Dafydd, the more powerful of the brothers, and ruler of East Gwynedd with the Perfeddwlad (modern Clywd) bordering on the earldom of Chester, was heavily defeated in battle on the lower Conwy by two rebel nephews late in 1194 and forced to divide his lands with them. Neither of these men had any English links or loyalties. The more dynamic of the two, Llywelyn ap Iorweth (born *c.* 1173), was the son of the disinherited eldest son of Owain Gwynedd, and was apparently already in rebellion against Dafydd in his mid-late teens, in 1188, according to Giraldus. He was also possibly hostile to some of the Marcher nobles from clashes with them as a boyhood exile in Powys with his mother's kin after his father was evicted from his lands and died. Allied to the equally resentful disinherited sons of Dafydd's late half-brother Cynan, who also had nothing to lose by rebellion, he defeated Rhodri, who had already been driven out of Anglesey by these youths in 1191 and had had to seek Viking help to return, in two battles in Anglesey in 1194. Thence he ruled part of the West. He defeated and reduced Dafydd to nominal co-rulership in a battle on the Conwy in 1195 and imprisoned and exiled him in 1197/8, driving him and his family into England as refugees to live on the lands Henry II had given them at Hales in Shropshire. King Richard was too busy regaining that part of the Norman frontier seized by his foe King Philip of France during his captivity in 1193 to help, and Dafydd died in exile in 1203. Llywelyn then set about removing his other relatives from their domains, aided by the death of his main rival, Rhodri's son Gruffydd (who he had bought off in 1195 by accepting his rule of Anglesey and Arfon) in 1200. His eviction of his cousin Maredudd ap Cynan, one of his 1194 allies, from Lleyn in 1201 and Meirionydd in 1202

1. Ludlow Castle, outer bailey, looking north. (Author's collection)

2. Ludlow Castle, Mortimer's lodgings from the keep, looking north. (Author's collection)

3. Ludlow Castle, keep looking north-east; royal apartments of Prince Edward (Edward IV) ahead. (Author's collection)

4. Ludlow Castle, west side looking north; where King Stephen rescued Prince Henry of Scotland from a grappling-iron during the June 1139 siege. (Author's collection)

5. Ludlow Castle, entrance to the great hall. (Author's collection)

6. Ludlow Castle, the Duke of York's apartments (Edward IV's & Richard III's father). (Author's collection)

7. Ludford Bridge, looking north into Ludlow. (Author's collection)

8. Coat of arms of Roger de Mortimer, 1st Earl of March. (CC Japse)

9. Wigmore Castle. (Courtesy of Humphrey Bolton / Creative Commons)

10. Hay Castle, looking south-east. (Author's collection)

11. St Quentin's Castle gateway, Llanbethlan Castle, from the east; home of the St Quentins in the twelfth and thirteenth centuries, located outside Cowbridge, Glamorgan. (Author's collection)

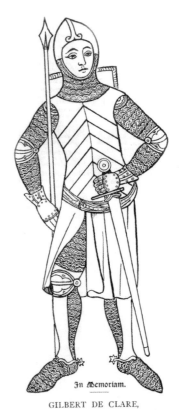

In Memoriam.

GILBERT DE CLARE,
LORD OF CLARE, EARL OF GLOUCESTER AND HERTFORD, ob. 1230.
After John Carter.
See GLOUCESTER, 110.

12. Gilbert de Clare, 5th Earl of Gloucester (d. 1230). (Courtesy of Joseph Foster, *Some Feudal Coats of Arms*)

13. Gilbert de Clare's coat of arms at time of sealing Magna Carta. (CC rs-nourse)

14. Raglan Castle. (Courtesy of Rob Farrow / Creative Commons)

15. Oystermouth Castle from the east. (Author's collection)

16. Carmarthen Castle's main gatehouse, from the north. (Author's collection)

18. Laugharne Castle, from the south; stronghold of the de Brians. (Author's collection)

19. Victoria Bridge from the Hereford Castle bailey, looking south-east down the River Wye to Dinedor Hill; this is the meadow where Prince Edward (Edward I) escaped from Simon de Montfort's guards on horseback to start the rebellion in July 1265. (Author's collection)

20. Godstow nunnery, looking north-east; burial-place of Henry II's mistress, Rosamund de Clifford. (Author's collection)

21. Ogmore Castle, looking north up the River Ewenny; headquarters of the de Londres and Chaworths – later to the Duchy of Lancaster (under John of Gaunt) and lordship of Glamorgan (Warwick, 'the Kingmaker', and Richard III). (Author's collection)

22. Hereford Castle gatehouse, looking north over river; site of the famous water-gate. (Author's collection)

23. Candleston Castle, looking north; interior of the fourteenth-century manor house of de Cantelupes. (Author's collection)

24. Edward II deposed by Queen Isabella and her army. (Courtesy of British Library, Royal 15 E IV, f. 316v)

25. Coronation of Richard II. (Courtesy of British Library, Royal 20 C VII, f. 192v)

26. Chepstow Castle. (Courtesy of Rob Farrow/Creative Commons)

27. Pembroke Castle, from a 1905 postcard.

28. Effigy of William Marshall, 1st Earl of Pembroke. (Courtesy of Joseph Foster, *Some Feudal Coats of Arms*)

29. Geoffrey, Count of Anjou. (Courtesy of Joseph Foster, *Some Feudal Coats of Arms*)

completed his triumph, and in 1201 the English government recognised his current possessions and allowed the supremacy of Welsh law in them. He was also aided by the military eclipse of his powerful neighbour Gwenwynwyn, of southern Powys, the possessor of the stronger of the two principalities into which Powys had been divided on the abdication and death of Madoc ap Maredudd in 1160. Gwenwynwyn attempted to use King Richard's preoccupation overseas to extend his lands south into the upper Wye Valley by taking over the Builth/Radnor area (historically part of Powys), but was defeated by the royal justiciar Geoffrey FitzPeter at Painscastle in 1198. Famously, his attempt to seize the eponymous castle at that location was driven off by a determined defence led in person by the lord, the younger William de Braose's wife Mabel – later to be nicknamed the 'Lady of Hay' from her association with nearby Hay-on-Wye Castle. She may have led her troops herself, probably built most of the extant buildings, and was to end up murdered by her husband's foe King John – and celebrated in fiction in modern times. While she rallied the defence, her messengers summoned the royal army in time to catch Gwenwynwyn outside the castle and rout him. In 1202 Llywelyn attacked Powys again to take advantage of his foe's recent losses, though decisive victory was prevented by the troops of the cantref of Penllyn refusing to aid him; he deposed their lord Eliseg in retaliation.

Gwynedd was still however unable to repel a sustained English assault on the lowlands by a royal army operating with its full strength, and once King John had temporarily abandoned his attempts to reconquer Normandy and Anjou – helped by a strike by some of his English vassals who refused to join his army of reconquest in 1205 – he turned to affairs in England and Ireland after losing almost all his Continental lands to Philip Augustus. In addition, he had some Marcher experience: he had previously been the husband of the current holder of the earldom of Glamorgan with its huge South Wales lands, Isabella, Countess of

Gloucester. He had divorced her on uncertain grounds soon after his accession in 1199, a move supposedly linked to his alleged paedophiliac lust for the underage heiress Isabella of Angouleme in Poitou, in western France. In fact, Isabella (d. 1246) was more likely aged fourteen or fifteen than the suposed twelve when he married her in 1200; marrying her had its strategic imperatives as her Angouleme lands were part of the endangered lands of Poitou, left exposed by the loss of Anjou as the northern frontier of the king's Duchy of Aquitatne in south-west France and under threat of conquest. Acquiring this territory with Isabella shored up the king's distant Poitou frontier – but it also infuriated her current fiance, Count Hugh of Lusignan, who defected to King Philip with his family and added to John's problems. The king's restless and brooding presence, a man of swift passions quick to punish insults and allegedly predatory towards his barons' womenfolk, who he seduced or raped at will, loomed large over his uneasy and increasingly hostile vassals. Nor did he have his father's and brother Richard's consistency, strategic genius, or ability to win lasting loyalty; though he was not devoid of military skills and has been praised as a methodical administrator by modern historians, he seems to have suffered from a degree of bipolar disorder and mixed periods of intense energy and active campaigning with other periods of lassitude and over-eating. Llywelyn loyally aided him against King William, 'the Lion' of Scotland, in person in 1209, but faced his suspicions – probably over links to rebellious Marcher lords such as William de Braose of Brecon and Radnor. After de Braose fled to Ireland in 1209 John pursued him there, while Earl Ranulf of Gwynedd and Bishop Peter des Roches invaded the coastal lowlands of Gwynedd. Llywelyn, who was building new castles in stone in the English style, most notably at Dolwyddelan in the upper Conwy Valley, had to pull down his new castle at Degannwy and retire into the mountains. John then invaded in person in 1211. Llywelyn had to take refuge in his mountain fastnesses as John occupied the Conwy Valley, and relied on the English running short of time and supplies to secure a reasonably favourable treaty through Joan's mediation with her father. He handed over the lands east of the Conwy but retained the heartland of Gwynedd, as his grandsons were both to be forced to do (1247 and 1277). He was lucky in that a challenge from his cousin Owain failed in 1212 – John could not invade again that year due to fear that his mutinous barons would seize him during the planned campaign, and the English barons' revolts kept John preoccupied thereafter.

Llywelyn was not the only Welsh ruler to take advantage of King Richard's preoccupation with overseas affairs. The bold claims of Gwenwynwyn ap Owain Cyfeiliog, who succeeded to the South on his father's abdication in 1195, as a national leader of the Welsh had to be displayed by military success, and he chose to try to to retake lost territory in the Builth and Radnor areas from William de Braose (*c.* 1152–1211), lord of the upper Monnow Valley and Brecon. As mentioned, this met met with a humiliating defeat at the Battle of Painscastle by the royal army in 1198. He survived Llywelyn ap Iorweth's planned invasion in 1202 as the Gwynedd ruler decided in favour of a treaty at the last moment after Church mediation and the defection of the cantref of Penllyn, but in 1208 he tried to take advantage of the disgrace of his principal English Marcher rival, the younger William de Braose (*c.* 1150–1211), with raids on disputed lands. De Braose, lord of Builth and Radnor plus Brecon and Abergavenny, was among the most powerful of the Marcher lords and dominated the lands to the south of Gwenwynwyn stretching into Gwent, where he was reliably supposed to have been a leader in the massacre of the lord of Gwent Uwch Coed (upper Gwent) and his neighbours and the seizure of their lands in 1177. He had been among Richard I's leading captains but had effortlessly transferred his allegiance to John – in 1189–99 his neighbour as lord of Glamorgan *de iure uxoris* – in April 1199, and had subsequently fought for the latter in Normandy as he sought to fend off the attacks of King Philip Augustus of France. Philip had backed the succession of John's deceased elder brother Geoffrey's son Prince Arthur, Duke of Brittany and stepson of the northern Marcher warlord Earl Ranulf de Blondeville of Chester, in 1199–1202, but the so far militarily ineffective John had risen to the occasion as they invaded Anjou. Aided by William de Braose and other veterans, they had hastened to deal with Arthur's siege of his grandmother Queen Eleanor at Mirabeau with a swift ride to the rescue and had caught the besiegers unawares, capturing Arthur – a deed done in person by de Braose – and so ended the threat of civil war for the moment. John had handed over Arthur to the custody of de Braose at the ducal seat of Rouen Castle, and some time around Easter 1203 Arthur had disappeared and never been seen again. The most reliable version of the story had it that the prince had had a stormy interview with the visiting king, who had murdered him in a fit of rage and thrown his body, weighted down, into the River Seine. But whether de Braose had been involved or not, he was supposed to know the truth – and even to be holding it over the king as he continued to be given lands and honours by the latter. These included in 1206 the south-eastern Marcher castles of Skenfrith, Grosmont, and the White Castle – the so-called 'Three Castles' – in the upper Monnow Valley upstream from Monmouth, south-west of Hereford and east of the de Braose lordship of Brecon. De Braose also had some major degree of influence in Irish affairs, outmatching the weight of his landed inheritance there, and was apparently the prime mover in the pardoning in 1202 of the disgraced senior lord Theobald Butler, principal landholder in what was to become Tipperary in northern Muster. The official decree reinstating Theobald as lord of the district's territories of Ely O'Carroll (Eile Ua Cerbhaill), Eliogarty (i.e. the area of Eile owned by the O'Fogartys), Upper Ormond, Lower Ormond, and Owney and Arra stated that they were in the hands of and were restored by William de Braose, who presumably had received them from John when Theobald was forfieted. De Braose also acquired the governorship of Limerick, previously held by his son-in-law Walter de Lacey, the lord of Meath, in 1206, though the latter continued to administer it for him. By this date John was complaining that Walter had been acting against his interests and seizing his assets in alliance with his brother Hugh de Lacey, Earl of Ulster, as of 1205 so trusted by the king then, and John de Courcy, the previous lord of Ulster. But it turned out that John could not trust de Braose to act for him either.

De Braose was believed to be the king's accomplice in the disappearance of Arthur in 1203, but whether or not this was true, the king quarrelled with him in 1208, apparently claiming that he owed large sums of money for rent on his lands. William's wife Maud de St Valery, a formidable lady of the same mixed reputation of piety (from Church sources) and avaricious ruthlessness (from more secular writers), was supposed by gossip to have boasted that John was Arthur's murderer and that she and her husband knew the truth. The story had it that John demanded that Maud hand over her younger son William to him as a hostage for the family's good behaviour, and she refused saying openly that she would not give him to a man who had already killed his nephew. Whether determined to end open defiance by an over-mighty subject, angry at having his guilt exposed, or aggrieved at slander, John firstly confiscated William's lands in Sussex (including the rape of Bramber with its castle) and then attacked and overran William's Marcher lands too, confiscating them with their castles before they could be used for rebellion. William was forced to flee to his lands in Ireland, and was joined by his family; his daughter Margaret was married to Walter de Lacey, lord of Trim Castle in Meath (and Ludlow in Shropshire) and brother of the royal adviser and Irish stalwart Hugh de Lacey, who gave them sanctuary. John then invaded Ireland, and landed at Waterford in June 1210. The documentary evidence of his stay has mostly been lost, but his troops advanced across Meath so the de Braoses fled; Mabel and the younger William ended up sailing to southern Scotland but were handed over by the local lord, Alan of Galloway, before they could ask King William for sanctuary. Meanwhile the alarmed Walter de Lacey sent envoys to the king in Dublin to surrender his lands as a loyal vassal and ask pardon, hoping now the de Braoses had left for confirmation of his current holdings as easier than John having to conquer and then reassign them. John, typically, refused and declared him forfeit; he was only able to regain his lands in 1215 when John was under pressure over the Magna Carta crisis and needed allies. His brother Hugh de Lacey also fled, and John occupied his main Ulster stronghold of Carrickfergus Castle. Mabel and her son William were sent back to Ireland by Alan of Galloway and brought to John at Carrickfergus, and when he left Ireland in August they were taken back to England – to the dungeons at the secure royal residence at Windsor Castle (autumn 1210). John then notoriously starved Mabel and the younger William (probably in his early twenties as he had a son) to death, either at Windsor or later at Corfe Castle, Dorset. This castle, John's favourite residence for hunting in the forests of Purbeck, was usefully isolated in the middle of a royal hunting range with only one road approaching it, from Wareham, and John used it throughout his reign as a prison for top-priority prisoners – more of whom were murdered too – and a secure place of internment for important hostages such as his niece Eleanor of Brittany, Arthur's sister, and the daughters of his reluctant vassal King William of Scots.

The elder William de Braose fled to France and died there in poverty in August 1211, but the Brecon/Radnor lordship was later to be regained by force by another of de Braose's younger sons, Reginald (*c.* 1190–1228), in the post-Magna Carta political chaos. The widowed Reginald also married Gwladys, the daughter of John's foe Llywelyn ap Iorweth of Gwynedd, in 1215 to add to the king's fury; his son by his first marriage was William (executed 1230) who was to succeed him as lord of Brecon, Abergavenny, Builth, Radnor, and the 'Three Castles' in 1228 and end up executed by Llywelyn for having an affair with his wife, John's daughter. Reginald's murdered brother William had married the daughter of Richard de Clare, third Earl of Hertford and relation to the late 'Strongbow'. Another of the de Braose sons, Giles, was Bishop of Hereford and was among those clerics who refused to back King John against the Pope and withdrew in protest to France, having their property seized; he was restored to his lands and rights in 1215 too but died before he could return. The political manoeuvres of their ambitious parents meant that some of the daughters were married off to prominent Marcher/Irish or Welsh lords, adding to the king's paranoia: as well as Margaret's marriage to de Lacey, her sister Maud was married to Gruffydd (d. 1201), one of the feuding sons of Rhys ap Gruffydd of Deheubarth. The latter's sons, who their paternal uncles Rhys Gryg ('the Hoarse') of Cantref Mawr and Maelgwyn of Ceredigion tried to elbow out of their share of the principality after 1201, were thus related to and usually allies of the de Braoses – but were enemies of their local Anglo-Norman rivals, William Marshal and his sons the lords of Pembroke. For the moment, John had defeated the seeming threat by the de Braoses and seized their lordships, but at the cost of what contemporary sources agree was increasing disquiet among his elite at what had happened to his latest victims and could happen to others too.

Having been summoned to the English court at Shrewsbury by the wrathful King John in 1208, Gwenwynwyn of southern Powys was deposed and his territories were briefly annexed to England; the king was thus considering advancing direct royal rule over the central Marches and was probably aimed at Gwenwynwyn's neighbours, the untrustworthy de Braoses, too. This bold move foreshadowed the plans of John's grandson Edward I in the 1270s, but John lacked the resources or ability to concentrate on this region long-term that Edward possessed, and he was also distracted by his unfortunate ability to stir up enemies unnecessarily and have to conduct several major campaigns, political as well as military, at once. His dispute with the papacy was coming to a head as he further refused to accept the autocratic and interfering Pope Innocent III's choice of archbishop of Canterbury; such disputes between the Angevins and their neighbours and the papacy were common – Philip of France had been excommunicated recently for illegally divorcing his unwanted wife – but John preferred bluster and extreme measures to negotiating. As all senior clergy who were unwilling to obey the king rather than the Pope were driven out of the realm and a papal interdict loomed, those barons who resented John's extortionate tax-raising (admittedly worse due to the unprecedented military threat from Philip and the loss of all revenues from Normandy, Maine and Anjou) could take heart from the probability of papal approval and Church blessing for rebellion. These were the years when John was to seize Church lands for alleged non-payment of fines and round up priests' concubines to hold them to ransom and fill his coffers for his wars – and allegedly to threaten to turn Moslem to defy the Church (possibly only one of his black jokes). The bolder and more autonomist Marcher lords, such as de Braose, duly took heart from the threatening king's troubles and meddled in plots to overthrow him – or so John alleged. In this worsening situation, even the bold and at times rash John could not add southern Powys, full of hostile Welsh lords objecting to English rule and with Gwynedd a potential ally if they revolted, to his lands. Grudgingly he restored Gwenwynwyn in 1210 as a counterbalance to his enemy Llywelyn, having surrendered to humiliating terms of political and jurisdictional dependence. John presumably realised that without Gwenwynwyn's presence in Powys the English were unlikely to secure much of it from Llywelyn's attacks if it came to a major war. Pope Innocent absolved Llewelyn from his oath to the king, who was currently under a papal interdict, in 1212, and he set up a new coalition of lords to regain lands that he had lost to John. Later in 1212 he entered into some sort of pact with the other princes of Wales (Powys, Deheubarth and Gwent) whereby they recognised him as their superior, and negotiated on their behalf with John's enemy Philip Augustus of France. But Gwenwynwyn's subsequent alliance with Llywelyn from 1212 did not last; in 1216 he was deposed by Llywelyn for allegedly plotting against him with John, and his lands were occupied by Gwynedd. In the meantime Llywelyn used the 1213 invasion threat, when John had to muster a huge army on the Kentish Downs near Dover and send his fleet to Flanders to destroy King Philip's invasion-fleet, to reclaim the disputed Perfeddwladd, the 'Four Cantrefs' east of the Conwy, in 1213. He then used the subsequent confrontation between John and his barons in 1215 (see below) to resume his authority in central Wales and lead a large army south into Deheubarth, one of whose feuding rulers, Rhys Gryg of Cantref Mawr, had arrived at his court asking for help against his nephews, the sons of his late elder brother Gruffydd, and the English. A mild winter then enabled him to retake Ceredigion and overrun the major English castles of Cardigan and Carmarthen, along with Gower, in 1215–16.

In Deheubarth, on the lord Rhys' death on 28 April 1197, aged around sixty-five, his princedom was split among his sons. He was buried at St David's Cathedral, but only after his body had been scourged as punishment for a recent outrage (possibly an assault on Bishop Peter de Leia, builder of the present cathedral). Maelgwyn also underwent a scourging to gain Church support and offset his lack of legal recognition by the clerics as a bastard, in the manner of the way that Henry II had done penance for the death of Thomas Becket. The senior of Rhys' legitimate sons, Gruffydd, described by Giraldus as devious, succeeded to Cantref Mawr, but was soon under particular threat from his half-sibling

Maelgwyn who gained Ceredigion. Maelgwyn, who was the most unscrupulous of the brothers, was under threat of disinheritance if Church law was followed as he was illegitimate – possibly accentuated by the recent removal of the illegitimate claimant to Gwynedd, Dafydd, by his nephew Llywelyn ap Iorweth in 1195. He briefly deposed Gruffydd with the aid of Gwenwynwyn of southern Powys in 1198, and when his victim escaped and drove him out of most of Ceredigion he deserted to the new English King John. The latter backed his return to Ceredigion as a royal vassal in 1199, and Maelgwyn handed over the crucial Cardigan Castle to the king's officials in an act regarded with fury by patriotic annalists. Meanwhile, Gruffydd also secured his younger brother Maredudd's realm of Cantref Bychan in 1201, but died weeks later. Maelgwyn secured most of his lands, but their dispossessed brother Rhys Gryg linked up with Gruffydd's sons Rhys and Owain. In 1204 the trio drove Maelgwyn out of Cantref Mawr, most of which fell to Rhys. Maelgwyn was also responsible for his men's murder of one of their excluded brothers, Hywel Sais, in 1204, but lost most of his remaining lands to William Marshal, Earl of Pembroke, later that year.

Rhys' continuing rivalry with his nephews, the sons of Gruffydd, led them to seek the patronage of Llywelyn Fawr after 1201. In response Rhys backed John in the confrontation between Gwynedd and England in 1210–11. He received no territorial reward and eventually decided that Llywelyn was a safer ally after John's failure to invade Gwynedd again and preoccupation with the Church, France, and rebellion after 1212. Turning on his English ex-patrons after John's troops had assisted his local power with an expedition against Maelgwyn to Ceredigion in 1211, but set up new castles there too, he sacked Swansea in 1212. Maelgwyn supported whichever side suited his purpose at the time. Both Rhys and Maelgwyn eventually became loyal vassals of Llywelyn Fawr against King John and their rivals, Gruffydd's sons Rhys and Owain. In 1213 the latter two assisted an invasion of Rhys' lands in Cantref Mawr by John's most notorious mercenary commander, Fawkes de Breaute (who had rebuilt Aberystwyth Castle in 1211 to restore royal power in northern Ceredigion), and he had to flee to Llywelyn's court.

The Marcher barons and the civil war and French invasion of 1215–17. William Marshal's finest hour: the Earl of Pembroke ends up as effective ruler of England

King John had granted the earldom of Gloucester, held by his recently divorced wife Isabella, to one of his Norman/French supporters, her sister Mabel's son by Amaury de Montfort, another Amaury, in 1200. This was as compensation for his having to give up his lands in France, held of John's foe King Philip under the Treaty of Le Goulet, which re-established a precarious peace between the two kings. The lands of the Gloucester lordship however remained with the acquisitive and paranoid king, to keep his grip on the turbulent southern Marches. Isabella and Mabel's younger sister Matilda (*c.* 1158–1220) was married to Richard de Clare (d. 1217), third Earl of Hertford and sixth lord of Tonbridge in Kent and Clare in Suffolk, a cousin of 'Strongbow' from the senior branch of the de Clare family, which had little current connection with the Marches but was to inherit the Gloucester earldom and the Glamorgan lordship via this link after Isabella's death. War soon resumed in Normandy and Anjou, and Amaury de Montfort continued to hold the earldom until his death in 1213. Isabella then regained the title, but John was currently busy trying to shore up his support among the nobility in the rising tide of discontent at his massive financial demands, administrative interference, capricious judical decisions, extortionate demands for 'recognizances', i.e. payment of sureties for good behaviour (which he frequently then called in when in need of money), and general unreliability. John had prevented the threatened papal-backed French invasion to enforce the interdict on his lands and his deposition in 1213 by the political coup of suddenly surrendering to the papal terms that he had been defying for six years, then accepting the papal candidate Stephen Langton as Archbishop of Canterbury, and

declaring himself a papal vassal in 1213 – though he could easily
have done this earlier as Pope Innocent was never going to back
down, and only desperation drove him to it. Now he planned to
invade France on several fronts with his hired European allies
(the expensive subsidies for which were infuriating his over-taxed
subjects), attacking Paris and thus retrieving Normandy from
Philip, though this was to meet with disaster at the Battle of
Bouvines in 1214. Isabella was now married off in January
1214 to one of the greatest nobles in south-eastern England
whose support John needed, Geoffrey (FitzPeter) de Mandeville
(c. 1190–1217), previously married to Isabella's sister Amicia's
husband Richard de Clare's sister Avelina. The son of John's late
Chief Justiciar from 1199–1213 and trusted senior administrator
Geoffrey FitzPeter, Earl of Essex (d. 1213) by the de Mandeville
heiress, Beatrice de Say from the Marcher dynasty of de Say
of Clun, Geoffrey was the elder brother of William FitzPeter
or de Mandeville (d. 1227), who was to succeed him as Earl
of Essex, and Maud, wife of the senior baron Henry de Bohun
(1172–1220), fifth Earl of Hereford as grandson of Earl Roger's
(d. 1155) sister Margaret; his half-brother was John FitzGeoffrey
(c. 1205–1258) of Shere in Surrey, Geoffrey FitzPeter's son by
a subsequent wife. The king was hoping to tie this young and
ambitious nobleman to his side in succession to his father, but
instead Geoffrey FitzPeter seems to have been more influenced by
his brother-in-law de Bohun, who John had granted the defunct
earldom of Hereford and the national High Constableship in
1199 by right of his descent from their earlier holders via his
grandmother, but was to be a leading light of the future rebellions
against John in 1215–16. Henry de Bohun was lord of Caldicot
Castle in the southern Marches through his father Humphrey
de Bohun (d. 1181), a loyal general of Henry II's who had led
the defeat of the invading rebels at Fornham in Suffolk in 1173;
his mother was Princess Margaret of Scotland (1145–1201),
daughter of Earl Henry of Huntingdon, granddaughter of King
David, and sister of King s Malcolm IV (d. 1165) and William
(d. 1214). Margaret had previously been married to Duke Conan
of Brittany, which made Henry de Bohun half-brother of Duchess

Constance and uncle to Prince Arthur who had disappeared in King John's custody in 1203.

The combined Breton/Arthur link, semi-royal blood, and possession of the Hereford inheritance no doubt served to boost de Bohun's combination of self-confidence when standing up to King John, plus resentment at the king's excesses and landed and familial backing to help him defy royal power, and in 1215 both him and his brother-in-law the new earl of Gloucester were prominent in the grouping of barons who raised an army and marched on London to force terms out of the king. The latter retreated to Windsor Castle but did not have enough support to fight back, and he was forced to open negotiations and then seal (not sign) the Magna Carta, an exhaustive list of royal administrative and judicial excesses, which were now to be banned. FitzPeter and de Bohun were on the panel of barons who were duly empowered to control the government and see that John carried out his promises – and were among those excommunicated for this by the Pope when John promptly broke his word and wrote to the latter asking for absolution from the Charter and his help in regaining his authority (supposedly in order to help the planned Papal Crusade). The fragile peace that had been arranged between the embattled king, his allies, and the rebel barons in the negotiations at Runnymede near Windsor in June 1215 broke down, and civil war resulted – with the main leaders and numerical weight of the rebel coalition based in northern England and East Anglia rather than the Marches, but including the East Anglian (and Tonbridge) de Clares, who were as seen closely related to the current FitzPeter/de Mandeville holders of the Gloucester/Glamorgan lands, as well as the latter whose heartland had been in Essex and Cambridgeshire since the days of the brigand warlord Geoffrey de Mandeville in the 1140s. Giles de Braose, Bishop of Hereford and son and brother of John's most famous victims in 1210–11, and William Marshal's eldest son and heir William (with the aid he could call on from family tenants in Pembrokeshire) were the main backers of the rebel leaders Gloucester (FitzPeter) and Hereford (de Bohun) in the Marches; at the moment the king's continued distrust of William Marshal was helping to keep the latter marginalised from the royal forces, and he probably disapproved of John's notorious and blatant breaches of faith, too. The rebel leaders, Robert Fitzwalter (lord of Dunmow in Essex) and the northern baron Eustace de Vesci (brother-in-law to John's reluctant vassal and soon-to-be foe King Alexander of Scots), were not famed for their honour and idealism like the Marshal, but seem to have been driven more by ambition and a desire to protect their own assets from the grasping king and were not spoken of warmly by contemporaries; FitzWalter had had his London residence of Baynard Castle and other property forfeited in 1212 for a plot to murder the king – allegedly after the latter tried to seduce his daughter – and according to a story by the gossipy 'Anonymous' chronicler of Bethune (France) had previously threatened him with violence over the indignity and insult offered to his family by putting his son-in-law on trial. The latter offender was indeed Geoffrey FitzPeter's younger brother William FitzPeter, later the Earl of Essex after Geoffrey (1216), who had murdered a servant while in attendance on the king and had thus broken the legally enforceable peace of the king's court – perhaps suggesting that William was an arrogant and impetuous baronial thug.

Geoffrey FitzPeter joined Fitzwalter at the initial, relatively small armed rally of the leading rebel barons at Stamford in April 1215 that initiated the rising and led to the march on London, suggesting that his brother's aggressive father-in-law rather than the more cautious de Bohun was the main influence on him at this point. After the breakdown of the Magna Carta truce, John called on and received the support of both William Marshal, commanding the resources of the earldom of Pembroke plus Leinster in Ireland, and Ranulf de Blondeville, Earl of Chester and dominant magnate of the northern Marches, and they seem to have kept most of the region loyal apart from the castles held by the rebel earls of Hereford and Gloucester, keeping the latter from serving as a springboard for more attacks by aggressive local action. FitzPeter's castle at Hanley (presumably the one in Hanley Chase near Great Malvern Priory, south-west of Worcester) was attacked by the loyal Roger de Clifford, lord of Clifford, on royal orders in a minor action later that autumn, while the main royal army concentrated on dealing with the rebellion in the south-east by besieging the crucial strategic point of Rochester Castle and closing in on rebel-held London. John himself headed off to attack and burn rebel lands in northern England in an attempt to dissuade the Scots from aiding them, and even crossed into Scotland; Earl Ranulf aided this campaign and duly received custody of the retaken castles in Lancashire. The hard-pressed rebels duly offered their leadership and the Crown to the young but militarily experienced Prince Louis of France, heir to the French throne and husband to John's sister's daughter Princess Blanche of Castile (later Queen of France and mother of Louis IX, St Louis the Crusader). His reinforcements forced John to fall back from the south-east, and as Louis and his invasion-fleet landed at Sandwich and proceeded to reinforce Rochester in May 1216, William FitzPeter joined his father-in-law FitzWalter to do homage to Louis as rightful King of England. The French-rebel army advanced on Reigate, Farnham, and Winchester, joined by the Marshal's eldest son William, though the latter insisted on being named its 'marshal' in place of Louis' chosen nominee in return for his allegiance, in a typical act of baronial self-advancement. The younger Marshal was nearly put off the rebel cause when his family's old castle at Marlborough was given to a Frenchman rather than to him, but instead he agreed to lead a rebel force to Worcestershire to take over the county town from the loyalist sheriff, and so annoyed his father for interfering in his region that the latter promptly told him to clear out of Worcester or face attack. The younger William obeyed, and Earl Ranulf reoccupied the city on 17 July – aided by the king's most brutal and effective mercenary captain, Faulkes de Breaute, whose atrocities in this war did much damage to John's reputation and who had already served a term as a notably harsh sheriff of Glamorgan. The king was able to maintain control of most of his castles outside the south-east, but had lost his capital and around a third of his kingdom (on an approximate line from the Wash to Hampshire) and the adherence of around two-thirds of the nobility (nineteen of the twenty-seven most important ones had defected) and was reduced to successive campaigns of ravaging his enemies' lands across the country rather than closing in on the rebel area, which may have been due either to prudent avoidance of a battle that could be lost in favour of ruining the rebels' resources or, less chaitably, to a mixture of inability to concentrate on a fixed objective or personal spite towards his foes. He was based in the Marches in August and vainly attempted to negotiate to persuade Llywelyn ap Iorweth and the other Welsh princes from expanding their territories at his Marcher allies' expense, and then moved off with his local reinforcements to relieve the rebel siege of Windsor Castle. This was successful, but in the meantime the rebels and Louis' main army had been vainly besieging Dover Castle – whose epic defence was led by Hubert de Burgh, Henry III's future chief minister and Marches strongman – and the teenage King Alexander of Scots had led his army all the way across England to join in. As the latter left the siege for home, John moved into East Anglia and made a vain attempt to intercept him; his subsequent campaign of burning and pillaging rebel lands in East Anglia into the East Midlands ended with his famous tidal disaster of losing his baggage-train in the Wash (11 October) and then his death, of dysentery, at Newark on 18 October.

However well the long-term consequences of his energetic but inconclusive campaign may be judged in military terms, in political ones the removal of the controversial and unpopular king with his talent for making enemies was a major bonus for his side, as his nine-year-old son Henry III was a boy innocent of his father's many crimes who could be regarded by those not incontrovertibly committed to Louis as the rightful king and a chance for a fresh start. The direction of the royalist military campaign now passed to William Marshal, the only other experienced and well-regarded royalist general being de Burgh who was under siege in Dover, and he took direction of the government too as the new king was brought from his safe haven at Devizes Castle to Gloucester to be crowned at the abbey there on 28 October by the papal legate Guala, who Innocent had sent to mediate. William Marshal also knighted the new king, as was appropriate for the most renowned knight in England if not Europe; the 'Histoire de Guillaume le Marechal' said that William promised that even if the entire world abandoned Henry he would carry him from land to land on his shoulders looking for help. The only post-1066 coronation not to be carried out at Westminster Abbey (Louis still held London firmly) was followed by a new military offensive led by William, while the new Pope Honorius III explicitly recognised Henry as king and called on Louis to withdraw and all the kings who supported him to back the new regime or face excommunication, a major diplomatic blow to the rebels. Major defections from the rebel cause now began – only once the vengeance-prone and unreliable John was dead and the capable and honourable William was in charge of the royal cause. But despite the usual narrative of a smooth progress of the royalist cause from the accession of Henry III to the royalist victory (the detailed contemporary chronicler Ralph de Coggeshall devoted only a couple of pages to the end of the war) and the major success of Louis soon abandoning the siege of Dover Castle, in fact the rebels continued to mop up more significant castles in East Anglia during the winter as initial negotiations stalled. William, based initially at Gloucester and Bristol and then at Oxford, did not move forward propitiously and instead trained his men and waited for defections, while the majority of barons who had deserted John in 1215–16 sat on the fence and the papacy proclaimed the war a Crusade – an ironic fate for Prince Louis, who only a few years before had been the papal champion leading the Albigensian Crusade against the Cathar heretics in south-west France to slaughter them en masse and confiscate their lands. In January 1217 William moved forward to Nottingham to close in on the major rebel base of Lincoln, which protected their links up the east coast route to the North, but he was distracted as the long-term guerrilla war by patriotic locals in the Weald of Sussex and Kent against the French led to revolt against Louis in the Cinque Ports, aided by Hubert de Burgh, who now that Dover was safe was commanding a royalist fleet at sea against Louis' admiral, the pirate-captain Eustace the Monk. The emerging port of Rye was seized by royalists, endangering the French control of the Kent coast, and Louis hastened to nearby (Old) Winchelsea in a vain attempt to retake it; in turn, William Marshal led his army south-east to Dorking in Surrey to mastermind its rescue and was joined by Earl Ranulf of Chester, Walter de Lacey, lord of Ludlow and Weobley, with his men from Meath and the brigand-like mercenary commander de Breaute. Louis was blockaded in Winchelsea as men he had sent to London to get help and then relief-troops from were ambushed by guerrillas in the Weald and killed. He faced being caught by William's advancing army, but his ships managed to drive off the English blockaders and embark his men at Winchelsea; he headed back to France to acquire reinforcements. In his absence, the younger William Marshal and William de Longespee, Earl of Salisbury and illegitimate son of Henry II, defected back to the royalists and showed their loyalty by leading the attack on rebel-held Winchester – though they were more noted for a mixture of ferocity and fondness for looting than for military skill, and the elder William had to send them off to retake Southampton and negotiate an end to the siege – which had repeated the devastation of the town in the 1141 siege. The younger William then proceeded to retake his would-be 1215 target of Marlborough Castle, and his father had to abandon Winchester again and retreat to Marlborough as Louis arrived back with a new army. But the pretender then sent part of his army north to help Saer de Quincy, Earl of Winchester, in Leicestershire by saving his castle at Montsorrel, which the Earl of Chester, sent by William Marshal the elder, was besieging. Short of men as a result, his second attempt to take Dover Castle in May was no more successful than the first, while Saer de Quincy and the rebel leader Fitzwalter led the rebel/French relief force to Montsorrel (whose siege Earl Ranulf duly abandoned, to William Marshal's irritation) and then on to Lincoln at an overconfident claim that its hard-pressed royal castle would fall with one more effort.

Hearing that the main rebel army was split in two, William Marshal decided to strike a decisive blow against their northern force and to march to relieve Lincoln – and is credited by his poetic biography with an inspiring speech to his captains, calling their cause that of justice and Holy Church, as well as rousing their families and the nation against truce-breaking invaders. A muster was duly called at Newark en route to Lincoln for 15 May, with local East Midlands chronicler Roger of Wendover saying that royalist castles were emptied of all but skeleton garrisons in a push to maximise the relief-force, with around 400 knights and 250 crossbowmen collected – 405 knights according to the 'Histoire de Guillaume le Marechal'. William Marshal was joined by the legate Guala, the late king's leading administrator (and extortionist) Bishop Peter des Roches of Winchester, much of the rest of the episcopate, and as assistant commanders the earls of Salisbury, Chester, and Derby, as well as Faukes de Breaute. The legate and the young king kept out of the battle at Nottingham, while William led the army to Lincoln on 19 May to avoid a risky attack over the low ground by the town (the rebel base, from which the castle to its east was being attacked) and approach from the north along a ridge instead that led directly to the castle. The rebels were taken by surprise as the royalists arrived at the castle on its far side from the town (i.e. the north-east) early on 20 May, and had to head uphill from the town to meet the attackers on the high ground outside the castle, whose bulk obstructed their view so they could not see the relief-force's size and had to send out scouts to check first. (The rebel army had 600 French knights and 1,000 French infantry according to the 'Histoire', plus an unclear number of English barons and their men; this was therefore an unusually large battle for the era.) The rebels planned to defend the town's northern walls from the royalists and at the same time to renew their ongoing attack on the castle from inside the adjacent part of the town, but the royalists both got into the castle – enabling them to place their crossbowmen on its battlements and open fire into the rebel-held town – and secured a northern gate into the town. (This is linked by an account to an initiative by the fighting Bishop Peter des Roches.) They then attacked the rebels from two sides at once and drove them back downhill through the town, with one notable French casualty being the young Count Thomas of Perche, a descendant of the Marcher family of de Belleme/Montgomery through Robert's (d. *c.* 1132) Perche marriage. The rebels and French alike were driven out of the town in a melee that lasted around six hours and fled – although heavy casualties might have been expected, the latter did not occur; some sources say only three to six men were actually killed. Apart from the useful protection of heavy mail for armed men and the usual hunt for lucrative prisoners to ransom, it appears from Roger of Wendover's version of events that many on both sides were fighting their own kinsfolk and friends and were keen to avoid killing them.

Whether or not there was a knightly freemasonry of arms and a mutual belief among the armies' leading ranks that this war was more a sort of enlarged tournament, contending for a crown rather than the usual trophies, the battle was thus unusually civilized – at any rate for the knights involved. Its outcome left the rebels' Northern army routed and most of its leadership, including Robert FitzWalter and the Marcher Henry de Bohun, Earl of Hereford, the earls of Winchester (de Quincey) and Hertford (de Clare), and 380 knights, rounded up for ransom and thus out of the war. The Marshal family apparently did particularly well from the ransoms. Around 200 French knights escaped back to London. The rebels abandoned the Midlands and their remaining castles there, which enabled the Earl of Chester to secure the abandoned Montsorrel Castle, which had led to the Lincoln expedition in the first place, and William Marshal led his forces south. Prince Louis had just suffered having his latest relief-force sent from France being destroyed in the Channel by the royalist navy, and he abandoned the siege of Dover at the end of May and returned to London; negotiations with the royalists followed with the Church mediating and a second, larger French relief-force sent by King Philip (probably around eighty ships not the three hundred claimed in the 'Histoire') was defeated by the English navy in a major naval battle off Sandwich at the end of August. William Marshal commanded his navy in person, and the series of hand-to-hand combats as the crews of the rival fleets boarded each other's ships ended with the French commander Eustace the Monk and many other invaders dead, many great nobles taken for ransom, and the French ships either taken, sunk, or escaped in what was subsequently played up as one of the early glories of the English naval tradition. Louis had to resume negotiations, and the subsequent Treaty of Kingston-upon-Thames in September gave him a very generous financial settlement (around a quarter of the English Crown's annual revenue) in return for abandoning his claim to the throne and returning home. William Marshal and Hubert de Burgh led the English negotiators, with the regent's ex-rebel son the younger William helping to cajole his former colleagues to agree, and royal hard-liners like the Earl of Chester excluded from the talks. The Marshal even pledged his lands in Normandy as surety that Louis would be paid in full, and kept his word. The result left him as regent of a reunited England and in effect the man to whom the young King Henry owed his throne, and he served loyally and honourably as the real ruler of England until his death at his estate at Caversham, near Reading, on 14 May 1219, aged probably seventy-three or seventy-four. He was buried at the Temple Church in London, having taken vows as a Templar knight on his deathbed as promised earlier. He was succeeded as regent by the legate Guala at his own request; his eldest son the younger William Marshal (1190–1231) succeeded as Earl of Pembroke and in 1225 was to marry, secondly, the young king's sister Eleanor who later married Simon de Montfort. The family's position and relationship with the monarchy it had saved was however to be far from straightforward.

The crucial year of 1217 also saw the ground laid for a major diversion of the crucial Marcher earldom of Gloucester, with the death of King John's ex-wife Isabella, Countess of Gloucester, on 14 October. Her rebel husband the Earl of Essex had died a year previously; as she had no children, the earldom now reverted to the descendants of her younger sister Avice (d. 1220), who had married Richard de Clare, third Earl of Hertford (d. 1217). Richard was one of the main noble landed proprietors in East Anglia and the South-East backing Prince Louis in 1216–17, as master of the 'honours' of Clare in Suffolk and Tonbridge in Kent plus most of his titular county of Hertfordshire, and had been among the baronial party who forced John to agree Magna Carta in 1215. So was his son and successor, Gilbert the fifth Earl of Hertford (1180–1230), who was indeed captured in person at the Battle of Lincoln by William Marshal. The latter then married Gilbert off to his own second daughter, Isabella, on her seventeenth birthday on 9 October 1217, as part of his using his huge family to create a network of links among the royalist and ex-rebel aristocracy to bolster his rule (normally something that a new and insecure king would do). It may have been an arranged marriage as was normal for the era, but it is said to have been extremely happy – and the death of the Countess of Gloucester a few days later meant that the said earldom was now transferred to the de Clares, soon making William Marshal's daughter a double countess. The rights to it passed to her mother-in-law Amicia, and in 1225 Henry III created Gilbert the (fifth) Earl of Gloucester; thus the de Clares made up for losing the earldom of Pembroke and the main landed 'bloc' in South-West Wales by acquiring the main landed 'bloc' in South-East Wales with the lordship of Glamorgan. Gilbert' s and Isabella's eldest son Richard (1222–1262), fifth Earl of Hertford and sixth Earl of Gloucester (1230), was in turn to play a major role in challenging the extortionate and incompetent rule of the current king in the 1250s, as co-leader in the baronial reform movement with Simon de Montfort (see next section) – but this time there was no overt talk of dethroning the king, merely constraining him. Richard was to be married off, firstly as a teenager to Margaret de Burgh (d. 1237), daughter of the then strongman Hubert de Burgh (co-leader of the resistance to Prince Louis with William Marshal), and after her death married (1238) Maud de Lacey, daughter of the head of that branch of the de Laceys, which held the earldom of Lincoln. Richard's younger brother William died unmarried in 1258; one of his sisters, Amicia, married Baldwin de Redvers, sixth Earl of Devon and lord of the Isle of Wight; and the other, Isabel (d. 1264), married the senior Scots peer Robert de Bruce (1214–1295), lord of Annandale and contender for the Scots throne in the 1292 dispute. By this marriage the subsequent members of the Bruce family, including the 'Contender's grandson King Robert Bruce of Scotland, acquired descent not only from the great William Marshal but also from the royal line of Leinster in Ireland via 'Strongbow's wife. This was not just a matter of genealogical interest: it gave the new Bruce dynasty of Scotland from 1306 a claim to the throne of Leinster plus the Irish High Kingship, and in 1315–18 King Robert's brother Edward Bruce was to use this to claim the latter throne in his invasion of Ireland after the eviction of the English from Scotland. The marital arrangements of the Marcher nobility in the early and mid thirteenth century thus impacted on international affairs in the following century.

The crisis years of King John's reign were also the setting for one of the most famous 'outlaw' literary romances of the medieval period, which centred on the concept of a heroic young man of aristocratic blood unjustly losing his lands and being forced into the wilderness to fight for his rights against the 'evil' King John and his grasping advisers. This in turn fed into the emerging legend of Robin Hood, who was to be placed (first by a Scots writer, John Major, in the early sixteenth century) in the time of King Richard's Crusade in 1190–3 but in his early incarnations was linked variously to events of the 1220s or 1260s. 'Robin' was originally a yeoman, that is a minor farmer, not the deprived rightful claimant to the earldom of Huntingdon (held by the Scots royal family at this time in real life), and was set according to the early poems about him either in Barnsdale, southern Yorkshire, or else in adjacent northern Nottinghamshire – the 'Sherwood' myth was not originally definitive. The possible prototypes for his activities who have been chased up by researchers include genuine 'Robert Hood's in trouble with the law in the 1220s (and also the later 1320s) and historical outlaws with names like 'Robin' who were victimised due to political misfortunes, such as men disgraced and outlawed after the defeat of Simon de Montfort's cause in 1265 (e.g. Roger Godberd). But although Robin and all his main prototypes were not connected to the Marches, there was one famous Marcher legend of an outlaw who fought for justice against the corrupt and vindictive King John and his elite, based on real events and turned into a literary epic. This was the tale of Fulk FitzWarine, in fact the real minor Shropshire baron Sir Fulk FitzWarin (*c.* 1160/5–1258), whose family were the hereditary lords of Whittington. His great-grandfather Warin or Guarin of Metz in Lorraine, after whom the family were named, was one of the incoming French landed elite of the Marches around 1100, a contemporary of the founders of the FitzAlans of Oswestry, and Warin's son Fulk FitzWarin of Whittington (d. *c.* 1120) was succeeded by his son Sir Fulk (d. 1197), the outlaw's father. This man crucially married Hawise de Dinan, or Dinant, the daughter and heiress of that Joce de Dinan who had held Ludlow Castle for King Stephen in the 1130s and who died in 1166 after losing that lordship and its lands to his rivals the de Laceys. Hawise's mother, Joce's wife, had been the widow of Henry I's local southern Marches strongman Payn FitzJohn, killed in 1137. Sir Fulk the outlaw, who married firstly Maud Vavasour (d. 1226) and secondly Clarice d'Auberville, thus inherited the de Dinan claim to Ludlow and the other lands of Payn FitzJohn, in opposition to the de Laceys who had regained this ancestral inheritance *c.* 1150–5 and were well-connected at Henry II's court (and bolstered from the 1170s by lands in Ireland, too). The whole issue of Sir Fulk's outlawing was thus connected to the long-running feud between his family, as heirs to Joce de Dinan, and the de Laceys – with the latter usually possessing more political clout at the royal court and quite ruthless enough to undermine their challenger by trying to have him disgraced. More provably, Fulk was also in dispute with King John early in his reign over the ownership of Whittington, which lay in the extreme north-west of Shropshire and had been fortified by William Peverel (from the major family of Peverel that were based in Derbyshire) on behalf of Empress Matilda in the civil war in 1138. The castle and its estate were subsequently abandoned to the resurgent power of adjacent Powys under Madoc ap Maredudd (ruled 1132–1160), and in 1165 Henry II recognised a Welshman, Roger de Powys, as its lord. The latter's heir Maurice (d. 1200) was in dispute over its ownership with Fulk's father, with the latter recognised as owner by Richard I's courts in 1195; but when Fulk inherited his estates in 1197 and paid £100 for the feudal relief (i.e. inheritance tax) for Whittington, its possession was not confirmed and in 1200 John granted it to his rival Maurice de Powis. Unable to secure possession despite his payments, Fulk ended up in rebellion against the king by spring 1201, and was cited as a rebel along with fifty-two followers and named in company with another rebel based in Somerset, William Marsh, who had pirate ships in the Bristol Channel. The king sent his trusted retainer Hubert de Burgh (soon to be put in charge of the king's captive nephew Prince Arthur) to deal with him. He was clearly driven out of his home region as he appears in 1202 as a refugee at Stanley Abbey, near Chippenham in Wiltshire. On 11 November 1203 he and his brothers William, Philip, and John, their cousins, and other rebels were pardoned – the revolt was clearly a family enterprise – and in October 1204 a payment of a fine of two hundred marks secured him his inheritance of Whittington, which he enjoyed for the rest of his life. This is the basic historical record, of a reasonably typical minor dispute over the inheritance and lordship of estates, which saw the unsuccessful party take to the hills and woods as an outlaw and eventually negotiate his pardon. In real life, Fulk was well-connected, and his list of noble sponsors who stood surety for his payment of the necessary fine to marry the de Vavasour heiress in 1207 included Earl Henry de Bohun of Hereford, the 'Constable of England', William de Braose of Brecon (d. 1211)'s grandson William (executed 1230), the king's half-brother the Earl of Salisbury, and some of the de Peverels, who had evidently given up any dispute between them over Whittington. Sir Fulk was subsequently summoned to serve in King John's campaign in western France in 1214, and was probably one of the landowners who joined the rebels in 1216–17 as his other main estate of Alveston in Gloucestershire was then temporarily confiscated. He subsequently struggled over control of Whittington with Llywelyn ap Iorweth in the 1220s. But his 'stand' of 1201–3 was literarily turned into a romance of an unjustly persecuted hero boldly and successfully defying a corrupt and brutal regime with 'people's justice' in the manner of Robin Hood. The original is lost, but appears to have been French – like the main contemporary thirteenth-century romances about King Arthur. In this version he was a youth brought up at Court as one of the young squires attendant on the future King John, who (naturally given the latter's reputation) was an arrogant and unpleasant young hooligan. When the prince cheated at chess, hot-headed Fulk objected and ended up knocking him out in a brawl, for which he had to flee from court, and years later John had his revenge by outlawing him. Fulk then lived in the 'greenwood' like Robin Hood with his loyal band of followers, helping the poor by robbing the rich and outwitting the blundering officers of the law, until his many noble deeds and the impossibility of capturing him drove the king to pardon him. Some of this may be grounded in reality, but the actual significance and impact of his career was very minor.

After the civil war: Gwynedd resurgent, and more tensions between the English monarchy and the Marcher lords. Llywelyn the Great, the younger Marshals, and Hubert de Burgh

The distraction of the Marcher lords by the civil war in 1215–17 enabled the Welsh to make their greatest gains for eighty years, this time under a more powerful state than that which had faced them in the 1136 crisis. This involved a major march south into Deheubarth by Llywleyn of Gwynedd in winter 1215/16, as invited by Prince Rhys Gryg to combat his nephews. Rhys duly assisted Llywelyn's southern campaign of winter 1215/16, when the large Gwynedd army used unusually mild weather to show its power across South Wales and to retake Carmarthen and Cardigan castles. All the local Welsh princes queued up to submit to Llywelyn, who enforced a division of Deheubarth between them at a summit at Aberdyfi early in 1216. Rhys was secured in Cantref Mawr and his brother Maelgwyn in Ystrad Tywi and Ceredigion, with Rhys (d. 1222) and Owain ap Gruffydd (d. 1235) restricted to minor principalities. In 1217 Llywelyn granted Rhys Gryg the custodianship of Swansea Castle under his authority as overlord. But the princes of Deheubarth were unable to hold onto Gower/Gwyr, dominated by the castle of Oystermouth, which the 1216 expedition had seized from the de Braoses. The new lord, Reginald de Braose, was initially in a precarious position as a foe of King John, who had driven his family out of their lands in 1210 and murdered his mother and brother, and was unable to save Gower but held onto his main bloc of lands around Builth, Radnor, Hay, Brecon, Abergavenny, and the 'Three Castles'. Llywelyn however agreed to hand Gower back to Reginald, as the latter married his daughter Gwaldys in 1220; both of them needed the other as potential foes and victims of the English government once the regency for Henry III ended. The English maintained a toehold on the coast east of the Tywi Estuary as well as holding out in southern Pembrokeshire. The powerful Marshal earls of Pembroke, of whom the aged Earl William was regent of England in 1216–19 and had a brood of aggressive sons, rallied the defence. His eldest son and successor (1219) Earl William returned from looking after his landed inheritance in Ireland after Welsh attacks on his Pembrokeshire lands and captured Carmarthen and Cardigan from Deheubarth in 1223, and then allied himself to the dissident Prince Cynan, son of Hywel Sais, whom he granted the commotes of Emlyn and Ystlwyf as his ally against the senior princes of the dynasty. The Marshals retook the offensive in Ceredigion under William, but his absence from Ireland had led to his local rival there, Hugh de Lacey, the lord of Ulster, attacking his lands, and in 1224 the king and his regents sent William back there as justiciar. He served a two-year term there, briging the de Laceys back under control, but lost royal support; as he was recalled in 1226 he was ordered to hand over Cardigan and Carmarthen to the king. In 1230 he joined Henry to be the military leader of the king's first overseas expedition – a typically initially bold but over-optimistic and ultimately shambolic attempt to reconquer Normandy with inadequate resources. The king landed in Brittany with an army to encourage a revolt in Normandy following the death of his late challenger Prince Louis (Louis VIII of France, d. 1228), but lost his nerve and refused to attack Normandy until a revolt actually occurred – which did not happen as his promised allies there were ironically too cautious to move until he was in their land. The campaign fizzled out, and as Henry went home William was left in charge of the remaining army in Brittany. He restored his influence at court by marrying off his widowed sister Isabella to the king's brother and heir Richard, Earl of Cornwall, in February 1231, but died soon after he returned to England in April 1231. (One story by the chronicler Matthew Paris later claimed his rival for power, Hubert de Burgh, had him poisoned, but this seems unlikely.)

This brought his brother Richard Marshal back from the family lands in France – lands which he had taken on instead of his elder brother as it was now illegal to do homage to both the King of England and the King of France – to become earl and take up the inheritance. William's widow Eleanor, the king's sister, took a vow of chastity, but broke this when in 1236 she unexpectedtly married the rising young nobleman Simon de Montfort (1208–1265), son of the leader of the Albigensian Crusade, who had returned like Richard Marshal from his family's lands in France to take up an English peerage to which he had rights – in this case, the earldom of Leicester. The marriage was secret and not approved by the king and his council as would be normal, probably due to the king preferring to marry off Eleanor to some useful foreign ruler, and its legality was disputed. Henry III subsequently claimed that Simon had deliberately had sexual relations with Eleanor before the marriage so that she was 'damaged goods', who another bridegroom would not want, and the king would thus have to accept Simon's marriage to her for lack of an alternative – even at this stage, the relationship between the two men was thus strained. The waywardness, extravagance, and unreliability of Henry, coupled with his excessive grants of land and office to resented royal favourites, was already causing criticism, and the Marshals and other Marcher lords were drawn into this political maelstrom – as was Hubert de Burgh, who his one-time royal protégé and ward was to alternately grant lands and power and just as suddenely he withdraw them. Luckily for Llywelyn of Gwynedd, his main potential Welsh challenger, Richard Marshal now ended up as de facto leader of the rash and favourite-prone king's critics, with his faction objecting to the power wielded by and grants given to the most acquisitive senior administrators, the clerics Peter des Roches (Bishop of Winchester, veteran administrator for King John, and civil war colleague of William Marshal the elder) and his relative Peter des Rivaux. The latter piled up a collection of county sheriffdoms that was unprecedented for a civilian courtier and was believed reliably to be living well off the financial proceeds, and the fault for this unbalanced concentration of offices ultimately lay with the king – and, in a visibly nationalist mood, the criticism focused on the two Peters and their court allies of overseas origin as being French Poitevins, as recounted by Matthew Paris. (The fact that the royal critics were led by two men of French landed origin themselves, Richard Marshal and Simon de Montfort, was ironical.) The king also piled up honours on Hubert de Burgh, giving him Cardigan (along with the 'Three Castles' of Skenfrith, Grosmont, and the White Castle in northern Gwent) in 1228 along with the castle and honour of Montgomery that had once been held by the earls of Shrewsbury. Hubert was thus meant to be the king's local enforcer and to create a large new lordship dependent on Henry, but his bold attempt to invade and take over the cantref of Ceri in Powys from his new lands in the adjacent upper Severn Valley in 1228 was an expensive failure. His new castle there was built at great effort but soon abandoned at the end of the campaign, and earned him mockery; nor was Henry's own campaign in the region successful. The resultant campaign into the South by Llywelyn ap Iorweth in 1231 to reassert his power complicated matters further, while Rhys Gryg recaptured Cardigan Castle in 1231, too. In 1232 Hubert's enemies prevailed on the king to dismiss him and seize his lands, and he was thrown into prison at Devizes Castle – but the lesson for other great magnates was that if the king took against them the same fate could befall them, too. As a result, when the king's trenchant critic Richard Marshal was summoned from his Welsh lands to court at Gloucester in 1233, he refused to come and was duly outlawed. He rose in revolt against the royal government and boldly sent his men to Devizes Castle to arrange the escape of his one-time foe de Burgh as another victim of royal injustice; the latter then joined him in an anti-Poitevin alliance that if unchecked might have brought in other barons in a 1215-style appeal to the idealistic against royal misrule. A truce in March 1234 provided for Richard to keep his lands and de Burgh to be pardoned with promises that Peter des Roches would be dismissed from court, but in the meantime a war had broken out in the Marshal family's Leinster lands between the rebels' younger brothers and the de Laceys, Walter, the lord of of Trim, and Hugh, the Earl of Ulster, with the Justiciar Maurice FitzGerald (1232–45), lord of Offaly to the north-west of Leinster, backing the latter. FitzGerald (d. 1258), who succeeded his father Gerald FitzMaurice in the Irish midlands barony of Naas in 1204 and inherited the barony (later county) of Offaly – the former Irish kingdom of the 'Ui Failghe' kindred – on the north-west borders of Leinster from his mother, Eva de Bermingham, was a major player in the Anglo-Norman Irish baronial elite too, and as such had plenty to gain from marginalising the Marshals there; and he was also the grandson and namesake of the Marcher adventurer Maurice FitzGerald, lord of Llansteffan (d. 1176), who had played a leading role in the conquest in 1170–6.

Richard Marshal was accused of encouraging the rebellion of his brothers in Ireland, though they were probably the victims of deliberate provocation by the king's men, and he fled to his Leinster lands rather than face a rigged investigation and forfeiture in England. Subsequently he was attacked and defeated at the Battle of the Curragh in Meath on 1 April 1234 by FitzGerald, who was accused of tricking Richard's men into leaving the battlefield on pretence of a truce and then attacking. Richard could have fled but preferred to rally those few men who stood by him (allegedly only fifteen knights) and attack the vastly larger royal forces, and was mortally wounded and captured. He died on 16 April, aged thirty-three or thirty-four, and was popularly regarded in England as a martyr of the oppressive Poitevin faction; his next brother Gilbert (1193–1241) succeeded him as Earl of Pembroke but had no children by his new wife (as of August 1235) Margaret of Scotland, sister of King Alexander II. The same applied to the youngest brothers who in turn succeeded to the earldom, Walter (1198?–1245) and Anselm (c. 1200–1245). Gilbert was killed in a freak accident at an illegal tournament at Ware in June 1241 after he took part against the king's orders and was thrown form his horse and dragged along the ground; his brother Walter was also present, and Henry did not confirm him in the combined role of Earl of Pembroke and Marshal of England until 1242 due to his anger. Walter married on 6 Janaury 1242 Margaret de Quincey, Countess of Lincoln (1206?–1266), a formidable heiress who in the complex world of thirteenth-century English elite politics was a major catch, being countess in her own right rather than as usual by marriage. The Lincoln title and lands had been held previously by her great-uncle Ranulf de Blondeville, Earl of Chester and the main northern Marcher warlord, who died without children in 1232; he passed on his property and titles to various heirs, and of these his niece Hawise gained the Chester and Lincoln titles. She then almost immediately passed on the latter with its estates (such as the honour of Bolingbroke) to her daughter Margaret, who married firstly John de Lacey, lord of Pontefract (d. 1240), and secondly Gilbert Marshal. The union of part of the Chester lands with the Marshal dominions was prevented as she had no children by Gilbert; instead he died young at Goodrich Castle, near Ross-on-Wye, in November 1245. Margaret took part of his lands, including Kildare in Leinster, as her inheritance. His brother Anselm then died a month after him, not having been confirmed as Earl of Pembroke by the king. The deaths of five brothers without children was unusual and was supposed to be due to divine punishment, as called for by an Irish holy man for their church-robbing in Ireland. This succession of deaths thus left their younger sister, Matilda (d. 1248), who had married the Earl of Surrey, and her sister Joanna's (d. 1234) daughter by Warin de Munchensey, Joanna (*c.* 1230–1308), as heiresses. Henry used this windfall of lands and titles to enrich his kin: he made Joanna Countess of Pembroke and married her off to his half-brother, William de Valence (1226?–1296), soon after 1248 to give the latter the Pembroke lands and title. William and his brothers were the sons of King John's widow Isabella of Angouleme by her second marriage, to her ex-fiance's son Count Hugh of Lusignan; the way that this group of sharp-elbowed young nobles leeched off their half-brother Henry III and collected lands and heiresses played a major role in stimulating baronial resentment against Henry in the 1240s and 1250s.

As of the late 1220s Llywelyn's elder, illegitimate son Gruffydd was his viceroy in the lands of southern Powys, taken from Gwenwynwyn, later being superseded by his younger son and heir Dafydd. The rulers of Deheubarth were weaker militarily and needed his help against the Marshals and occasional royal expeditions. But the self-declared 'Prince of Wales' lacked his eleventh-century predecessors' full control of Wales as he could not either regain the south coast from the Anglo-Norman settlers or depose the remaining rulers of Deheubarth and Powys – nor did his marriage to Joan (Siwan), born *c.* 1190, the illegitimate daughter of King John and a certain Clementia, mean that either John or the adult Henry III after 1230 would allow Llywelyn to build up an unchallenged position in Wales. His marriage brought him into a major incident in Marcher politics, when his unfaithful wife had an affair with the baron of Brecon, Hay-on-Wye, the 'Three Castles' of the upper Monnow Valley, and Totnes – William de Braose, son of Llywelyn's late ally Reginald (d. June 1228) by the heiress Grace de Briwere and stepson of Llywelyn's daughter Gwladys, who Llywelyn captured in 1228 and 'invited' to his court as a potential ally. William was now required to hand over Builth to Llywelyn, who thus gained a valuable foothold on the upper Wye. But he was found in compromising circumstances with Princess Joan in Llywelyn's bedchamber in February 1230 and was executed in a famous scandal. William's death meant the division of the huge de Braose lordship among his four daughters as he had no son – the eldest, Isabel, was married to Llywelyn's son Dafydd, so Builth was passed on to this couple; second daughter Maud and her husband Roger de Mortimer of Wigmore (d. 1282) gained Radnor lands; third daughter Eva (*c.* 1226–1255) and her husband William de Cantelupe (d. 1254) gained Abergavenny; and the fourth daughter, Eleanor (d. 1251), and her husband Humphrey de Bohun (d. 1265) gained Brecon with the peninsula of Gower. Humphrey de Bohun was the son of another Humphrey (d. 1275), second Earl of Hereford (of the de Bohun line) and Earl of Essex after his father Earl Henry, but predeceased his father so his son by Eleanor, Humphrey (d. 1298), succeeded. The great de Braose lordship was thus split up permanently, to the king's political benefit – no one heir was now well-resourced enough to challenge him. Indeed, the de Cantelupe line that now gained Abergavenny (not a Marcher dynasty but owning Calne in Wiltshire and Aston Cantlow in Worcestershire) were to die out in the main line with Eva and William's son, also William, in 1273; his sisters then divided it up. The elder William who married Eva was usefully the son of the king's steward, hence the gift of a valuable heiress to keep the Abergavenny lands in the hands of a royal trusty from a loyal service family; his brother (St) Thomas, Bishop of Hereford, was however more independent-minded, an idealistic Christian reformer closely associated with Simon de Montfort.

Llywelyn's ambitious marital diplomacy saw his daughter Helen married off to Earl Ranulf of Chester's (d. 1232) principal heir John 'the Scot' (1207–1237), son of the earl's sister by the new Scots King Alexander II's uncle Earl David of Huntingdon. John took over the earldom of Chester after Ranulf's daughter Hawise but died childless in 1237, bringing the earldom of Chester back to the Crown; Helen was now forced by Henry III to marry an English baron, Roger de Quincey. Her widowed sister Gwladys (d. 1251), married secondly in 1230 Ralph de Mortimer (*c.* 1190–1246), lord of Wigmore and successor in 1227 of his childless elder brother Hugh. She was the ancestress of the later Mortimers who became Richard II's heirs and as such posed a threat from 1399 to the House of Lancaster; her son by Ralph, Roger de Mortimer (1231?–1282) the seventh lord of Wigmore, as seen above married Matilda, the daughter of the William de Braose who Llywelyn had executed in 1230. This alliance of 1247 thus aligned the Mortimers and de Braoses together as central Marcher allies. A third daughter, Margaret, married (in 1219) the nephew of the executed William de Braose, John de Braose, whose father William and grandmother Mabel had been murdered by King John so he was nicknamed Tadody ('the Fatherless'). The girls were thus used to further Llywelyn's dynastic links to major Marcher families.

Gwynedd's period of greatest authority among the other Welsh princes (1212–40 and 1258–77) notably coincided with English preoccupations elsewhere, and depended on the personal prowess and power of the two Llywelyns rather than any permanent acceptance by the other Welsh princes of legal and military subordination to any ruler of Gwynedd. But in the youth of Henry III, Llywelyn Fawr was temporarily able to build up as much dominance over Wales as was practicable for a realm much weaker in resources than its English neighbour, and could even have one son – his son by John's daughter, Dafydd, not the elder Gruffydd – recognised as sole heir to avoid a repeat of the civil wars after 1170. In defiance of Welsh custom, he chose to avoid the division of his lands between his legitimate and illegitimate sons, and secured papal approval in 1222 for following the Europe-wide practice of inheritance solely by his legitimate son, i.e. Dafydd. The Welsh lords were duly summoned to assemblies in 1226 and 1238 to swear fealty to Dafydd. Gruffydd was given two cantrefs in the early 1220s, took an army to help drive the earls of Pembroke out of Ceredigion in 1223, and became his father's sub-ruler of annexed Southern Powys (Gwenwynwyn's former lands) in 1226, but was imprisoned at Degannwy from 1228–34 and as of 1238 was only allowed to rule Lleyn.

The civil war in England in 1216–17 gave Llywelyn the chance to seize the territories of his enemy Gwenwynwyn in Southern Powys in 1216, and in 1217 he made a major progress through South Wales unopposed, receiving the submission of Swansea and marching through Deheubarth as far as Haverfordwest. His subsequent treaty with the regency government of England at Worcester in March 1218 granted Llywelyn the custody of Cardigan and Carmarthen castles for the king's minority and recognised his annexation of Southern Powys in return for his fealty. The two castles, and Montgomery, were regained by the English in 1223 as the newly adult Henry and his principal South-West Wales Marcher lords, the Marshals of Pembroke, turned their attention to restoring their local power. But the aggressive new Earl of Pembroke (1219), the ex-regent's son William, and his brothers Richard and Gilbert all died young, and for much of the late 1220s and early 1230s they were at odds with the king's government and in semi-revolt, so they lacked royal aid to tackle Gwynedd. Llywelyn's strong position in central and southern Wales remained intact for his lifetime, and the English sought his help in ordering lords such as Rhys Gryg of Cantref Mawr to return disputed territories in 1220. One of these areas, Gower, was handed over to Llywelyn's new son-in-law (1219), John de Braose, lord of Bramber in Sussex, of the senior line of the lords of Brecon, whose family retained it throughout the thirteenth century.

When he executed William de Braose early in 1230 the latter's lands passed to his daughters (Builth to Dafydd's wife), and King Henry granted Brecon and thus the most powerful southern Marcher estates to his senior minister and commander Hubert de Burgh, who had successfully defended Dover Castle against the French in 1216. In retaliation Llywelyn used the convenient deaths of two major Marcher earls who held the main estates in South-West and South-East Wales, Pembroke and Gloucester, to join in a revolt by their tenants and by the local princes – who had to seek his permission to break the peace with the English first. In June–July 1231 he retook Montgomery, Radnor, Hay, Brecon, and other central Marcher castles and then moved on south to Neath and west to retake Carmarthen and Cardigan, reasserting his power in the South, while the inexperienced Henry moved up the Wye to retake Painscastle (but then stayed inactive there for weeks). A truce was finally arranged with the English at Brocton in Shropshire in March 1234, and renewed in June the following year at Myddle – as it turned out, permanently. Llywelyn was left supreme within those lands held by the Welsh rulers, and in 1234 the English government relied on him to return some lands in northern Glamorgan seized by local rebels. He tied his Welsh junior princes to him by bonds of fealty and by requiring legal suits to appear in his courts. The difficulty – apart from the lack of any historical tradition or legal precedents to back up these initiatives – was that Llywelyn's supremacy rested on personality rather than long-recognised rights, and he had restive junior princes, particularly in Powys. He sought to play up the supposed tradition of primacy by Gwynedd in Wales with promotion of the overlordship of his ancestor Maelgwyn within Wales in the sixth century. As of the late 1230s he was weakening after a stroke in 1236 and his wife's death in 1237, and it is probable that the oaths taken to his son Dafydd in October 1238 implied that the latter was now effective co-ruler.

6

THE MARCHER APOGEE?
1235–1295

How the Marcher lords helped Simon de Montfort constrain the king's power and then turned on de Montfort and destroyed him; the rivalry of the king's poitevin kinsmen; the Marchers threaten to overshadow young Edward I; the king hits back

The last princes of Gwynedd/Wales were closely connected to current English politics, not least from Llewelyn Fawr's marriage to King John's illegitimate daughter Joan. Their son Dafydd succeeded on 11 April 1240 when Llewelyn died, aged around sixty-seven. His elder half-brother Gruffydd was superseded. Dafydd had been recognised as heir by all the principal men of Wales, who Llewelyn required to do fealty to him at Strata Florida Abbey in October 1238. (He had intended a full ceremony of homage, but Henry III protested that this was illegal as he was a royal vassal.) Dafydd arrested and imprisoned Gruffydd and his eldest son Owain either before or after their father's death, but Gruffydd's wife Senena escaped to England and persuaded – and paid – Henry III to intervene on the prisoners' behalf. Dafydd was Henry III's nephew but was still rudely treated as an ordinary vassal, rather than a sovereign prince, at his post-accession meeting with Henry at Gloucester in May

1240 – even his knighting there emphasised his dependence on his patron. He had to restore Gruffydd and Owain to their lands, but the former was promptly removed to England as a hostage. His lack of power was shown up as his father's dependents and enemies mockingly reasserted their power, the Marshal family (earls of Pembroke) seizing Cardigan, and the mid-Marches baron Roger Mortimer, Dafydd's cousin, seizing Maelienydd and Gwerthyrion in southern Powys. A royal military campaign into Gwynedd saw Dafydd submitting to a new treaty at Gwerneigron (29 August), and in its confirmation later in London was required to give up Degannwy, Mold, and the eastern section of Gwynedd to England to curtail its power. Dafydd had married (in 1229) Isabella de Braose, daughter of William de Braose, who his father had executed in 1230 for adultery with Dafydd's stepmother Joan and Eva Marshal, daughter of the English 'regent' of 1216–19 William Marshal, Earl of Pembroke, but they had no children. Gruffydd, deported to the Tower of London as an English hostage in 1241 to be used against Dafydd if the latter displeased Henry, died on 1 March 1244 when a rope gave way as he was trying to climb down from a window in the White Tower. This led to a major revolt by angry Welsh tenants of the Marcher lords, from which Dafydd was able to regain some territory.

Gruffydd's eldest son Owain succeeded Dafydd when he died, aged under forty, on 25 February 1246 at Abergwyngregyn. He was forced to surrender as Henry's new lieutenant of Cardigan and Carmarthen castles, Nicholas de Molis, led a royal army north from Carmarthenshire along the coast right to the new English fortress on the Conwy at Degannwy that summer (a template for Edward I's attack in 1277). Owain had to surrender much more territory to Henry – the entire Perfeddwlad east of the Conwy – in the treaty of Woodstock in April 1247.

The earldoms of Pembroke and Gloucester and Simon de Montfort in the late 1250s crisis: one a royal ally, one a royal critic

The reassertion of royal control in Wales at the expense of both

Marcher lords and Welsh princes was however temporary, and was to be brought down by Henry's own rashness, extravagance, favouritism to his Court intimates (now dominated by the Lusigans, his half-brothers, led by the new Earl William of Pembroke), and lack of skill at handling his nobles. He had learnt nothing from the turbulence of the early 1230s, and added to the disquiet of alienated nobles by the taxation arising from his bold European ambitions – probably stimulated by his marriage of 1236 to Eleanor of Provence, one of the four co-heiresses to that county but also niece to a new set of ambitious and office-seeking incomers, her Savoyard uncles. One of these North Italian semi-royal nobles acquired the Archbishop of Canterbury (Boniface), another the London land on which he built the eponymous Savoy Palace (Peter). In addition, they helped to embroil Henry in Italian politics as he accepted an offer of the Kingdom of Sicily (and Naples) from the papacy for his second son Edmund, provided he helped to evict its Hohenstaufen rulers, arch-foes of the papacy – which entailed hugely unpopular new taxes on the English Church to raise an army. Meanwhile the king's brother Earl Richard of Cornwall was also engaged on an expensive mission to acquire the Holy Roman Empire, vacant after the deaths of emperors Frederick II (d. 1250) and Conrad IV (d. 1254) of Hohenstaufen. The English elite fulminated at the expense and uselessness of the king's plans and his being dominated by a small clique of foreign favourites, among whom the Franco-Italian Peter d'Aigueblanche had acquired the Bishopric of Hereford to the irritation of the Marchers – and now Earl Gilbert (de Clare) of Gloucester, who had spoken up against royal extravagance and favouritism in the Great Councils and embryonic Parliaments of the 1240s, was joined by alienated former royal favourite Simon de Montfort, Earl of Leicester. Married to Earl William of Pembroke's (d. 1231) widow Eleanor, the king's sister, Simon was certainly at odds with the king's acquisitive uncles-in-law and half-brothers. He was supposed to have said in 1252 that if the king confiscated his lands as a result of the Gascons' lawsuit against him over his misrule as their recent governor, some Savoyard or Poitevin would receive his earldom of Leicester, indicating who he saw as out to ruin him. In May 1257 Simon and William of Valence, Earl of Pembroke and royal half-brother, had a furious quarrel that nearly ended in a fight at the King's Council over William's men allegedly raiding Simon's lands and then having their loot recovered by Simon's steward. At the time of the major crisis over a stand by part of the elite against Henry's unwise governance in spring 1258, William was accusing Simon of putting his enemy Llywelyn of Gwynedd up to raiding the earldom of Pembroke.

As events turned out, it was personal disputes among the great magnates which brought a substantial faction of them into the opposition ranks in spring 1258. A split occurred in the ranks at Court and a fear among those opposed to the king's favourites that they would not secure justice from their sovereign – always a danger for a narrowly based regime. Already even two of the queen's uncles, Peter of Savoy and Archbishop Boniface, had been in dispute with the king's half-brothers, and on 1 April 1258 a dispute between the ex-Justiciar of Ireland, John FitzGeoffrey, and the king's half-brother Aymer de Valence (Bishop-elect of Winchester) over the revenues of the church of Shere in Surrey (lands held by FitzGeoffrey) led to their retinues brawling. Aymer's men were the aggressors, but when John complained to the king he was ignored. John was closely related to the FitzPeters, who had been involved in the 1215–16 rising (his father and half-brother), so a defiant response to the king was to be expected. This latest example of royal partiality sparked off demands for widespread reform at the Parliament that met at Westminster around 9 April, with the threat of excommunications and an interdict hanging over the realm if the money for the Sicilian expedition was not found. On 22 April seven leading magnates – Simon de Montfort, the fourth Earl of Norfolk (Roger Bigod, *c.* 1209–1270) and his brother Hugh Bigod (d. 1266), the Earl of Gloucester (Richard de Clare), the king's half-uncle Peter of Savoy, John FitzGeoffrey, and Peter de Montfort (Simon's retainer and Warwickshire neighbour but no relation) – committed themselves to a sworn oath of confederation. They then confronted the king, weapons in hand, to demand that he expel alien courtiers and accept reform of the realm by a committee of twenty-four; Henry had no loyal magnates with troops to hand to defy them and had to agree to this. Norfolk, who had been involved in the Parliamentary demands for a reformed constitution in 1244 and led a delegation to the Church Council of Lyons in 1245 to complain at papal taxation of the clergy, and Gloucester (who had personal experience of the abuses of royal patronage and fiscal extortion as an unwilling ward of Hubert de Burgh on royal orders after his father died in 1230), were cousins, the sons of 1230s rebel Richard Marshal's sisters. Roger's mother was Matilda Marshal (1192?–1248), the eldest daughter of William Marshal. He had indeed inherited the role of Marshal of England after his Marshal brothers-in-law all died in 1231–45, and had also fought briefly in Richard's rebellion; and by normal rules of inheritance he could have expected more of the Marshals' lands than he had been given by the acquisitive king. He had violently quarrelled with the king and been threatened with the ruinous demand to pay all his debts at once in retaliation (1255) and had since been in dispute with Aymer de Lusignan, the new Earl of Pembroke – probably aggrieved that Aymer had some of 'his' rightful Pembrokeshire lands. Norfolk thus had experience of royal capricousness and unrealiability, like Simon, and had reason to fear the Lusignans' malevolence. Both these senior earls were dynastic rivals of William de Valence to lands which the latter had acquired by his marriage to a Marshal co-heiress, and had claims on the earldom of Pembroke estates; they had practical reasons to turn to the opposition cause rather than continue to rely on the king. As heirs to long-established regional dynasties, the de Clares (southern Marches) and Bigods (East Anglia), they had family pride to consider and would have regarded their families' role as senior advisers to the king as being usurped by greedy parvenus – and the future course of their loyalties was to show that Norfolk at least was prepared to swing back to the king's side once the initial tranche of reforms had been achieved. The motives of most of these figures were personal as much as ideological. The committee of twenty-four that they now set up consisted of twelve men nominated by the king and twelve by the confederate magnates, and prepared measures to be brought before a Parliament at Oxford in June. In the meantime Simon had another personal confrontation with William de Valence, over the latter's accusations that he had encouraged Llywelyn of Gwynedd to attack the earldom of Pembroke's lands; he was called a liar and a traitor, and had to be restrained from assaulting him in public.

A wide and representative meeting of the nation's political classes met at Oxford on 9 June 1258. This duly provided the opportunity for a much wider airing of grievances and demands that these be met in a legislative framework, extending the April 1258 confederates' demands into a broader move for reform of decades of complex abuses. Parliament was already accustomed to debate such issues as a prelude to granting the king taxation for war – and not to grant him taxes or troops if not satisfied. The military and Marcher factor in calling a Parliament should not be forgotten, as it followed alarming advances made against the embattled Marcher lords in South Wales by Llywelyn ap Gruffydd, who had evicted his elder brother and co-ruler Owain from his lands in Gwynedd in 1255 and was aggressively expanding his principality into territories to the south, which were either ruled by minor local Welsh princes or by English barons (including the refomers' target William de Valence in Pembrokeshire). The expanded but precarious 'super-state' of Gwynedd set up by Llywelyn's grandfather Llywelyn Fawr ('the Great'), with areas to its south as far as Carmarthenshire under his control or titular overlordship, had briefly created a tentative Principality of Wales from 1216–40, with Llywelyn using that title, but had been driven back by Henry into a smaller state consisting of eestern Gwynedd alone in 1240–1. Llywelyn ap Gruffydd was now resuming his work, overthrowing some of the princelings of Mid- and South Wales, and reducing others to vassalage and evicting English settlers from disputed lands; a repeat of Henry's large-scale campaigns of the 1240s to keep Gwynedd in check was urgent. Thus the June 1258 Parliament was supposed to provide a muster for a new Welsh campaign, with the king concentrating on his near territories, rather than Italy for a change, and helping out his embattled Marcher barons. A muster was to follow at Chester on 17 June for the war, with a larger than usual complement of landowners called up for the latter. The fact that the bulk of the de Clares' lands lay in Glamorgan, in the path of Llywelyn's expansion, is an important factor in explaining why the Earl of Gloucester was keen to see Henry diverted from Italy to Wales in his military interests. The gathering at Oxford took the opportunity to draw up what was known as the 'Petition of the Barons', a collection of grievances variously attributed to the earls and barons (i.e. the major landowners) or knights and freeholders (i.e. lesser landowners). This contained demands for controls on the Crown's intrusive and oppressive local agents, a less dilatory and biased judicial system, and an end to extortion by assorted leading beneficiaries of royal patronage on their estates. The committee of twenty-four, or parts of it, drew up the 'Provisions of Oxford', probably a series of 'working draft' memoranda of their plans rather than definitive published proposals. This envisaged systematic and permanent control of the royal government by people other than the king and his nominees, a first for English government (the controlling committees of barons set up in 1215 had been temporary, to achieve specific objectives in a fixed period). The committee of twenty-four would be superseded during this Parliament by a committee of fifteen, chosen by a complicated electoral system and crucially including seven of the twelve reformist baronial nominees on the twenty-four and only three of the king's twelve.

It was thus meant to give the reformers a permanent majority and end the current veto that the king's twelve could impose on progress (and apparently were doing). It would oversee all the royal officials and appoint the leading ones – an advance from the measure proposed in Parliament in 1244, which had only the leading ministers to be subject to Parliamentary choice and veto. It would have to approve all non-routine royal writs, thus controlling grants of money, offices, and other favours, and it was to remain in being for an indefinite number of years (perhaps twelve). It would cooperate with Parliament, which was now to meet regularly at prescribed times thrice yearly, with the council meeting there with a board of twelve elected representatives of the estate of landowners holding baronial rank. The justiciarship, the chief judicial/administrative office held by the king's most powerful ministers in the twelfth century and last used as the basis of Hubert de Burgh's power, was to be revived in favour of Hugh Bigod, Norfolk's brother. This in effect institutionalised politico-administrative control of the Crown's powers by the senior landowners, with a mechanism for making it semi-permanent and for overriding royal objections and controlling all the king's grants of office and wealth – in a form which was still to be contentious and resisted when something similar was attempted by Parliament in 1641, to be reversed in 1660. It was a stark comment on the political nation's lack of trust in Henry III and his chosen intimates. The attendees at the Oxford Parliament proceeded to take an oath to observe the Provisions before they dispersed, in accordance with the precedents of 1215 and serving to affirm the religious nature of their action, but also as a means of 'smoking out' objectors and prosecuting those who agreed to this but subsequently defected. The Lusignan brothers refused to take the oath to a plan that would undoubtably have deprived them of their ill-gotten gains, were duly deprived by a second Parliament which met within weeks at Winchester, and fled overseas, William included. This effectively decapitated the king's faction, and the council of fifteen and a subsidiary committee which was set up to negotiate a financial settlement for the king were dominated by reformists and their allies.

At this juncture the chroniclers identify Gloucester and FitzGeoffrey as well as Simon de Montfort as the reformist leadership; Thomas Cantelupe's uncle Bishop Walter Cantelupe of Worcester's participation in the vital council and committee suggests that he was the Church representative. The main danger of the administrative coercion of the king in June 1258 was that it would turn the latter irrevocably against the reformers and cause him to seek to restore his freedom of action by any means necessary – encouraged by greedy courtiers who had lost their ability to loot the nation's resources due to the reforms. This was a problem for any coercive reform of the royal administration, and was to overthrow the initial achievements of reformist barons in Edward II's and Richard II's reigns – and was to present a (literally) fatal threat to the chance of compromise between Charles I and his Parliamentary defeaters after 1646. Could the king be trusted to abide long-term by any agreement that was forced out of him, and if not what was to be done to save the victors from a royalist counter-coup? Henry's father John had not stood by the concessions forced out of him at Runnymede in June 1215, and this route might well have been taken by Henry, who had a reputation for capriciousness and untrustworthiness; the fate of ex-justiciar and royal mentor Hubert de Burgh (sacked and forced to flee to sanctuary, then imprisoned) was a warning to the king's potential foes. The reformers sought to prevent any papal intervention on Henry's behalf by sending a mission to Rome asking for approval of their actions, the appointment of a papal legate to bring on-the-spot papal legal backing to their work, the cancellation of the grant of Naples and Sicily to Edmund, and the dismissal of Aymer de Valence from the bishopric of Winchester. The only one of these requests granted was the cancellation of the Sicilian grant. The reformist measures enacted by the council and Parliaments notably included judicial action to remedy abuses of office by officials on the baorns' own estates. Gloucester was to resist this early in 1259 – and Simon was to insist on it and quarrel with him over it, showing his greater idealism (and probably a religious element of virtuous self-denial). The absence of Simon for several months while he was negotiating the Anglo-French peace treaty of Paris in 1259 (which finally abandoned Normandy and Anjou to Louis IX), the death of FitzGeoffrey, and judicial work across the country by Justiciar Bigod left Gloucester as the most determined reformist magnate. When the next Parliament met in February 1259, the Ordinance of the Magnates' that was issued envisaged the magnates and other baronial holders of manors allowing complaints against their judicial malpractice. The judicial rights of the baronage were laid out and regulated in the 'Provisions of the Barons' and published so the wider political public would be aware of them. On one level this was a morally approvable act, expressing a Christian self-denial and putting the barons under the same restraint as the king – no doubt under pressure of potential demands for this action in Parliament. On another, it separated the more altruistic (or ultimately realistic) leadership from those who preferred to act in their own self-interest and would be scared off this act into preferring a royalist 'revanche'. The initial planned text was altered to the barons' interests, and allegedly helped to cause a quarrel between Simon and the less generous Gloucester about the reformers becoming self-serving. Queen Eleanor and the king's brother Earl Richard were always ready to push Henry into confrontation – and as the hot-headed Prince Edward (born June 1239), from 14 February 1254 the king's Marcher deputy as the new Earl of Chester, lord of the 'Three Castles', and owner of Builth, Carmarthen, and Cardigan castles and so with a massive Marcher landed base and vassals to fight for him, emerged into political maturity, he could be expected to join this faction too, to regain his lost rights and prevent himself from being held in tutelage by a baronial committee once he was king. In March 1259

Edward formed a formal alliance with Gloucester to look after each other's interests, with the earl promising to help Edward get back lands lost in 1258 – though this alliance had had an awkward preliminary, as an earlier dinner held to consider terms with the two men at Winchester in June 1258 had left Gloucester (whose hair fell out) and his brother William (who soon died) extremely ill amidst the usual rumours of poisoning; Gloucester's steward was blamed and hanged.

The uneasy admiration of Edward for Simon was a factor in national politics from 1258–65. The two vigorous and ruthless warriors and political operators certainly had attitudes in common (including their mixture of self-serving greed, piety, and abrasiveness). Was it possible for Simon to have won him over long-term? But in a crisis Edward was always to put his family first. As of spring 1260, Edward's support for Simon led to someone spreading rumours that he was planning to depose his father in a revolt, presumably as Simon's ally – possibly a malicious plan by Gloucester to discredit both men and make himself indispensable to the alarmed king. Henry now returned to England from a visit to Louis with a force of mercenaries to add to his military power, and left Simon and various allies of his off the list of tenants-in-chief who were summoned to bring their troops to London for a meeting in late April. Simon managed to arrange the meeting of a Parliament at Westminster despite the king banning it, but Earl Richard of Cornwall held the City militarily for the king and when the latter and his troops arrived, an uneasy reconciliation was arranged beween Henry, Edward, and Gloucester. Having failed to get Justiciar Bigod to ban the king from returning or bringing mercenaries, Simon – who had thus shown his lack of conciliatory intent – faced the king putting him on trial. The trial, held during the July Parliament, saw Simon accused of obstructing both the French treaty and Henry's return, attempting to do the latter by armed force, and him in turn boldly denying it all and making sarcastic comments. The need for adjournment for another campaign against Llywelyn of Gwynedd, who was attacking Builth in mid-Wales, held up a resolution, and the trial was abandoned. The senior ministers were changed, Bigod – who had crucially denied Simon any legal support for coercing Henry earlier – being replaced as justiciar by Hugh Despenser. But the autumn Parliament now gave the power to remedy the misdeeds of lords' own officials to the lords themselves, a setback to the grass-roots demands of the reformers; the new general 'eyre' (i.e. a touring legal investigation into abuses) also lacked powers to correct these misdeeds and enforce the Provisions by its own fiat. In political terms, this watered down the achievements of 1258 and reasserted the lords' own rights. It was a betrayal of what had been achieved, or at the least a practical acceptance of the need to satisfy the alarmed, depending on the viewers' standpoint.

Both Simon and Gloucester ceased to attend the Council in midwinter 1260/1, and royalist adherents purged in 1258 returned unchallenged to Court. The initiative may have been Henry's or his relatives', and it had the political skill to keep moderate Montfort allies Bigod, Hugh Basset, and Despenser in office. Henry now sent an envoy to Rome to seek papal absolution from the Provisions of Oxford, using his father's tactic against Magna Carta in 1215 – a move attributed by the chroniclers to Earl Richard, the queen, or the queen's kinsmen. Summoning armed assistance from loyal barons to the February 1261 Parliament, he addressed the latter in tones of virtuous indignation to complain that the post-1258 regime had failed to reform his finances, had enriched itself, and had treated him as its minister not its lord. The king (or his prompters) did not attack the Provisions head-on but made accusations of misrule and personal gain that were less easy to brush off as arbitrary royal 'special pleading'. Once Henry was ready in May, he marched into Kent and Sussex to take over strategic castles (especially Dover) and the Cinque Ports, receive oaths of fealty from the locals, and secure the region for his army and potential foreign aid. Returning to London at the head of his vassals, he ousted the opposition governor of the Tower, and a papal bull of absolution from Henry's oath to the Provisions (June) enabled him to declare the latter invalid and to absolve others from their oaths to the Provisions. A mixture of promises and bribery, plus probably the desire to avoid a risky war, led to Gloucester and other opposition magnates drifting back to the king. Simon summoned three knights from each country to his headquarters in St Albans to discuss the situation, to receive reactions to the local initiatives in his favour and to moot a possible move for a Parliament free of royal leadership, but the king summoned a rival meeting with more attendees. As a result Henry had the military muscle to be able to impose terms on the opposition in the resulting talks held at Kingston-on-Thames, and a treaty on 2 November 1261 agreed that three representatives of each faction would negotiate on the future of the Provisions and the disputed sheriffdoms. If they failed to agree, firstly Richard of Cornwall and then Louis IX were to arbitrate. The opposition leadership duly accepted this and took part in the resulting arbitration processes, except for Simon who refused and left for France, apparently saying that he would rather be landless than perjured. His estimate of how far Henry could be trusted was more realistic, and the new Pope duly upheld the king's absolution from the Provisions while the baronial Council lapsed and the Lusignans were allowed to return to Court. In the interim, Earl Richard of Gloucester unexpectedly died at the manor of Waltham, near Canterbury, on 15 July 1262, aged only thirty-nine, and so was prevented from having to make a decisive choice to back either the king or the de Montfort faction. He was interred initially at nearby Canterbury Cathedral, and later at Tewkesbury Abbey once his grand tomb there was complete. His surprise death followed a dinner with the queen's uncle, Peter of Savoy, and the latter was rumoured to have poisoned him, but this seems unlikely; it is not known if this was seriously believed by his elder son and successor, Earl Gilbert (born September 1243), who succeeded him, but the latter gravitated towards the opposition. The complexities of Marcher inheritance meant that Earl Gilbert's mother, Maud de Lacey (1223–1288/9), Earl Richard's second wife, was the inheritor of the barony of Usk as her section of the vast Marshal inheritance – her mother Margaret de Quincey, Countess of Lincoln, referred to earlier, was the widow of the elder William Marshal's son Earl Gilbert of Pembroke (d. 1241), and had received a fifth of the earldom's lands. But Maud was an aggressive and litigious woman, aggrieved that her mother had not passed on more of the land to her and they spent most of their lives quarrelling over it. Earl Gilbert, nicknamed 'the Red Earl' because of his hair, was to be equally hot-tempered and assertive.

The next outbreak of a successful Welsh revolt in the middle Marches in November–December 1262 (probably partly to take advantage of the accession of a new and untried young Earl of Gloucester), which Llywelyn backed up, acted as a precipitator for the next round of domestic confrontation in England. As in 1258, Welsh politics – in particular the presence of a united and aggressively expansionist Gwynedd under Llywelyn – thus indirectly aided Simon and the reformers. Revolt by Welsh tenants against their alien and oppressive lords – in the case of 1262 the Mortimers of Wigmore – was not restricted to times of English weakness and Gwynedd strength, as a large-scale revolt had broken out in 1244 despite English military supremacy, after Llywelyn's hostage father Gruffydd had fallen to his death in an escape bid while trying to abseil down the wall of the White Tower in London. But revolt was always more dangerous with Gwynedd to take advantage of it and aid rebels. Needing military support from reliable royal tenants-in-chief in a new campaign, Henry prudently reissued the Provisions on 22 January 1263 and sent them around the country for publication by his officials, with assurances that he was reissuing them out of his altruistic goodwill. The imminent

Welsh war then led to Edward's return from France with a large mercenary army of Burgundians, Champenois, and others from central France, whose leaders he promoted over the heads of his aggrieved English tenants (these latter included the men recently targeted by Henry). This army was supposed to be aimed at the baronial opposition as well as at the Welsh, though Edward's interests on the eastern flanks of Gwynedd make it unlikely that he only used the Welsh war as an excuse. (John had used overseas mercenaries against domestic opponents in 1215–16, as had Henry II in 1173–74.) But the grant of lands and offices within Edward's estates to the newcomers' leaders alarmed the prince's excluded Marcher allies. Some disgusted English lords from Edward's estates thus linked up with other, more definitely Montfortian objectors to the alleged threat than Edward's troops – who should not have been brought in without Council permission according to the Provisions posed to the king's opponents. A 'leadership group' from these factions, combined with the Welsh war and Edward's recruitment of mercenaries, thus provided the spark to turn discontent into an armed challenge to Henry again, though if this had not occurred there would have been others. Simon was able to return with a basis of support for criticism of the king that led some of Edward's close associates, such as John de Warenne and the Marcher leader Roger Clifford, and even Earl Richard of Cornwall, to join him for a meeting at Oxford – the symbolic site of the Provisions. They reaffirmed their oath to the Provisions, and sent Henry a letter demanding that he publicly adhere to them too, and denounce all the enemies of the Provisions as mortal enemies. This was followed by direct action in the Marches, always a region suited for military acts of defiance to a challengeable king, as by Richard Marshal in 1234. The Montfortian faction of Marcher barons, including Edward's affinity, proceeded to arrest the unpopular Savoyard royal favourite Peter d'Aigueblanche in his own Hereford cathedral and ravage the local estates of royalist hardliners such as Robert Walerand.

Strategic towns were seized to cut the Marches off from a royalist attack, with sporadic attacks on royalist barons' lands and goods occurring elsewhere. Simon appears to have made approaches to Llywelyn for help, an alliance that coincided with their common interest in the military defeat of Prince Edward (Earl of Chester so a local foe of Gwynedd), whose castle at Diserth was attacked by the Welsh. Apart from securing Sussex and Kent – his route for Continental help – the king did nothing to challenge the opposition rampage across the Marches and disorder elsewhere. Instead it was Simon who moved forward once he had secured the Marches, leading his men round to the south of London to take over Guildford and Reigate castles and then to secure the Cinque Ports in July. The proudly semi-autonomous civic authorities at the latter defied the king and declared in favour of the Provisions, and there were hopes that the civic authorities in London would do so, too. Once Dover Castle had surrendered, Simon could advance on London; despite Edward's mercenaries at London and Windsor, Henry preferred to negotiate rather than fight. This time the balance of numbers of armed barons – plus the lack of cooperation for royalist sheriffs from the county elites – was on Simon's side, and the resultant negotiations and settlement (16 July, London) reflected this. All the Provisions were now to be enforced, except those found objectionable by an arbitration panel, but corrections could be made; all aliens were to be excluded from government, which targeted the Savoyards and Lusignans but also Edward's recently rewarded mercenary captains. The disturbances in London included the famous occasion when the (French/Savoyard) queen's barge was pelted with refuse by the City crowds at London Bridge as she attempted to head upriver from the Tower to Windsor. This and the country-wide attacks on 'alien' clergy who her faction had secured posts in the English Church gave a personal element to her hatred of Simon.

The most effective resistance against the encroaching English (whose power was now enforced by the creeping extension of the remit of the king's courts) was from Owain's younger brother and co-ruler Llewelyn 'the Last'. Already a semi-autonomus dynast in Dyffryn Clywd in Dafydd's later years, in 1250 he secured a secret alliance with Gruffydd ap Madoc of northern Powys, and in 1252 allied with Maredudd ap Rhys Gryg and Rhys Fychan of Deheubarth. If they stood by their promises they could widen any war with Henry, whose relations with his barons were deteriorating over his rash promises to aid the Pope in taking over Sicily and his favouritism for his French relatives so England might be distracted from an assault. Owain was defeated in battle at Bryn Derwin and deposed by Llewelyn in 1255. The latter regained most of the Perfeddwlad from England late in 1256, and exploited Henry's troubles with his barons to improve his position. He stalled Henry's invasion in 1257, gained his acceptance of Gwynedd's reconquest of lands that Henry had handed back to Gwynedd's Welsh and English Marcher rivals in 1258, and was recognised as Prince of Wales by an assembly of the senior Welsh lords called to conclude a treaty with the Scots in March 1258. He then seized Builth (with the cantref of Gwerthyrnion) from the Mortimers in 1260, took over Cedewain (on the upper Severn in northern Powys) when its ruler Owain ap Maredudd died in 1261, and in November 1262 accepted the opportunity of an attack by locals on the new Mortimer castle of Cefnllys in Maelienydd to overrun that territory, too. Maelienydd was annexed to Gwynedd; in the north the royal castles of Diserth (August 1263) and Degannwy (September 1263) fell, and in December 1263 Gruffydd ap Gwenwynwyn of southern Powys submitted. Llywelyn now allied himself with the baronial coalition led by Henry III's brother-in-law Simon de Montfort, Earl of Leicester, in 1263–4, and sent his troops to capture Bridgnorth for de Montfort (June 1263) and in 1264 to compel royal garrisons at Montgomery and Worcester to surrender to the earl. Usefully for him, the earl had by then taken control of the earldom of Chester from Henry's aggressive heir the Lord Edward.

In spring 1264 events moved towards a climax in the struggle between the king and the Montfortians, as the king and his army invaded the pro-Montfort region of the Cinque Ports in coastal Kent after successes in the Midlands. Once the region was overrun, Henry would have the option of using the Cinque Ports' fleet to blockade London immediately or waiting for reinforcements to arrive from the Continent first, and so it was best for Simon to challenge him before this potentially overwhelming threat developed. Thus the rebel army moved out of London into Sussex, and Henry headed west to the security of the castle at Lewes, held by his ally John de Warenne, sixth Earl of Surrey or 'Earl Warenne' (1231–1304), who was the son of William Marshal senior's daughter Matilda Marshal (d. 1248), the widow of the sixth Earl of Norfolk, and thus half-brother of the current earl. On 12 May Simon and his army – outnumbered by about three to one in cavalry – arrived at Fletching, a Montfort manor north of Lewes, en route to intercept him. The location of the resultant clash on the Downs immediately north of Lewes was thus due to the success of the king's unhindered campaign in Kent and the fact that Simon had avoided an earlier clash over the royal threat to relieve Rochester Castle. The Montfort army was the smaller force, and he was apparently waiting unsuccessfully for the arrival in London of Robert de Ferrers and his Derbyshire allies – who had enough to do that April coping with attacks on their lands by Prince Edward and his northern Marcher troops from the earldom of Chester. The failure of Simon's eldest son Henry de Montfort to capture or rout Edward earlier in a clash at Gloucester thus inhibited the full strength of the rebels from collecting in London. Simon had consulted his episcopal allies in the past few weeks about possible peace-terms offering the king compensation for his financial losses if Henry would uphold the Provisions, a sign of willingness to compromise. A second attempt to mediate by the Bishop of Chichester and local friars with Henry at Lewes now failed, with Simon again requiring the king's adherence to the Provisions and the withdrawal of 'evil counsellors' but prepared to submit all other issues to a panel of learned clerics.

During the night of 13/14 May Simon moved his army forward from his initial position at Offham, in the Weald on the north side of the Downs, to climb the steep northern slope of the ridge and occupy the summits. He would thus be fighting downhill southwards towards Lewes, giving him the advantage of momentum and cancelling out the royalist advantage of numbers. The king and his men, quartered in and around the town to the south, had to advance uphill – though on a reasonably gentle slope. Simon's address before the battle gave it an aura of moral righteousness; according to the 'Song of Lewes' he said that they were about to fight for the kingdom of England, the honour of God, the Blessed Virgin and all the saints, and for the Holy Church. They then prostrated themselves on the ground, confessed their sins and were absolved by the two bishops, and donned the crosses of Crusaders – which also helped to distinguish them from the foe as both armies would have been wearing similar mail coats or padded jerkins, with the higher social classes adding tabards adorned with their heraldic emblems. The battle then commenced, with the Montfortians drawn up neatly in four divisions and fighting with a coherent strategy arranged by an expert leader who retained control of his men. Unlike the inexperienced king, he was able to react to events and keep control of his subordinates – though due to his literally keeping the high ground he could also look out over the sloping battlefield easier than the king (on lower ground) could do. The impression of the royalists failing to use their advantage of numbers is reinforced by the crucial muddle on their right wing, the east side of the battlefield. Here, the ground fell away from the hillside into the Ouse Valley, and Edward was in command. Already a capable cavalry commander and in command of a force including his personal household intimates, other young aristocrats and gentry from the earldom of Chester, plus the hated 'alien' royal kinsmen William de Valence (with his Pembrokeshire troops) and Guy de Lusignan, he faced the London infantry and broke through their ranks with the force of his charge. This fate was to be expected when relatively inexperienced volunteer infantry without a compact 'hedge' of pikes met a charging force of cavalry; as yet there was no concept in England of arranging a tightly packed body of infantry with pikes to present a bristling barrier to nervous horses. Simon had not trained his infantry to withstand a charge, and regarded this danger as containable – as it turned out, correctly, but due to Edward's rashness not his own skill. One chronicler also has it that as Simon had had to travel by litter recently due to a broken leg he cunningly placed a cart with the de Montfort banner on it in the Londoners' wing to act as a magnet for Edward, who duly attacked it to target him and so wasted time on a futile mission. The impetuous prince pursued the Londoners off the battlefield for miles, keen to avenge the insult they had done his mother (by pelting her barge with refuse) in blood, and chased them across the river and up the Ouse Valley. According to local legend, he then slaughtered a body of trapped and exhausted Londoners on 'Terrible Down' at Halland, five or six miles up the Roman road. But while he was conducting his private feud, the absence of his right wing of cavalry from the battlefield enabled Simon's men to press the royalists back elsewhere, and neither King Henry nor Earl Richard were capable of steadying their flanks on the royalist centre and left. Eventually the royalists broke and fled back downhill into Lewes. The king took refuge in the Priory in the town, and Richard of Cornwall was trapped on the battlefield, hid in a nearby windmill, and was mocked by rude opponents as they surrounded him and shouted for 'Sir Miller' to surrender. By the time Edward returned it was too late to fling his cavalry into the fight and rescue his allies, and he had to fight his way back into Lewes to join the king at the Priory. The king's position was not entirely hopeless, in that he might have lost his army but he was in sanctuary under the protection of the Church; it would not look good for a self-proclaimed Crusader to defy the Church, and if the Priory was blockaded to starve the king's party out, the royalist garrison at Tonbridge might try to rescue them. As a result Simon needed recognition by the king that he had won and royal orders to demobilise his remaining followers, and Henry was able to negotiate his surrender, albeit on weak terms. The resulting 'Mise of Lewes', which can be reconstructed from chronicle accounts, provided for the king to pardon the rebels and assure them of their lands and goods, restoring all goods and hostages seized so far in the war. Henry would uphold the Provisions of Oxford in full and dismiss 'evil counsellors': a panel of arbitrators – four English bishops or magnates – would consider amendments to the Provisions and if they could not agree hand over arbitration to Henry's (and Louis') brother-in-law, Charles of Anjou, and the Duke of Burgundy. The other issues outstanding – including the long-running saga of the money owed by Henry to Simon and Eleanor regarding Eleanor's dowry – was to be dealt with by two French arbitrators, named by a panel of six French nobles and prelates free from Louis' veto on their membership, and one English arbitrator. Edward and his cousin, Henry of Almain, Richard of Cornwall's son but known for his admiration for Simon until he put family loyalty first in 1263, were to be hostages for the implementation of the deal, but those 'Edwardian' Marcher barons captured at Lewes were to be freed. The latter was probably necessary to win the clannish and violent Marchers' goodwill, but events were to show that they could not be trusted.

The terms of Simon's settlement with Edward in March 1265 required him to hand over his main source of landed power in the Marches, the earldom of Chester lands, plus

Newcastle-under-Lyme and his Peak District lordship to Simon, in return for lands of an equivalent value elsewhere The town and castle of Bristol were to be held by Simon as a pledge that Edward would implement the agreement, for five years. Edward was to restrict his household and council to men approved by the King's Council and refrain from bringing any aliens into England, and was to remain in England (not setting foot in the Marches) for three years. This prevented him from seeking Marcher or Louis IX's support in person, or bringing in another army of mercenaries; if the agreement was kept, Edward should be politically neutered and his threat held in check. The wild card in all these arrangements remained disputes within the baronage over lands, which could easily turn into factional confrontations and provide would-be rebels with an army if not defused. As events turned out, the first open threat to Simon came from the predictable source of the Marchers, who apparently formed a plot to rescue Edward in autumn 1264 with the involvement (or at the instigation of?) the exiled Queen Eleanor, who had fled to France after the Battle of Lewes to join her sister Queen Margaret. Edward's mother's agents had discovered the layout and defences of Edward's prison at Wallingford Castle, and according to one account a band of rescuers led by one Robert Walerond got as far as breaking into the outer bailey; the defenders rallied, held their prisoner at sword-point, and threatened to throw him over the walls until he called out to the royalists to persuade them to leave. Edward and the other royal hostages were moved to 'top-security' Kenilworth, which indicates how seriously the threat of rescue was taken. The Marchers went ahead and defied the regime in an armed assembly of their tenants: Roger Mortimer of Wigmore, Roger Clifford, and Roger Leyburn (stalwarts of Edward's following since 1258) were the ringleaders.

Simon ordered a summons of the feudal host for 25 November at Oxford, and after the offenders failed to obey a summons to meet him at Warwick moved into the Severn Valley with his forces. The would-be rebels were persuaded to obey a summons to meet him at Worcester, and under an agreement – which they were allowed to discuss with Edward as he was their feudal superior – Simon was to take their lands into custody for a year and a day while they went into temporary exile in Ireland (the usual refuge for Marcher lords in trouble with the government who had lands there, e.g. de Braose in 1211 and Richard Marshal in 1234). In return, Edward was to be liberated and to settle with the government at the February 1265 Parliament, which was duly carried out, unlike the Marchers' promises to leave England. There are two crucial pointers for future events and 'what ifs' at issue in this incident. Firstly, the armed assembly west of the Severn and plan to rescue Edward directly foreshadowed what happened in May–June 1265; and in this first episode Simon acted with vigour and speed, unlike in 1265, despite it being winter. Llywelyn of Gwynedd aided him by threatening the Marchers' rear.

A second challenge came from the Derbyshire magnate Robert Ferrers, Earl of Derby, who was in dispute with Edward (lord of the 'Peak' lands and of Peak Castle) as of 1264 and who had used the civil war as an opportunity to seize Peak Castle and other lands of the prince's. Simon now took the right to these over in the March 1265 agreement. It apparently added to grievances felt by Gloucester, who had the leading role in pressure on Simon in the February 1265 Parliament to dismiss his own mercenaries (ironically, aliens like Edward's much-criticised army of 1263) and hand over custody of assorted royal castles from his own personal nominees. Both a private army of mercenaries and trusted castellans were militarily useful security-measures for Simon, but could be seen as autocratic and a sign of double standards by the regime's leader. Was he behaving any better than Edward had done in 1263? Gloucester, whether out of ambition or out of principle, was able to seize the moral high ground on the issues, and later that spring he accused Simon openly of failing to observe the Provisions and 'Mise of Lewes'. At the least Simon was becoming politically careless, and after Gloucester's personal dislike of Simon's sons led to a threat of a planned tournament at Dunstable ending in a brawl, Simon cancelled it and infuriated him. Gloucester left Court for his Marcher estates, where he could plot and collect troops if so inclined. As in the 1250s, the head of Court and government had allowed his loyalist entourage to break up into faction – but given the presence of assorted hot-headed young nobles with rival ambitions and sharp tongues (and swords), this was probably inevitable at some point. According to the Chronicle of Guisborough, when Simon faced destruction by Edward's army at Evesham a few months later he was to tell his eldest son Henry that he and his brothers were to blame for this – but by then it was too late.

Gloucester failed to turn up as expected for a new tournament at Northampton on 20 April, a warning that he expected to be arrested like Ferrers had been. The danger of armed tenants being massed by him and his ally John Giffard in the southern Marches (possibly at St Briavel's Castle in the Forest of Dean) brought Simon's entourage to Gloucester at the end of April. The uneasy mixture of de Montfort household and royal court that accompanied Simon everywhere included both the king and Edward, which was necessary for security – neither could be trusted away from their unwelcome controller – but was yet another breach of the supposedly inviolable peace settlements. The move to the Marches was to end up with Simon trapped west of the Severn by rebellion, but was logical enough at the time to keep an eye on and possibly confront the Earl of Gloucester; as the regime's leader and best general, Simon could not trust the campaign to anyone else, and bringing the king along gave it royal authority. Negotiations between Simon and the earl followed, albeit with Simon's choice of arbitrators (all his close allies) so Gloucester had every reason to distrust the outcome. But now the exiled John de Warenne and William de Valence landed in the latter's Pembroke lordship with troops ready to join a rebellion, presumably with Gloucester's encouragement as he now held the lordship on Simon's behalf, and a plot for rebellion seems to have taken shape at Wigmore Castle, base of the Mortimer lordship in northern Herefordshire. Simon remained inactive for vital days at Hereford, planning for a new Parliament for June and seemingly unperturbed by the nearness of Gloucester's armed retainers to the town in hostile mode. Gloucester's brother Thomas de Clare, still trusted by Simon, negotiated between the two earls.

Simon was overconfident at this point, and failed to appreciate that Gloucester's approach was more than a negotiating tactic and did not heed what was going on at Wigmore. He was thus wrong-footed by a brilliant rebel coup on 28 May, as Edward was allowed to ride out of Hereford Castle to exercise his horse across the Wye in company with Thomas de Clare, an old friend, and some Montfortian knights. Instead, waiting Marcher rebels quietly arranged for Edward to change to a fresh horse once his accompanying Montfortian guards had worn their own horses out racing against him and so could not easily catch a fresh, fast horse. The prince then made a successful break for freedom, racing off across the meadows away from the riverside westwards, and was joined by de Clare; they out-galloped their pursuers, whose horses were tired out from the recent races. Edward rode north to Wigmore for a rendezvous with the Mortimers and then on to join Gloucester at Ludlow, who insisted he agree that he would respect the ancient laws and customs of England and that the king would remove all aliens from his council and kingdom and govern through natives once he was restored. This enabled them to present themselves as enemies of the self-seeking and autocratic de Montfort faction, innovators who were constraining the king for their own advantage, rather than enemies of the Provisions and 'just' government, and to reassure backers of the 1258 and 1264 reform programmes who might be persuaded to join them.

As a result of this Simon was left without the principal

figurehead for potential revolt by his own carelessness, facing a major Marcher revolt now reinforced by Warenne and de Valence. Edward was a quick learner as a general, and had a reconstituted and aggressive affinity of Marcher lords at his back. In the following ten days or so they proceeded to take Shrewsbury, Bridgnorth, and Worcester, break the bridges over the Severn, and take all the boats, and on 14 June the town of Gloucester fell, too (followed by the castle on the 29th). This left Simon and the Court cut off in Herefordshire with no easy route back to his headquarters at Kenilworth. But his talks with Llywelyn resulted in the 'Treaty of Pipton', a village on the middle Wye near Hay-on-Wye, which Simon, the captive Henry, and Llywelyn signed on 19 June. In return for military aid and a subsidy of 3,000 marks a year for ten years, Llywelyn had all his gains from his rival Welsh princes and from royal lands since his accession recognised; the native-ruled regions of Wales, considerably expanded into the outer Marches by Llywelyn, now passed under the rule of the Prince of Gwynedd or his vassals, reversing the king's policy of breaking up Gwynedd (and occupying what he could of its eastern lowlands) and making the other Welsh rulers vassals of the English king. Simon had to return quickly to the lands east of the Severn to link up with his gathering troops there. Instead, he moved south from Hereford to Monmouth (24 June) and took Usk Castle (2 July) en route to Newport to take ship for Bristol. Edward and Gloucester moved in undetected, retaking Usk en route, to burn the Montfortian ships in the River Usk at Newport before they could embark. This left them stranded and they had to move back to Hereford on 16 July.

The sight of the Montfortian ships burning in the Usk Estuary under the windows of the castle at Newport was a reminder that military expertise in English politics in the 1260s was not restricted to Simon, caught unawares. Also the Montfort army would not have been able to join up with their second main force under Simon's eponymous second son even if it had crossed the Bristol Channel. He had been raising troops in friendly

London and had headed not directly for Bristol but south-west on a diversion to Winchester, which he sacked on 18 July; he then headed for the family stronghold at Kenilworth Castle, a meeting-place for their assembling vassals, rather than hanging around the Cotswolds or Avon Valley waiting for his father to arrive. He was probably afraid of meeting Edward's army, which could have been anywhere south-east of Worcester if Edward was marching to intercept him. He arrived on 31 July, but chose to camp his army outside Kenilworth Castle's walls not within the protection of the outer bailey – allegedly the troops wanted to enjoy the comforts of the town, such as its baths. Two nights later Edward mounted his third daring move, marching swiftly east from Worcester to storm the town and take many of the younger Montfort's army's leadership prisoner, killing or dispersing their men. The younger Simon fled into the castle so he was not killed or taken hostage and a substantial body of men joined him, but his army was broken up and he did not dare to risk venturing out with the survivors to try to reach his father before Edward did. He was unable to come to his outnumbered father's aid as the latter finally crossed the Severn at the ford of Kempsey, near Worcester, on 2 August. Worse, Edward took the rebels' banners as he withdrew and was able to parade them before the elder Simon's army when they met at Evesham, fooling them into a false sense of security so they did not have time to prepare a defensive position.

The elder Simon arrived at Evesham from the Severn crossing at Kempsey early on 4 August, expecting to meet his son's army soon, and was buoyed up by seeing an approaching force bearing the de Montfort banners. Instead this turned out to be Edward's larger army, carrying the banners they had taken at Kenilworth, and it was clear that there would be no rescue. The psychological effect of this was a major boost for Edward, as was the capture of the bridge to the south of the town by Mortimer's men; the rebels were now trapped on the north bank of the Avon. Simon boldly marched out of the town northwards to attack the royalists head-on, but his army was overwhelmed in a fierce hand-to-hand struggle and he was cut down along with his eldest son Henry and many others. The fallen rebel leader's body was hacked to pieces by vengeful royalist knights, probably Marchers with a grudge – his head and genitals were sent as a trophy to the attackers' leader Roger de Mortimer's wife. This was a sign of the personal nature of the hatred that some felt towards Simon and his arrogant sons, and possibly showed contempt for the jumped-up foreign intruder who had amassed a substantial landed endowment to their detriment. The mutilation was seen as shocking by chroniclers on both sides, and even if Edward did not instigate it he did not bother to halt it; possibly he thought that a harsh example made of the leading traitor would encourage others to surrender. The bitterness felt in the civil war was also reflected in the fact that around thirty knights of Simon's entourage were killed in the savage battle – usually men of such rank were carefully taken alive to be held profitably for ransom and a code of ethics inhibited killing people of high rank. Very few knights had fallen in the crucial battles of the civil wars in 1141 and 1216–17 – so did the killing reflect an ideology as well as personal clashes over power into a civil war? (The devotion of the reformists to controlling royal power and to observance of the Provisions as just and Christian implies this.) The savagery may also be due to Edward's personal vindictiveness, a trait seen throughout his career.

The restored Royal regime was so weak they had to confirm his arrangement with Simon at Montgomery on 25 September 1267. His title and his control over all but one of his vassals were confirmed, provided that he paid fealty and homage to Henry, and he retained most of Maelienydd and Elfael. The claims of his dispossessed brother Dafydd to a share of his lands were to be resolved by impartial, Welsh arbitrators by Welsh law and not by the king's men. He was able to enforce his control over restive vassals like Maredudd ap Rhys of Deheubarth, who was imprisoned and forced to hand over castles in 1259 as punishment for abandoning their alliance, although in 1267 the English succeeded in keeping Maredudd as their's not Llewelyn's vassal. Gruffydd ap Gwenwynwyn had to acknowledge Llewelyn as his – hereditary – overlord in late 1263, as did Maredudd of Machen in South Wales in 1269; in 1269 Llewelyn supervised a division of northern Powys among rival heirs and in 1273 he built a new castle, Dolforwyn, in annexed Cedewain in southern Powys, threatening Gruffydd ap Gwenwynwyn's capital at Pool. Edward's typically brutal plan after his triumph at Evesham was to outlaw all the de Montfortians and seize their lands, and this was duly implemented without his father having the wisdom to procure a more cautious settlement that would not alienate so many people. As a result, assorted disinherited landowners took to the greenwood as outlaws and fought the government. This was the second occasion where such well-regarded rearguard actions by the victims of a vengeful royal regime produced figures that entered heroic legend, and may have influenced the extant legend of Robin Hood, such as in the case of Roger Godberd. Nor would Simon's surviving sons and their followers surrender the well-fortified, well-provisioned Kenilworth Castle; due to the poor state of current siege-technology the vengeful Edward was forced to blockade them and could not breach the walls. A period of chaos, political instability, and sporadic guerrilla attacks by the disinherited followed, but eventually common sense prevailed and Edward's cousin Henry of Almain and the papal legate Ottobuono were entrusted with mediation. The 'Dictum of Kenilworth' in October 1266 authorised the government to allow all rebels to buy back their confiscated lands on payment of a fine – larger for those closest to the rebel leadership in 1264–5. The hardline rebels at the Isle of Ely (emotive strongpoint of heroic Hereward's resistance to the Normans in 1070) under John d'Eyville refused these terms, and their continuing resistance plus extortionate fines levied on ex-rebels duly led Earl Gilbert of Gloucester to turn on Edward and in April 1267 ally his own faction to the Ely rebels to demand easier terms. They marched on London, which rose in their support, and Edward was forced to negotiate and agree to easier terms of reconciliation whereby more rebels were pardoned without any fines, more land was returned, and the Ely rebels were pardoned. This time he kept to his agreement, and the civil war ended – but the fact that Gloucester, greatest of the Marchers, had blackmailed him into abandoning his vengeance no doubt added to the distrust between the two men. Their continuing legal disputes (e.g. over control of Bristol and of some of the earl's mother's lands) rumbled on after Edward came to the throne in October 1272, and when Edward departed on Crusade in 1270 he tried to insist that the earl did so too – presumably for fear of a coup in his absence. In the event, Edward did go and most of his Marcher allies (including Gloucester's brother Thomas de Clare, Clifford, and Leyburn) did so too, but Gilbert backed out of it on the excuse of attacks on his lands by the insurgent Welsh.

Edward clearly awaited his chance to reverse the humiliation of the Treaty of Montgomery and reduce Llywelyn's lands and status to that of his uncle Dafydd in 1241–46, as he was to do in 1277. Llywelyn's continued efforts to marry Simon de Montfort's daughter Eleanor (probably arranged in 1265) in the 1270s showed his sense of honour but could not have been better calculated to arouse Edward's distrust. Eleanor's brothers, in exile in France like her, had murdered Edward's cousin and close aide Henry of Almain in church at Viterbo in Italy in 1271, which led to Edward seeking vengeance, and when they sent Eleanor by ship to Wales she was intercepted and taken to the English court as a prisoner. Nor was Llywelyn helped by his treacherous brother Dafydd, who had already been exiled once for plotting (1263), was restored to his lands in 1269, but in 1274 joined Gruffydd ap Gwenwynwyn of southern Powys to plan his brother's murder. They were discovered and fled to Edward, while Llywelyn seized their lands. He had also refused to attend Edward's coronation in 1274 to do homage or to turn up to a meeting with the king at Chester in 1275, probably fearing arrest but enraging Edward. In the spring or summer of 1277 a massive English invasion was coordinated, with one army marching across northern Powys to the Bay of Cardigan, a second taking the usual route west from Chester to the Conwy and Caernarfon, and separate local Marcher campaigns reducing Llywelyn's castles in Cedewain and Builth and forcing the princes of Deheubarth to submit. The prince, a refugee in the mountains of Arfon with his lowland possessions overrun, was forced to submit, and in the Treaty of Aberconwy was reduced to the status of vassal prince of West Gwynedd and forced to return lands to his dispossessed brothers, Owain and Dafydd (the latter in Rhos and Rhufoniog, east of the Conwy). Their other brother, Rhodri, had his claims bought out.

This time, taking no chances, the methodical Edward started building a string of massive new castles in the occupied lands – firstly at Flint, later at Rhuddlan, Aberystwyth, and Hawarden – and left his foe the homages of some minor northern Powys princes for his lifetime, and started to use English-law courts to put pressure on the autonomy of local Welsh law and its princely guarantor. The courts of the royal bailiffs extended their jurisdiction over the locals, while the Perfeddwlad east of the Conwy was controlled by the royal earldom of Chester; captured ex-princely castles remained under royal control. Even Llywelyn was forced to appear before the new royal judges as an ordinary litigant; as with the dispossessed or vassal princes of south-central Wales, the lesson was emphasised that Edward was in full legal control of all of Wales. It is likely that Edward used a legal dispute between Llywelyn and Gruffydd ap Gwenwynwyn over who owned the Gwynedd/Powys border cantref of Arwystli to tighten the screws on or even provoke Llywelyn, as the case – now under the jurisdiction of his courts – was repeatedly delayed and dubious manoeuvres occurred. But Llywelyn was not guiltless either, as he secured local Church agreement that his claim of overlordship over Gruffydd ap Gwenwynwyn was still legal so he may have planned to depose him again. Llywelyn was allowed by Edward to marry Eleanor de Montfort at Worcester Cathedral on 13 October 1278, with the king in charge of proceedings as overlord, but she died in childbirth in 1282; under Welsh law their child Gwenllian (1282–1337) had no rights to Gwynedd and her father's heirs were properly his younger brothers, but by English feudal law (as imposed on Wales by Edward) she was the valid heiress, so he deported her to a remote East Midlands nunnery and refused to let her marry. An attack by Dafydd on English-occupied East Gwynedd and his capture of Hawarden Castle on the night of 21 March 1282 sparked off another round of warfare, apparently coordinated with risings in Mid- and South Wales where Llywelyn ap Gruffydd Maelor, prince of northern Powys, attacked Oswestry and some princes of Deheubarth retook Aberystwyth, Llanmyddfri and Carreg Cennen. The cautious and realistic Llywelyn was probably forced unwillingly into a war that he was likely to lose by Dafydd, who had a history of such gambles, but the Welsh enjoyed some early successes despite Edward's inevitable advance to the Conwy Valley, and the revolt spread south to Mid-Wales. After rebels there defeated Gilbert de Clare, Earl of Gloucester, at Llandeilo Llywelyn, they moved south, while the king's forces in the North recaptured Ruthin and Denbigh (in September). Roger de Mortimer (1256?–1326), lord of Chirk Castle on the border and younger brother of the new family head Edmund Mortimer of Wigmore (1254?–1304), put down the rebellion in the Montgomery area, and in the South the rebel castles were recaptured by Robert Tiptoft. Archbishop Peckham of Canterbury attempted to mediate as Edward prepared his forces to move in on Arfon, but all the king would offer Llywelyn was land to the value of £1,000 in England – his principality was now earmarked for confiscation.

Llywelyn was campaigning in the upper Wye Valley when

he was killed on 11 December 1282 at Irfon Bridge, Cilmeri. The exact circumstances are unclear but he was facing a local Marcher force under his cousin Edmund, lord Mortimer of Wigmore, who had only just succeeded his father Roger (1231?– 1282) and had usually been on friendly terms with Gwynedd. The elder Roger was the son of Ralph de Mortimer of Wigmore (d. 1246) by Gwaldys, daughter of Llywelyn ap Iorweth and the younger Llywelyn's aunt. The hiatus in local leadership following Roger senior's death probably enticed Llywelyn to intervene in Arfon while he had a suitable window, as the king's men had met with disaster as they attempted to construct a bridge of boats from occupied Anglesey to the mainland to invade. Llywelyn was ambushed with a few companions while separated from his main force by English troops under John Giffard of Bromfield, in Shropshire, who caught him by surprise by crossing a nearby ford, and he was run through in a cavalry attack on his group and beheaded. Possibly there was a trick offer of a truce to lure him into a false sense of security and then to attack him, but his identity was not recognised in the confusion so he was not targeted personally by a party of defenders who knew the value of their opponent being killed. His body was only identified next day, whereupon Edmund Mortimer sent his brother Roger, lord of Chirk, to present the prince's head to Edward I. Dafydd was forced into flight into the mountains and was captured hiding in a cave in April 1283, being publicly executed at Shrewsbury as a traitor to the crown of England. To the victorious Edward there was no question of David being an independent prince; like the executed Bruce brothers later in Scotland, he was a treacherous vassal to be treated with contempt. A chain of huge coastal castles, the largest on the legendary site of Maximus' fortress at Caernarfon, were constructed for Edward by his Savoyard master-mason to hold Gwynedd down – and are ironically now major tourist magnets. New English-style fortified boroughs were created on the coast with Welshmen banned from residing there, both at older settlements such as Caernarfon and Conwy and at strategic new sites such as Beaumaris (1295). Now the former principality of Gwynedd and those Powys lands that it had seized were incorporated into the lands directly ruled by the king, together with his extant holdings of the earldom of Chester and the castles of Cardigan and Carmarthen with their dependencies, and the king was made the pre-eminent lord of the Marches, English and Welsh lands alike. This new region of direct royal power was to be turned into a formal Principality of Wales for the king's eldest son in July 1301 – but before the heir was so created, and while he was underage, the king would rule it directly and take in all the revenue. From now on the royal family would overshadow the power of the Marcher lords, though this was not a sign of total dominance when a king was weak or preoccupied elsewhere.

Southern Powys remained a dependant English client, its rulers regarding Gwynedd as the greater threat. Gruffydd ap Gwenwynwyn, restored to his lands by Henry III on strict terms of vassalage in summer 1240 and paying the king 300 'marks' for his father's lands in 1241, was a useful ally for the English Crown against Gwynedd. In 1244 he was one of only three major Welsh magnates to remain loyal to Henry in a rebellion that followed the accidental death of Gruffydd of Gwynedd at the Tower of London, and was besieged by his angry vasslas at Tafolwen Castle until rescued by the English. In 1263 he was forced to accept Llywelyn as his overlord in the terms for peace, but in 1274 he joined Llywelyn's brother Dafydd in a plot to murder his overlord, probably alarmed at Llywelyn's recent construction of a new castle at Dolforwyn within his lands, and had to flee to England. He owed his restoration to Edward I's massive invasion of North Wales in 1277, and this time the balance of power shifted permanently to England and saved southern Powys from further attacks from Gwynedd. It became a prosperous vassal under strict royal legal jurisdiction, whose Anglicisation and loyalty saved it from the depredations of Edward I until Gruffydd's death in 1286. His son then became an English tenant-in-chief as 'Lord de la Poole/Powis'. An English trading-borough developed at its lords' principal residence of Poole, later Welshpool. Meanwhile the commotes of Ceri and Cedewain in the North were passed by Edward I in 1282 to Roger Mortimer of Chirk, the man who had presented the head of Llywelyn ap Gruffydd to the king. He had previously been guardian to their former lords, the underage sons and heirs of the late lord Madoc Cripyl (d. 1277) of the royal house of Powys, and the boys' mysterious deaths in his care were reckoned to be no accident: one story had it that he had drowned them in the River Dee where their bodies were found. His open adultery was said to have led to a local priest rebuking him and being thrown in his dungeons; at best he was the sort of man who attracted unsavoury stories. The similarly confiscated lordships of Bromfield and Yale went to the king's distant cousin and loyal follower John de Warenne, sixth Earl of Surrey (1247–1304), lord of Lewes in Sussex and later 'colonial' governor of Scotland after the 1296 conquest; after his family became extinct in 1347 the neighbouring Fitzalans inherited the title. A new Marcher lordship was created within the Perfeddwladd of Clywd, over which England and Gwynedd had fought, for Reginald de Grey (d. 1308), Sheriff of Chester and later of Nottinghamshire. Later ennobled as Lord Grey of Wilton, his son John's younger son would found the Cheshire/Clywd line of lords Grey of Ruthin. Despite the continuing inter-noble feuds the end of the Welsh wars led to an era of mostly greater security, with the emergence of such new mercantile dynasties as that of Lawrence of Ludlow, the spectacularly successful sheep-farmer who built Stokesay Castle (half-castle, half-manor house) near Ludlow in the 1280s.

Gruffydd ap Gwenwynwyn married Margaret Corbet, of the Marcher line of Corbet of Caus (called after the founder's Norman home at Caux). His daughter Margaret married the local Marcher baron Fulke Fitzwarin of Whittington, scion of the family of a famous rebel/outlaw of King John's reign. His son Owain, an English baron, succeeded him in 1286 and endowed his four younger brothers with lands in 1290, with the proviso that if they had no heirs the lands reverted to his children. Owain died in 1293, leaving a three-year-old son, Gruffydd, second Lord Powis/ de la Poole, who died in 1307. The latter's sister Hawise (d. by 1353) married John Charlton, ancestor of the lords Charlton, who duly acquired Poole/Welshpool Castle on their marriage in July 1309 and built the current Powis Castle.

The end of Deheubarth also saw division of its lands, and a mixture of some lords cooperating with the English and being reduced to minor landowners and others choosing eventually to fight and being overwhelmed. On Rhys ap Gruffydd's death in 1197 his three older sons, Gruffydd, Rhys Gryg, and Maelgwyn, secured most of the kingdom; Gruffydd also secured his younger brother Maredudd's realm of Cantref Bychan in 1201, but died weeks later. Maelgwyn (ruling Ceredigion) took most of his lands, but their dispossessed brother Rhys Gryg linked up with Gruffydd's sons Rhys and Owain. In 1204 the trio drove Maelgwyn out of Cantref Mawr, most of which fell to Rhys. Maelgwyn was also responsible for his men's murder of one of their excluded brothers, Hywel Sais, in 1204, but lost most of his remaining lands to William Marshal, Earl of Pembroke, later that year. Rhys' continuing rivalry with his nephews led them to seek the patronage of Llywelyn Fawr, and in response Rhys backed John in the confrontation between Gwynedd and England in 1210–11. Turning on his English ex-patrons after John's troops had assisted him against Maelgwyn in Ceredigion in 1211 but capitalised on the opportunity to set up new English castles there too, he sacked Swansea in 1212. Both Rhys and Maelgwyn eventually became loyal vassals of Llywelyn Fawr against King John and their rivals, Gruffydd's sons Rhys and Owain. In 1213 the latter two assisted an invasion of Rhys' lands in Cantref Mawr by John's most notorious mercenary commander, Fawkes de Breaute (who had rebuilt Aberystwyth Castle in 1211 to restore royal power in northern Ceredigion), and he had to flee to Llywelyn's court. He assisted the latter's southern campaign of winter 1215/16, when the large Gwynedd army used unusually mild weather to show its power across South Wales and to retake Carmarthen and Cardigan castles. All the local Welsh princes queued up to submit to Llywelyn, who enforced a division of Deheubarth between them at a summit at Aberdyfi in 1216. Rhys was secured in Cantref Mawr and Maelgwyn in Ystrad Tywi and Ceredigion, with Rhys (d. 1222) and Owain (d. 1235) ap Gruffydd restricted to minor principalities. In 1217 Llywelyn granted Rhys Gryg the custodianship of Swansea Castle. Despite the reannexation of Swansea, the princes of Deheubarth were unable to hold onto Gower/Gwyr, dominated by the castle of Oystermouth, which the 1216 expedition had seized from the de Braoses. Llywelyn agreed to hand it back to the latter in 1220. William Marshal (d. 1219)'s eldest son Earl William (d. 1231) recaptured Carmarthen and Cardigan from Deheubarth in 1223, and then allied himself to the dissident Prince Cynan, son of Hywel Sais, who he granted the commotes of Emlyn and Ystlwyf as his ally against the senior princes of the dynasty. Rhys Gryg died, aged around sixty, of wounds suffered in a failed attack on Carmarthen in 1234, and his lands passed to his son by Matilda de Clare, Rhys Mechyll. After this and the eclipse of the Marshal dynasty in the early 1240s Owain's sons, particularly the eldest, Maredudd (d. 1265), were able to extend their rule over much of Ceredigion; Maredudd supported Llywelyn ap Gruffydd, aiding his invasion of the South in 1256, and became his main ally in South-West Wales. But the tradition of dividing lands among all of a ruler's sons prevented consolidation, and his territory was divided between his underage sons Owain (d. 1275), Cynan, and Gruffydd in 1265. The younger two, surviving longer, and Owain's son Llywelyn were all loyal to Edward I in 1277 but joined in the 1282 revolt and were deported to England.

Maelgwyn of Ceredigion died in 1230; his reduced principality duly passed to his son, Maelgwyn ('Fychan') ap Maelgwyn of Ceredigion (d. 1257), who married Angharad, the daughter of Llywelyn Fawr. Rhys Mechyll ap Rhys of Cantref Mawr (d. 1244) was succeeded as senior ruler by his brother Maredudd, but his own son by Matilda de Braose, Rhys Fychan, inherited some lands, too. The last princes ended up as clients of Edward I holding much-reduced lands. Rhys Wyndod of Ystrad Tywi, lord of Dinefwr, Carreg Cennen, and Llanmyddfri, was dispossessed of Dinefwr and other estates by Edward I in 1277 for opposing the king's invasion; it became the main centre for English administration in the confiscated lands of northern Carmarthen. Rhys Gryg's grandson Rhys ap Maredudd of Dryslywyn retained most of his estates for the moment and received much of his cousin Rhys Windod's lands in Ystrad Tywi in 1282; he backed Edward in 1277 and 1282, but considered that the king had cheated on a promise to award him Dinefwr in 1277. He was treated slightingly by the local English judges and castellans, particularly John Tiptoft, the new Justiciar of Carmarthen, and in response tried to argue that he should be legally subject to the Pembrokeshire district court instead. In 1287 he refused a summons to court in Carmarthen and attempted to resist dispossession by a revolt; he seized Llandovery and Carreg Cennen castles in July but was hopelessly outnumbered as a huge army was assembled at Carmarthen. Rhys was besieged in Dryslwyn and then fled into the hills; he re-emerged to take Newcastle Emlyn in November after Earl Edmund's army went home but it was retaken in January 1288. He was caught in the Tywi Valley and was executed at York on 2 June 1292.

The rising power of the de Clare lords of Glamorgan, controlling the earldom and the Anglicised lowlands, gradually extended northwards over the upland principalities of Morgannwg in the mid-thirteenth century. The lords of Glynrhondda were dispossessed in 1246 and Afan effectively reduced to vassalage in 1247; in 1267 Gilbert de Clare, the 'Red Earl', arrested Gruffydd of Senghenydd, son of Rhys (d. 1256), confiscated his lands for alleged links to Llywelyn ap Gruffydd of Gwynedd, and built the impressive Caerphilly (Caerffili) Castle in his lands to hold the locals down. The alleged treason was an excuse for a naked land-grab. The castle was soon sacked as the dispossessed dynasts sought the aid of Llywelyn of Gwynedd, but the annexation was made permanent as Edward I destroyed Gwynedd's power. Gilbert always had an uneasy relationship with Edward, whom he had defied in the late 1260s; he broke a pledge to go on Crusade with him without repercussions. There were rumours that the collapse of his first marriage, arranged by the king in 1253 to bind him to the royal family, to Alice de Lusignan in 1267, was due to her partiality for Edward instead; the earl then remained unmarried until in 1290 he married a much younger princess, the king's daughter Joan of Acre (1271–1307), who had been born on Edward's Crusade in the Holy Land. The terms of the marriage, as arranged by Edward, provided for the earls' lands to pass only to the children of this marriage, thus disinheriting Gilbert's two daughters by his first marriage – Isabella (1262–1333), who married Maurice, Lord Berkeley, and Joan, who married the seventh Earl of Fife in Scotland. Gilbert seems to have spent his latter years asserting his authority as a landholder and intimidating his neighbours; he had a famous dispute with the Bishop of Hereford over the boundary between their rival hunting-grounds on the Malvern Hills and constructed the still extant 'Red Earl's Dyke' to mark the border and stop his animals escaping into the bishop's territory. He died on 7 December 1295 and was succeeded by his son by Joan of Acre, the second Earl Gilbert (1291–1314), who was killed at Bannockburn in June 1314. This divided the huge de Clare estates in the southern Marches among Gilbert's three full sisters and their husbands.

7

FROM THE TOWER TO THE QUEEN'S BED, FROM REGENT TO THE GALLOWS

Roger de Mortimer, 1st Earl of March, challenges King Edward II's strongmen and ends up in the Tower; his escape to France and relationship with Isabella of France; his invasion of England to depose Edward II; his journey from regency to execution at the hands of the new king.

Edward II was the first king since the Conquest to be deposed, by means of a forced 'voluntary' abdication at Kenilworth in January 1327 following his wife Isabella's invasion of the country in his elder son Edward's name. Despite his unquestioned legitimacy as sovereign unlike many predecessors, his excessive grants of lands and honours to a small and widely disliked group of favourites had sparked off violent political opposition throughout his reign, and led to attempts by leading nobles to force him to remove the offenders and govern according to their guidance instead. The hatred shown by the leading earls towards the 'low-born' royal favourite Piers Gaveston, a young Gascon knight who Edward's father had initially welcomed as a knightly exemplar for his unmilitary son but then banished as a bad influence, was centred on the new king's blatantly loading patronage onto him. Edward's lack of interest in his overbearing father's warlike pursuits was shown by his failure to pursue the royal campaign against Robert Bruce on which Edward I had died in July 1307, and his own preference for spending his leisure lay in unseemly manual crafts, which the nobility regarded as only suitable for the lower classes. He was as keen on horses as many young nobles, possessing a notable stud-farm at Ditchling in Sussex, and his arrogance, spendthrift nature, and violent antipathy to his critics as a prince were not particularly unusual or regarded as reprehensible. (Edward I had been guilty of lawless assaults as a young man.) His sporting pursuits centred not on tournaments or combat but on activities such as rowing; he also enjoyed digging and building walls, regarded as fit pursuits only for labourers. The change of tone at Court at Edward's accession, with a manly warrior-king who had been a Crusader hero replaced with an unmilitary young man, was always going to alienate a number of important peers but might have been without drastic political implications, but for the new king's open showering of power and presents on his objectionable close friend. Gaveston was given the earldom of Cornwall (traditionally kept for the royal family) and governorship of Ireland, and played an important part in the coronation in 1308. He openly flaunted his monopoly of royal patronage and made no effort to conciliate other nobles who had made the most of their relationships with and the right to give advice to the king under Edward's father, and were now ignored. But he also entered the complex and sometimes violent field of Marcher politics, as the latest royal favourite (like the older Hubert de Burgh under Henry III but far less well-prepared or acceptable) to be intruded into the region as a strongman. Already Edward I had given him the wardship of the underage new head of the dynasty of Mortimer of Wigmore, Roger Mortimer (1287–1330), when the latter's father Edmund died in 1304, at the Prince's request – so Gaveston was familiar with the region. In this case, Gaveston was married off by the king on 7 November 1307 to the latter's sister Joan's daughter, Margaret de Clare (1293–1342), second daughter of the late 'Red Earl' Gilbert of Gloucester and co-heiress to her brother the current Earl Gilbert. (The latter was also married off in 1308 to an heiress, Maud de Burgh, the daughter of Earl Richard of Ulster and sister of Robert Bruce's queen, but had no children.) Margaret's elder sister Eleanor (1292–1337) had been married in 1306 to the rising and aggressively ambitious young Court official Hugh le Despenser, the Younger (1286?–1326 executed); her younger sister Elizabeth (1295–1360) was married to Richard de Burgh's son and heir, John de Burgh (d. 1313), and by this marriage was ancestress of the later Mortimers of Wigmore/Ludlow. Firstly Gaveston and then Despenser were to be selected by their admirer (some said sexual partner) the king to take over the lead role in the Marches for him, to the fury of the local barons.

The displays of affection between Edward and Gaveston gave rise to anger, exacerbated by Edward's lack of interest in or granting of traditional funds and a separate household to his admittedly underage teenage bride Isabella of France. Gaveston showed open contempt for the uncouth and militaristic leading peers at Court and used his cutting wit on them with every sign of royal approval, leading to a first coup by his infuriated victims and enforced restraint of the king in 1308. The king's cousin Earl Thomas of Lancaster (1278?–1322 executed), who probably felt that given his rank he should have had the role of the king's leading adviser, led a faction of nobles determined to remove Gaveston, and was joined by the king's sister Elizabeth's husband, Humphrey de Bohun (1276?–1322), fourth Earl of Hereford and tenth Earl of Essex – son of the third Earl of Hereford (d. 1298), who was in turn son of Eleanor de Braose, daughter of the William de Braose executed by Llywelyn ap Iorweth in 1230 and heiress of Brecon. The other major Marcher warlord involved in the anti-Gaveston clique was another close royal relative, Aymer de Valence (1275?–1324), Earl of Pembroke and son of that William de Valence, Henry III's half-brother, who had married the heiress to the earldom of Pembroke. A trusted and skilful general who Edward I used as governor of Scotland and on various French campaigns, he was seen as honest, honourable, less crude and ruthless than Thomas of Lancaster, and not driven by grudges unlike another member of the group, Guy de Beauchamp, Earl of Warwick (1275?–1316), lord of Elfael in Powys but also himself the latest head of a dynasty based in Worcestershire as lords of Elmley Castle. He was hereditary Sheriff of Worcestershire, another trusted general of Edward I elbowed aside by his successor, and had possibly at one time been engaged or married to one of the late earl of Gloucester's (d. 1295) daughters – and was known as 'The Black Dog of Arden' by the sniggering Gaveston. (Due to Pembroke's fondness for money, Gaveston nicknamed him 'Joseph the Jew'.) The other major peer involved was John de Warenne (1286–1347), seventh Earl of Surrey or Earl Warenne. This 'junta' of peers had never forgiven Gaveston for taking over management of the coronation from them and carrying the Crown himself, an intolerable insult to men who felt their ancestral rights had been insulted, and in March 1308 they used Parliament to arrange a demand that the low-born intruder be banished – having apparently taken an oath to drive him out of England. Only the young Earl of Gloucester remained neutral among the great peerage, and his brother-in-law Hugh Despenser's father, the elder Hugh (Warwick's son-in-law), stood by the king and was accused by the opposition of toadying in return for hopes of gain – commencing the downward path of their relations that was to lead to disaster in 1326. Notably, the future rebel Roger Mortimer. former ward of Gaveston. also stood by the king and joined him as he remained defiant at Windsor when the barons gathered an army in London. Backed by Philip IV of France (the new Queen Isabella's father), Edward had to send Gaveston away, and chose to give him the lieutenancy of Ireland as an honourable alternative to banishment. He recalled him in 1309, but the favourite was no less uncompromisingly assertive in pursuing influence and riches – and insulting to his opponents – than he had been before, and in February 1310 the baronial junta returned to the attack at the next Parliament. Gaveston was banished to evident widespread approval among the upper classes, and a committee of 'Lords Ordainers' seized power to usurp the king's executive authority and control all appointments and politial decisions, as had been done to Henry III in 1258. The king was bluntly told that unless he cooperated he would be deposed as he had violated his coronation oath. The devious or obsessive king sent Gaveston north to arrange the campaign in Scotland against Robert Bruce and joined him there later in 1310, but the Ordainers struck back and in August 1311 a new Parliament proceeded to diminish the king's powers further and banish Gaveston from the realm forever. Edward had to sign up to this, but later that year Gaveston returned secretly from banishment to visit the king at Westminster and in January 1312 the latter took his court – and his favourite – to York, out of the regime's reach, and there proceeded to nullify the latter's recent ordinances and restore Gaveston to all his lands and titles. This time the insurgent peers raised an army in London and set out to recapture the king and Gaveston by force, and the sovereign and his wife were put in the humiliating position of scurrying from place to place across the North-East to evade the baronial army and try to keep Gaveston safe. Thomas of Lancaster led the task of hunting down the king and trapped him at Newcastle, but the royal party escaped by sea, minus their baggage; the king then sent Gaveston to Scarborough Castle for his safety but the latter was hunted down there, forced to surrender, and promised a proper trial in an agreement on 19 May 1312 with the king's cousin, Aymer de Valence, the Earl of Pembroke, who was commanding the rebel army. But his arch-enemy the Earl of Warwick promptly ambushed his escort en route to his promised place of detention at his own castle of Wallingford, seized him, and had him subjected to a kangaroo court for returning from exile illegally. The honourable Pembroke had given his word that Gaveston would not be executed and objected to the death-sentence, but Warwick ignored him, and on 19 June Gaveston was beheaded on nearby Blacklow Hill to provide a permanent solution to the problem.

The king's subsequent and equally disastrous relationship with the more politically effective and ruthless Marcher baron Hugh le Despenser the Younger in the 1320s was less easy to portray in purely sexual terms as, although Edward deferred to his favourite's advice and showered him with offices, Despenser was a capable political leader and administrator. (The charge of homosexual relations in this case was first made, hesitantly, by the later fourteenth-century chronicler Froissart.) Despenser, unlike the Gascon squire Gaveston, came from the Marcher nobility, albeit a minor family, and his rise to fortune had begun under Edward I, who granted him the hand of his de Clare niece Eleanor (not yet co-heiress to Glamorgan as her brother was still alive, but semi-royal). He was politically valuable to a king who was seemingly incapable of governing without relying heavily on one trusted character from outside the traditional circle of royal advisers, though the blatant monopoly of patronage that his family received was a sign of Edward's failure to realise or care about the inevitable reaction. The locality of Despenser's base of power was particularly problematic, as it centred on his marriage to the king's niece as heiress to the vast estates of the de Clare family in Glamorgan and Gwent, the south-east region of the semi-independent Marcher lordships on the former Welsh frontier. When Earl Gilbert was killed at Bannockburn on 25 June 1314 the earldom's lands were divided among the last earl's sisters, with the eldest, Margaret, being Gaveston's widow (which argues that if Gaveston had still been alive then he would have been given the title and bulk of the lands and been the target of furious condemnation). The king's new favourite Despenser, husband of the next sister (Eleanor), now received the most important part of the inheritance, the lands of Glamorgan and later the title of Earl of Gloucester; and Edward did nothing to stop him pressuring the husband of the other de Clare sisters, Hugh Audley (who married Gaveston's widow Margaret de Clare in April 1317) and Roger Amory, to surrender the rest. Despenser also secured extra local lands, such as Gower, by a blatantly rigged legal process – it was clear that the only way to curb his acquistiveness would be by violence, given the king's favouritism. The Marcher lords had been given extensive military and judicial autonomy by the earlier

Anglo-Norman kings to defend and push back the border, and were accustomed to acting with minimal royal supervision; they also had large private armies of tenants accustomed to following their orders. Despenser's aggregation of lands and power in the Marches aroused the antipathy of a body of rival lords who were accustomed to call on their tenants to raise armed revolt and had little respect for the king's power. For the moment, the only major violence in the Marches involved the dispute over the rightful inheritance of the mini-principality of southern Powys when the Anglicised underage lord, Gruffydd de la Poole, second Lord Powis and grandson of Gruffydd ap Gwenwynwwyn (d. 1286), died as a royal ward in 1307. As chief justiciar of North Wales, Roger Mortimer's eponymous uncle Roger Mortimer of Chirk adjudicated on the inheritance and awarded it to the heir under English law, the late lord's elder sister Hawise and her new husband (1309), John, Lord Charlton, a friend of Gaveston's. This excluded the rights of their uncle, Sir Gruffydd ('Griffin' to the English) de la Poole, who objected that under Welsh law he should inherit, and when ignored besieged his rivals in their main residence, Welshpool Castle, in 1312. Sir Gruffydd also successfully sought the support both of Thomas of Lancaster and of the Mortimers' local rival on the mid-Wales borders – Edmund FitzAlan (1285–1326), eighth Earl of Arundel, whose grandfather John FitzAlan (1223–1267) had in 1243 inherited the lands of the D'Albinis of Arundel in Sussex from his mother's childless brother Earl Hugh of Arundel. By this match the FitzAlans of Oswestry in Shropshire, who had inherited the lordship of Clun from the de Says by the marriage of William FitzAlan (d. 1210) to Isabel de Says *c.* 1160, added a major English earldom to their lands – though this move up the pecking-order also diverted their centre of attention away from the Marches. The elder Roger Mortimer thus ended up on the side of the king and Gaveston against Lancaster as the great nobles feuded in the 1310s, a threat to the family until Lancaster was executed by the king in 1322, and meanwhile his nephew the younger Roger served the king in Ireland as a senior military commander in Meath and Leinster in 1308–9, defeating the rebel Irish lords Dermot O'Dempsey and the O'Byrnes of Wicklow. Crucially for Roger's and the family's future, in 1301 he had been married off to the major Marches/Irish heiress Joan de Geneville (1286–1356), daughter of the French knight Sir Peter de Geneville (died 1292 and related to the chronicler of Louis IX's Crusades, Jean de Joinville/Geneville) who had taken over Ludlow Castle in 1283 through his father Geoffrey's earlier marriage to Maud de Lacey (1230–1304), heiress of the de Laceys of Ludlow. Maud, Joan's grandmother, lived to April 1304, and from then on Joan was lady of Ludlow – Roger was by marriage lord of Ludlow and had added that major barony to the Mortimer estates. The de Lacey inheritance also included Trim Castle in central Ireland with its lordship in Meath, plus other Irish lands that Maud de Lacey had inherited in 1241 from her grandfather Walter de Lacey (d. 1241) – so the Mortimers now gained a major lordship and influence in Ireland, too.

In May 1315 Robert Bruce, having secured control of the remaining English garrisons in Scotland by his victory at Bannockburn, sent his brother Edward (descended from the kings of Leinster via 'Strongbow's wife Aoife) to invade Ireland and detach it from England. This was played up in Scots propaganda as a pan-Celtic war for both peoples to gain revenge on the hated English conquerors, and involved risings across Ireland by the native population, which were to seriously undermine the Anglo-Norman baronage there in the central and western provinces. Roger Mortimer may have heard rumours of the plan as he left Court to return suddenly to his Irish lands in April after making recent plans not to do do for another year or so; after the Bruces' invasion of Ulster he faced the self-proclaimed 'King Edward' heading south-west into Meath. Early in December Roger lost a three-hour battle against the Bruce army at Kells on his lands' frontier after two of the de Laceys either fled or (less likely) betrayed him, with the Scots burning the town around him and most of his men being killed. Roger was sent back to report the disaster to the English king, but now the incessant rain and famine of 1315, which had undermined Anglo-Irish troops' fitness, supplies, and morale (and tax-revenues), struck Marcher politics too as the famine caused a revolt in Glamorgan. Governed by royal officials on behalf of its co-heiresses since the death of Earl Gilbert at Bannockburn, it had recently been taken over by a harsh new sheriff, Payn Turberville of Coety Castle, who was more interested in keeping up the king's revenues – by extortion if necessary – than in famine relief. The starving and robbed rural populace rallied to the ambitious Llywelyn Bren, hereditary lord of Senghenydd in the hills and valleys inland from Cardiff, and in January 1316 he and his sons led them to storm a meeting of the lordship's court at Caerphilly to take him and his officials hostage. The formidable castle, rebuilt by the 'Red Earl' as one of the strongest fortresses in Wales, held out, but the rebels rampaged across the district and the king authorised Roger Mortimer (as lord of Ludlow, Wigmore and Ewais Lacey) and the Earl of Hereford (as lord of Brecon) to raise their men and attack them. Henry of Lancaster, loyal younger brother of the king's enemy Earl Thomas and husband of Maud de Chaworth (d. 1322), the heiress of Ogmore and Kidwelly, and John Giffard, lord of Brimpsfield in Shropshire, also assisted. The rebels were chased out of Caerphilly and back up into the hills, and Llywelyn surrendered to avoid a massacre and was escorted to the earl's castle at Brecon en route to London. Apparently Hereford and Roger Mortimer successfully persuaded the king to commute his sentence from execution to imprisonment, and Roger even helped his stepson to escape revenge attacks by English settlers and secure royal aid; Payn de Turberville was sacked and replaced by Giffard, which showed unusual English moderation toward rebels.

Roger's subsequent rise to Court semi-prominence as a capable and loyal official was cemented by his marriage alliance with the other rising star, Bartholemew de Badlesmere, whose small daughter Elizabeth (1313–1356) was married off to his son Edmund (*c.* 1308–1331) in 1316 as the famine raged, and in November Roger was appointed as royal Lieutenant of Ireland to drive out the Bruces, who had secured around a third of the country. The famine had struck both sides, and with the Anglo-Norman lords holding onto their 'Pale' heartland around Dublin and most of the south-west, the tide was turning against an invader who had been welcomed at first but by his death was to be seen as bringing an unwinnable war and ruin. Roger duly won many new recruits to add to his small army despite Robert Bruce's arrival to help his brother, though it is unlikely that this army was really 15,000 strong, and his careful avoidance of a major battle kept the Bruces on the march, unable to capture the well-walled castles and short of food due to the famine. Once King Robert had turned for home, Roger proceeded to defeat the treacherous de Laceys, who had been acting as guides to the Bruce army in Leinster, in a major battle on 3–4 June 1317 and so regained full control of Meath. He had driven the invaders out of all they held except for Ulster and secured the allegiance of most of the Irish lords who had deserted to them before his recall in spring 1318, and the main honour of the campaign thus belonged to him, though the final victory in Ulster, at the Battle of Faughart near Dundalk where Edward Bruce was killed, did not occur until 14 October. In 1319–20 Roger was back in Ireland, this time as justiciar, to rebuild wrecked towns, castles, and the administrative structure, but after this interlude his political star waned as back in the Marches he came into conflict with the acquisitive Younger Despenser, now lord of Glamorgan by right of his de Clare wife and trying to gain the rest of the late Earl Gilbert's lands from his wife's sisters' husbands, Hugh Audley and Roger Damory. As royal chamberlain from 1318 he had the king's ear, and the latter became his eager – and some said suspiciously – fond friend and patron. Edward's partisanship to his new Lord Chamberlain now led to him handing over more of the de Clare lands, led by Gwynllwg east of Cardiff, to him, and in autumn 1320 the king confiscated Gower from its lord John de Mowbray (1286–1322), an ally of the royally hated Earl of Lancaster, who had inherited it via his marriage to a de Braose heiress (Aline) in 1298. Llywelyn Bren, who had been promised his life, was executed by Despenser in contempt of the terms of his surrender. Hugh Audley was now forced to sell his portion of eastern Glamorgan/Gwent, the lordship of Newport, to Despenser in return for some inferior English manors, and with Earl Aymer of Pembroke leaving the country rather than having to take sides with the unjust king or the rebels, Roger, Audley, Damory, and others under threat from the Despenser land-grab withdrew from Court and prepared their castles and men for revolt.

Confiscations of their offices and the mustering of a royal army followed early in 1321, and with Lancaster believed to be about to come to the rebels' aid, the latter refused to come to the king at Gloucester and sent demands to him to sack and exile Despenser. In May Roger led a central Marcher army into Glamorgan to storm Newport, Cardiff, and other places now owned by Despenser and set about looting or burning his property, as the favourite's agents indignantly detailed to the king; Roger's replacement as Justiciar of Ireland, Sir Ralph Gorges, was kidnapped en route to take up his office and carried off to Wigmore as a hostage. He then besieged the loyalist Earl of Arundel's castle at Clun, and it appears that his supporters – whether local ones or Marchers sent in by him – attacked and sacked manors owned by Despenser and his father across over a dozen counties in southern England. The official royal legal account of these enormities, exaggerated or not, blamed Roger and his Marcher army in person, but it is unlikely that they had the time to visit so many sites, let alone do damage worth two-thirds of the king's annual income. Backed up by a meeting of seditious (or patriotic) Northern barons in Yorkshire led by Thomas of Lancaster, they now marched on London (joined by the earls of Hertford and Surrey) and encamped at Kennington to negotiate with the Court, boldly demanding the exile of the Despensers, and although their rising was not as strongly backed as the 1258 and 1263–4 ones against Henry III and his favourites, the king lacked a strong army and was advised by his clerics and the returned Pembroke to give in. In August 1321 a formal treaty duly saw the Despensers exiled and all the rebels pardoned and restored to confiscated lands and offices, but this was almost immediately ruined by a new dispute involving Roger's son's mother-in-law Lady Badlesmere. Obeying her husband's orders not to let anyone into their Leeds Castle in Kent during disturbed times, she refused hospitality to the passing Queen Isabella and her entourage in October, and the Badlesmere retainers scuffled with the queen's men and killed several of them. The furious king promptly attacked Leeds Castle demanding vengeance, and as Lord Badlsemere appealed to Roger for help the latter agreed and set out for Kent, only to be stopped at Kingston Bridge by the Earl of Pembroke and the Archbishop of Canterbury. They promised to mediate, but the king rejected this and went on with the siege, subsequently executing some of the garrison and carrying off Lady Badlesmere and her children to the Tower of London as an example to insolent subjects. Roger and his ally Hereford promptly allied with Lancaster and his army, but the latter were too far off to help them, and in the New Year the full weight of the royal army, collected at Cirencester, was flung against them. They tried to block the Severn crossings and held the bridge at Worcester, and on 5 January Roger and his uncle Roger Mortimer of Chirk drove the arriving royal army back out of Bridgnorth and set fire to the town. But loyalist Welshmen had meanwhile overrun Chirk and were attacking Mortimer-occupied Clun, and after the Earl of Hereford left to join Lancaster Roger and his uncle agreed to negotiate, as arranged by the Earl of Pembroke. They duly arrived at the great hall of Shrewsbury Castle on 22 January 1322 to meet the king after a promise of their lives and pardons by Pembroke, but the latter had no authority and/or was bamboozled by the king. Instead, the two Mortimers were arrested and dragged off to the Tower of London as traitors, and their estates were subsequently confiscated and looted by the Despensers' men. Roger's wife was forfeited too and removed to a Hampshire nunnery, and her older children ended up with Hereford's in Windsor Castle. On 16 March the royal army defeated Lancaster's at Boroughbridge in Yorkshire. Using the tactics of a compact infantry 'schiltron' as learnt from Robert Bruce and William Wallace, the loyal Sheriff of Carlisle, Andrew de Harclay, defeated Hereford's cavalry charge on his men over the eponymous bridge, and Hereford was skewered from under the bridge by a pikeman and mortally wounded. The death of the king's brother-in-law and lord of Brecon, plus Sir Roger Damory, was followed next day by the rout of the rest of the rebel army, and Lancaster was taken prisoner and executed. For the moment, the younger Despenser was left supreme in the Marches and at court – and to round off his victory he forced Damory's widow, the king's niece Elizabeth de Clare, to hand over her lordship of Usk to him and gave her Gower, which he later had confiscated, too.

Unlike the arrogant Despenser, Roger Mortimer seems to have had the knack of attracting support and was able to make the most of his victimization by the Despensers – as a resourceful adventurer he did not accept his dispossession and imprisonment in the Tower of London. On 1 August 1325, the Feast of St Peter ad Vincula when the miraculous release of St Peter from Roman custody was celebrated (appropriate for Roger's situation), his ally Gerard d'Alspaye, sub-lieutenant of the Tower, got his guards drunk and then arrived with a crowbar to help Roger dig his way out of his cell as the keys could not be found. He and his cellmate and their rescuer then escaped through the nearby royal palace kitchen with the help of a cook, climbed up the chimney onto the battlements, and made their way to a quiet part of the outer wall to let themselves down a rope onto Tower Wharf outside. Waiting accomplices with a boat ferried them down to Greenwich, where horses were waiting to take them into Kent, and within a few days they were on the Continent. There Roger was sheltered by his de Fiennes kinsmen in Picardy amidst royal fury and a rising heroic reputation for his escape, but he was no major threat until the queen, angry at her husband's involvement (political or sexual?) with Despenser, who was further treating her with contempt and urging Edward to divorce her, used the excuse of a diplomatic mission to her French homeland to defect. Once she was safe in Paris with the king's eldest son Edward, in 1325, she started to raise an army to overthrow her husband. Supposedly in Paris to do homage to the French king for Gascony on the king's behalf under the new Anglo-French treaty (which Isabella had helped to arrange), the prince instead was to be Isabella's nominee as figurehead to overthrow his increasingly hated father and the Despensers – and at this juncture Roger Mortimer, who had mortgaged his lands in France to the Count of Hainault (in Flanders) to raise troops to invade England, arrived in Paris to join the exiles. He and Isabella became lovers, and to the scandal of Europe the queen and her open lover were to lead the subsequent invasion of England in 1326 to overthrow her husband. The way that the pair lived openly together in Paris – albeit at a rather 'free and easy' court where several princesses had recently been arrested for adultery – shocked the era, and it seems that the passionate Isabella infinitely preferred her competent and ruthless new partner to her wayward, fickle, moody husband, whatever the truth of the stories about Edward being homosexual.

The king was only following the precedent set by Henry III in 1264 and his son Edward in 1265 in seeking to overthrow his enforced tutelage, raising a royal army to meet his aristocratic critics on the battlefield in 1322, and in heavy punishment of the defeated offenders. But the royalist reaction in 1265–7 had been followed by a period of wiser reconciliation in Henry III's last years. On this occasion, the king's success in reasserting his position against aristocratic intimidation from 1322 led to a repeat of the offences he had committed in lavishing patronage on Gaveston, this time in favour of the even more greedy and monopolistic Hugh Despenser the Younger and his family. As the small army of (at most) a few hundred Hainaulter mercenaries landed in the Orwell Estuary in Suffolk in September 1326, Edward's orders to his sheriffs to raise an army were ignored across the country and hundreds (possibly thousands) instead hurried to join the invaders, including a substantial section of the nobility. In London, the king faced riots against his greedy and corrupt officials and was forced to flee the Tower of London for the Severn Valley to try to raise an army of Welsh tenants; once he had left the hated treasurer, Bishop Stapledon, other ministers, and the sheriff were lynched by a mob. Roger and the queen chased the king into the West, and as Bristol fell the hated Despensers were captured and publicly executed as traitors. The Younger Despenser was eviscerated while still alive before a baying crowd before being beheaded; his castration may imply that the usual penalty for homosexual acts was meted out. Deserted by his leading subjects, the king was forced to flee into Wales and was eventually captured near Llantrisant in Glamorgan and taken to Kenilworth Castle. The triumphant rebels, headed by the queen, could not trust Edward II to keep any promises after what he had done in 1310 and 1322 and removed him permanently. Technically he abdicated voluntarily, though this left the possibility that if he escaped from custody he could claim that it had been invalid as done under duress – the Pope could absolve rulers from legal promises, as Innocent III had done for John over accepting Magna Carta.

As Edward III was only 14, Isabella and Mortimer assumed control of the government, though their relationship remained prudently discreet. Isabella was the effective regent as holder of the royal seal and Mortimer no more than her unofficial adviser, though he clearly exercised enormous influence as well as securing large grants of land and local office, and a degree of hubris soon became apparent. The technical head of the Council as the king's guardian, Edward's oldest male blood-relative, Henry, Earl of Lancaster, had little political power and matters of political patronage were decided solely by the acquisitive Isabella. Lancaster was swiftly rebuffed when he endeavoured to secure real power by taking custody of the new king. Obviously Isabella owed a debt of gratitude to Mortimer, was greedy for lands and riches as her acquisitions in 1327–8 show, and could not trust Lancaster – or any chief adviser but Mortimer – to keep her in her new position. But no queen had exercised such an important role in government before, the titular and de facto regents of the young King Henry III (who lacked close adult male kin) having been instead experienced warrior-nobles such as William Marshal and Hubert de Burgh. The prominence accorded to Mortimer – not a senior peer and only a minor Marcher lord until his accession to vast estates in 1326–7 – presented dangers to her regime, although it would appear that their sexual liasion was discreet. The very fact of the affair was however enough to blacken her reputation in subsequent centuries, adding to the unease felt about her improper action in overthrowing her husband. Edward's follies and misrule might have justified his removal, but unlike in other medieval English revolts the queen rather than his nobles had taken the lead in removing him and then had proceeded in a liasion with her principal male associate. The shocking nature of both occurrences was added to by the rumours of her involvement in Edward's murder, and her behaviour was seen as being worthy of total condemnation as an affront to the natural order of things – and thus to God. The literary genius of Christopher Marlowe provided the final touches to her reputation. In his 1592 tragedy on Edward II's reign Isabella was presented as a vengeful and over-sexed harridan who had unnaturally betrayed, deposed, and murdered her husband in association with her lover, and this picture was not seriously challenged for centuries. In 1757 the poet Thomas Gray transferred the epithet 'She-Wolf of France', used by Shakespeare for that other unatural Queen Margaret of Anjou (who had also led armies), to Isabella. The supposition that her long residence away from Court at Castle Rising in her son's reign was not voluntary but in fact a punishment – that is, imprisonment for murdering her husband – followed. Lurid legends grew up that she had gone insane through remorse, an appropriate fate for an adulteress and mariticide. The subsequent interpretations of the events of 1327 owed much to this unusual and sensational aspect of the rebellion, combining sexual license and wifely betrayal by a brazen – and foreign – queen with the subsequent violent death of her husband.

Edward II, removed from his initial prison at Lancaster's Kenilworth Castle on 3 April by Mortimer's trusted agents headed by Thomas, Lord Berkeley, was transferred around the country in disguise in great secrecy in evident fear of a rescue. Presumably the massive fortifications of Kenilworth, former stronghold of Simon de Montfort's sons as they defied Henry III in 1265–6, were not thought adequate to protect Edward from rescue, as Isabella and Mortimer did not trust Lancaster's loyalties. Berkeley's brother-in-law Lord Maltravers was Edward's official custodian and in charge of his escort, and they proceeded in unobtrusive secrecy around the South-West Midlands. Edward's whereabouts are unclear after his initial move in early April to isolated Llanthony Priory in the south-eastern Welsh Marches, with stories linking him to Corfe Castle in Dorset near Maltravers' estates. This was probably the safest stronghold in southern England, was isolated from easy approach in Purbeck so that visitors could be watched more easily than at Kenilworth, and had been used as a prison for dangerous political enemies by King John. According to the chronicler Bishop the ex-king was given poisoned food in the hope that he would die and solve the problem of what to do with him. He ended up at Lord Berkeley's eponymous castle near Gloucester, an isolated and near-impregnable fortress, though this was probably as much due to the security threat after the alleged plot at Bristol as it was a planned prelude to an already-decided murder. The evidence of the contemporary chronicler Adam Murrimuth and the stories collected by Froissart later in the century indicate that Lord Berkeley treated Edward well although Maltravers did not, and the ex-king's traditional chamber in the castle was not the noxious dungeon, susceptible to foul smells that the gaolers hoped would poison their captive, of Baker's story: it was a reasonably sized room on an upper storey in residential quarters. The supposed pit full of rotting bodies, which was intended to spread noxious vapours, was certainly not adjacent to the king's chamber as the legend would have it. The lurid stories reported decades later of passers-by hearing sobbing and screams from Edward's apartment may well have been invented to generate sympathy for the 'martyr' ex-king, at a time several decades later when the reasons for his overthrow – his favouritism and incompetence – had faded from the public memory. Alternatively, if the writers had heard rather than invented the stories, it would have been from local witnesses – staff at the castle, tenants on the Berkeley estates, or passing travellers on the Gloucester–Bristol road. Any screams heard from Edward's chambers could have been due to a nervous breakdown; the emotional Edward had had fits of depression before, notably on Gaveston's murder. Edward was a constant threat to the regime from devoted loyalists trying to free him, however willing the 'political nation' had been to be rid of him earlier that year. On 1 July a warrant was issued for the arrest of the outlawed Edwardian partisan Thomas Dunheved, along with members of his gang, for what a letter by Berkeley on 27 July makes clear was a successful infiltration by raiders into Berkeley Castle. Thomas' brother Stephen, a Dominican friar of dubious reputation, had been the ex-king's envoy to the Pope a few years before – apparently concerning a divorce from Isabella – so he was a natural choice for a plot to free his old employer and had reason to fear Isabella's rule. The guards had been overpowered by the gang and the ex-king had been carried off, probably aided by the current building-work at the castle, which could have enabled the raiders to disguise themselves as labourers and smuggle weapons into the buildings. The letter does not mention Edward's recapture, which therefore must remain uncertain, but the next plot to free him by Rhys Gruffydd in early September indicates that the latter's South Wales conspirators believed Edward to be back in custody then. One theory has been raised that the Dunheved raid was the occasion of Edward's permanent escape from custody, as is argued by Ian Mortimer in *The Greatest Traitor: The Life of Roger Mortimer, Rule of England 1327–1330*; others prefer a later date for any escape.

Edward was officially declared as having died conveniently at Berkeley Castle on 21 September 1327, the news being delivered to the Court at Lincoln on the 23rd by one of his guardians, Thomas Gurney. On the 24th Edward III wrote to his cousin, the Earl of Hereford, saying that he had heard the news the previous night. The date announced to the public is confirmed as being the 21st by contemporary chroniclers; a grief-related illness was blamed, as was to be the case for the equally sudden and convenient death of Henry VI in 1471. His body was kept for several months under guard by Mortimer's underlings at Berkeley Castle – suspiciously, the royal sergeant-at-arms in charge, Willliam Beaucaire, arrived there on the day of his death, not after it had been reported to the Court, as if it was anticipated. In December the body was escorted to Gloucester for a quiet funeral, attended by the Court; the delay was not unusually long by mediaeval standards as the pageantry of the ceremony had to be arranged in detail and preparations made. But the circumstances were dubious, both because he was only forty-two and in good health and because there was no public viewing of the body as was usual. Only one Mortimer partisan had been in charge of the body for several months. Further, only one party of visiting clerics had been allowed to view Edward, and then from a distance. Claims were duly made that he had escaped or been freed in disguise. The secrecy surrounding his captivity was such that an escape was plausible. Two years later his half-brother Edmund, Earl of Kent, could believe stories that he had really been kept alive at remote Corfe Castle under the care of its custodian (from 1329) Lord Maltravers, his captor at Berkeley. He accepted a statement from two friars that they had seen a man resembling the ex-king dining in the castle's hall, and apparently the castle's custodian in 1328-9, Sir John Pecche, also backed up the claim. Ian Mortimer points out that the terminology of the subsequent treason charge accused Kent of trying to free an alive Edward II, not a known fake – did this slip let out the fact that Kent's accuser Roger Mortimer knew the Corfe resident to be genuine? Besides, was it treason to free a 'fake' king rather than a real one? For the charge to be proved as treason, the ex-King who Edmund wanted to free surely had to be genuine. Kent is usually assumed to have been fooled by an insubstantial rumour, viewed as so desperate to overthrow Roger Mortimer that he would believe anything. But it should be said that other important people believed the rumours too, notably Archbishop Melton of York, who wrote in 1330 that he had heard definite news that the ex-king was still alive. Could Kent have been the sole source for their beliefs? Kent mounted a plot to free and reinstate Edward, which swiftly leaked out to the government resulting in his arrest. The stories are usually presumed to have been invented or used by Mortimer as a means of luring his enemy Edmund to his doom and to provide an excuse for executing him. It remains uncertain if the friars were in his pay or if they were genuine partisans of the ex-king – linked to friar Stephen Dunheved? – whose indiscretions enabled Mortimer to discover Edmund's intentions. They may have genuinely heard gossip on a visit to Corfe that an unknown guest, who they saw dining in the hall but only at a distance, was the ex-king; or Mortimer or Maltravers may have told their men at the castle to spread this story to encourage any spies who Edmund sent there to report back to him favourably.

The official charges against Mortimer at his trial in 1330 claimed that he had had Edward II killed, and Gurney and another henchman sent to join the guard-party at Berkeley, William Ockley or Ockle/Ogle, were also indicted for it in their absence. There was no mention of Lord Maltravers, who had formal charge of the ex-king. It is apparent from a 1331 court case that Mortimer – then at Abergavenny – sent Ockley to Berkeley around 14 September, with orders to its custodians to take appropriate action to forestall a reported plot to rescue Edward.

This was presumably the Rhys ap Gruffydd plot – the timing of Dunheved's arrest warrant at 1 July indicates that his raid had occurred some time in late June. The geographically nearest of the contemporary Church chroniclers, Adam Murrimuth, resident in the South-West in autumn 1327, reported in his text in the mid-1330s that it was commonly said then that Gurney and Maltravers suffocated Edward with Mortimer's connivance. He was the only local chronicler, and is thus the most crucial witness – at least as to what was rumoured at the time. The subsequent despatch of Beaucaire from Court to take charge of Edward's body before he was known to be dead would indicate that Mortimer knew what was to happen and when. The body was then displayed superficially to visiting clergy at Berkeley, standing at a distance, as proof that Edward was dead. The chronicle of St Paul's Cathedral and the shorter of the two versions of an ongoing chronicle of contemporary events, known as the Brut Chronicle, give little detail on Edward's death. The longer version – recorded a little earlier than Murrimuth, and written by a sympathiser of the anti-Mortimer Earl of Lancaster – presents the famous story that Gurney and Maltravers murdered him with a red-hot poker. It is confused about the site, naming it as Corfe at first and as Berkeley when dealing with the subsequent enquiry in 1330, and also calls Lord Berkeley 'Maurice' not Thomas. The reference to Corfe may be due to confused memories of the later Kent plot that centred on Edward II being at that castle, or reflect real stories that Edward had been at Corfe not Berkeley in 1327. Ranulph Higden's *Polychronichon*, written at Chester by 1340 at the latest, agrees with this version, apart from giving the means of death as a 'burning rod' not a 'spit' inserted through a 'horn' as in the Brut. Other chroniclers (e.g. the prior of Bridlington, who refers to 'common stories' which he scrupled to describe) seem to have been aware of the rumour. After *c.* 1340 accounts that mention the poker, such as the Northern *Historia Aurea*, can be taken as using the earlier version. Some invented or had heard of new details – Geoffrey le Baker, *c.* 1356, made the king's captivity and death even more lurid. This elaboration probably reflects the growth of myth about the event.

A case has been made out for possible sightings of Edward in Europe in the 1330s, possibly as the 'William de Waleys' who Edward III apparently had tracked down and met at Cologne in 1338. It has also been suggested that Mortimer's unexplained long visit to Abergavenny in September 1327, when he surely should have been preoccupied at Court, was connected to Edward's escape and flight to the loyal Welsh borderlands. The famous 'Fieschi Letter' (see below), which clearly had some private information on the ex-king's circumstances, does not refer to him being rescued by a gang but escaping on his own – probably with a captor's (Berkeley or Maltravers?) connivance. It would seem unlikely that a 'genuine' Edward II, as the man who recounted the escape story to Fieschi or his source, would need to hide the fact that he was rescued – the motive for lying would have been to safeguard the rescuers, but the man who would have punished them, Mortimer, had already been executed. Mortimer's long sojourn at Abergavenny in September suggested to Ian Mortimer that he was carrying out an intense hunt for the ex-king that he needed to command in person, it being more important to him than matters at Court. If he had recaptured Edward already by this date, why the long delay in returning to Court? The truth of what happened during and after the Dunheved attack on Berkeley Castle – or another plot to free Edward later – largely depends on the veracity of one written statement apparently made to Edward III by a member of the Genoese trading dynasty of Fieschi around 1340. This bizarre story, which a French archivist called Alexandre Germain found in the episcopal records at Montpellier and had privately printed in 1878, was examined by and mystified earlier English historians – Bishop Stubbs in his edition of the chronicles of Edward I and II's reigns (Rolls Series, 1882–3) and Thomas Tout in 'The Captivity and Death of Edward of Carnarvon'

(*Bulletin of the John Rylands Library*, vol vi, 1921). It was taken more seriously by an Italian scholar, Anna Benedetti, who claimed to have identified the North Italian sites involved in Edward II's hiding – Cecima and Milazzo – in 1924, though her research was shown to have been flawed. Manuele Fieschi's letter to the ex-king's son gave a garbled account from 'Edward II' himself, now living in an isolated hermitage at Cecima in Lombardy, of how he escaped from heavily guarded Berkeley Castle by changing clothes with a lookalike attendant who had warned him that Lord Gurney had arrived from Mortimer to kill him. He killed one porter, and wandered around England and then Ireland with a 'keeper', probably the attendant who had helped him escape, who was apparently keeping an eye on him for his protector – a mysterious 'Lord Thomas'. He was at Corfe Castle for eighteen months, which would take in the period 1328–9 and thus make it seem that he was at Corfe at the time that the friars hired by Edmund of Kent reported seeing him dining in the castle hall; then he sailed to Dublin. From Dublin he travelled back to England, sailed across the Channel from Sandwich to Brabant disguised as a friar, and called on the Pope at Avignon in 1331. He then pursued his devotion to the cult of the 'Three Kings' with a pilgrimage to Cologne, which is where Edward III sought out a man pretending to be him a few years later. After two years at Melasci/Milazzo in northern Italy he moved to Cecima, where Fieschi found out about him. Critics have pointed to this account's inconsistencies, particularly the difficulty of the tall and well-known Edward getting out of Berkeley Castle, which had a moat, even in disguise. But the Fieschi story contains much precise information that can be verified about the king's capture and captivity in 1327, details not then available in chronicles that an Italian writing some time between 1335 and 1338 (with no apparent contacts in Edward II's entourage) would have found out for himself.

The eminence of Roger Mortimer as effective co-regent from January 1327 onwards placed him on a political pinnacle as the most successful Marcher lord ever – and with Isabella's help he was a kingmaker, too. But his financial and landed gains from the revolution were limited, and he was seemingly content with the return of all his property, the justiciarship of Wales (an office held previously by his uncle Roger, who had died in the Tower in 1326) for life, the wardship of his late foe Despenser's widow and her lands (which he soon returned to her), and control of the disputed Marcher lands of Audley and Amory that Despenser had acquired. Unlike the shameless and spendthrift Isabella, whose annual revenue was raised from around £4,500 per annum to £13,333 (twenty thousand marks) plus grants of assorted castles, he clearly saw the danger of being seen to be as acquisitive as the Despensers. He also had had Church backing, especially from the local Bishop Adam Orleton of Hereford, ever since 1321, and now posed as the honourable upholder of justice and tradition against the feckless, spiteful, and incompetent ex-king. He preferred to operate behind the scenes, and although the great offices of state from January 1327 were mostly controlled by his own supporters or sympathisers (e.g. Orleton as Treasurer), this was normal for the effective head of government, and the number of grants of land and office to him and his family was no more than would be expected or than any great magnate with access to power would insist on – as was needed to reassure his affinity that he could deliver on rewards and was worth backing. His control over the appointment of sheriffs and custodians of royal castles did escalate as his position became more secure, but had its political reasons – and his marginalisation and eventual removal of the new king's personal guardian, Henry of Lancaster, was a political disagreement over Henry objecting to his and Isabella's decision to agree peace with Robert Bruce and so recognise Scotland's independence, not the act of a control freak crushing all opposition. Indeed, as the glory-seeking teenaged king and the majority of magnates wanted one more attempt to defeat Bruce and bring a stop to his damaging raids on northern England, the regime did carry out another campaign in 1328 after Edward

III's marriage to the invaders' backer Count William of Hainault's daughter Philippa. Bruce had a far better-prepared and motivated army and first-class generals led by the guerrilla expert Sir James ('the Black') Douglas, and the campaign in Durham was a disaster as the Scots raided the English camp at night, overturned the king's tent and may have tried to kidnap him, and sent the English fleeing – inside their own country – in a panic. The inevitable treaty, at Northampton, and recognition of Scots independence followed, as Roger seems to have wanted earlier. But this surrender to the long-term national foe was seen as a humiliation, and the subsequent marriages of Roger's daughters to two major peers, teenagers who were his wards (James Audley and the new Earl of Warwick, Thomas Beauchamp), in grand celebrations at Ludlow in May 1329, were followed by Roger assuming the title of Earl of March in October. His new eminence reflected his political eminence and raised his social status accordingly, but was bound to arouse jealousy and rumours of abuse of power, and was followed by more high-status marriages for two more Mortimer daughters (to the new young Earl of Pembroke, Aimery of Valence's nephew Laurence Hastings, and the king's cousin John, heir of the Earl of Norfolk) and a spectacular 'Round Table' tournament in the Arthurian manner at Wigmore Castle. The episode of the alleged attempted rescue of Edward II from Corfe and trial and execution of the king's uncle Earl Edmund of Kent followed, and a mixture of resentment at Roger's grandiose pretensions and his destruction of a royal prince was added to by personal anger from the king who had pleaded unsuccessfully for Edmund's life. Isabella seems to have been oblivious to the risks and Roger for once overconfident, though they did increase their personal security. On 19 October a royal visit to Nottingham Castle, with Roger in charge as usual, ended abruptly when the king arranged for a group of his friends, led by William Montague (soon to be Earl of Salisbury), to sneak up a secret passage (still extant) from a nearby inn underneath the castle rock and emerge into the inner bailey with the royal apartments. Heavily armed, they stormed Isabella's apartments and arrested and removed Roger, with the queen screaming to no avail to her watching son, 'Have pity on the gentle (i.e. nobly born) Mortimer! Do not harm him, he is a worthy knight.' This effective coup ended with Isabella removed from court and all political influence, while Roger Mortimer was tried in London (the king had apparently wanted him hanged without trial but Henry of Lancaster insisted on a legal process) on 29 November for treason. The trial was somewhat hypocritical and politically risky as the entire current regime – not least Isabella – had either participated in or tacitly approved of the removal of Edward II, the most obvious act of treason in recent memory, and had not objected to the grants of titles and honours to Roger and the subsequent dismissal of Lancaster; and the apparent murder of the ex-king had presumably been known, if not arranged, by Isabella. The charges did include murdering Edward II – though as seen above this may have been a sham – and Edward III's indignation at his being used as a puppet presumably lay behind the accusations that he had been forced by Roger to ennoble him, give him offices, and sentence his uncle Edmund to death. The charges of usurping royal authority and killing Edmund were the most just, and notably Roger was gagged so he could not make a reasoned defence that he had acted with the support of the queen and others – or desperately let out assorted embarrassing facts that the king preferred to keep hidden. Roger was sentenced to be hanged (i.e. as a commoner not an earl), which was carried out three days later at Tyburn – with him kept gagged again. Was he silenced to stop him revealing that Edward II was still alive? His widow was also forfeited for treason, though her lands were returned to her in 1336, and the death of their eldest son and heir Edmund in 1331 seemed to mark the fall of the House of Mortimer from its brief eminence. But events were to show that their most remarkable successes were still to come.

8

CHEATED OF THE THRONE?

A 'near miss' for Roger Mortimer's great-grandson Edmund, cheated of the throne by Henry of Bolingbroke; Edmund's alliance with Owain Glyn Dwr and the Earl of Northumberland to depose the new king and carve up England.

The overthrow of Richard II in 1399 and the choice of the next king; an unjust exclusion of the Mortimer claim by the new king?

The reversal of Mortimer fortunes from disgrace and execution to a place in the royal family had to wait for some decades under Edward III, but the latter was a fair-minded man who made much of his graciousness and openness to appeals for mercy, and it does not seem that he transferred his grudges against his mother's lover and his uncle's murderer to the later generations. Roger's eldest son Edmund had died a year after him, still in his early twenties; his son by Elizabeth de Badlesmere, Roger Mortimer (1328–1360), was restored to ownership of Wigmore in 1343 and inherited the Ludlow and Irish (Meath) estates from the elder Roger's widow Joan de Geneville in 1356. The family affinity was also usefully bolstered by the elder Roger's marriage of his daughters into useful Court-allied noble families – the elder Roger's daughter Agnes (d. 1368) and her husband, Earl Laurence of Pembroke (1320–1348) were succeeded by their son John (d. 1375) as earl while Agnes' sister Catherine's son was Thomas Beauchamp, twelfth Earl of Warwick (1339–1401), who was one of the 'Appellants' who forcibly coerced King Richard II into removing his favourites in 1387–8. Their sister Beatrice Mortimer (d. 1383) had married Edward III's uncle Thomas of Brotherton, Earl of Norfolk's (d. 1338), son Edward but he died before his father. The younger Roger was restored as second Earl of March, showing royal forgiveness for his father's presumption as King Edward had previously condemned this peerage as forced upon him by the elder Roger, and in August 1369 his son and successor Roger (1352–1381) married the great catch of Philippa (1355–?1381), only child of the king's recently deceased second surviving son Lionel, Duke of Clarence (1338–1368). The reasoning behind this was that Roger Mortimer owned a large part of Meath in Ireland and this would help Lionel's heirs to assert royal power as the king's lieutenants in Ireland; the widower Lionel had been lieutenant there in the 1360s but had died unexpectedly in Italy in October 1368 after his remarriage to local heiress Violante Visconti, daughter of the ruler of Milan. As Lionel had previously been married to Elizabeth de Burgh, heiress of the earldom of Ulster and in effect governor of that province, that role now descended *de iure uxoris* to Roger, who was to become Lord Lieutenant of Ireland in 1379–81. As of this point the king's vigorous and militarily successful eldest son Edward of Woodstock, known to later generations as the 'Black Prince', was the heir to the throne, but he fell ill following his Castilian campaign in 1369 and died before his father in 1376. His surviving second son succeeded the king as Richard II in June 1377, aged ten – who was the boy-king's heir, and if he died childless (neither of his marriages produced children and his second wife was a small girl, Isabella of France), who would succeed him? This put the Mortimers in the frame for succession as the heirs of the deceased next son of Edward III after the 'Black Prince' – but an adult younger son (John) had won out over the underage child of a deceased elder brother (Arthur) in 1199. By this reckoning the late king's third surviving son, Duke John of Lancaster, nicknamed 'John of Gaunt' (i.e. Ghent, his birthplace), head of the regency council for Richard after 1377, could claim the heirship – and the paranoid Richard seems to have feared this, as several times he apparently plotted to murder him. The Mortimer claim was also weakened by the death of Philippa's husband Roger, aged twenty-four, in a skirmish near Cork on 27 December 1381; his elder son by Philippa, another Roger (1374–1398), succeeded him and duly became Earl of Ulster, too. In 1388 he was given in marriage to the king's half-brother Thomas, Earl of Kent's (1390?–1397) daughter Eleanor Holland; this had been agreed legally when Thomas was made the boy's guardian in 1381. Roger seems to have been treated as the king's heir in the 1380s, though it is unclear if he was formally mentioned as heir in the 1385 Parliament when his claim was discussed. He was later made nominal Lord Lieutenant of Ireland in 1392 and probably commenced his actual rule when he accompanied the king's expedition there in 1394, but fell into disfavour in the mid-late 1390s after becoming too close to the king's critics. He had annoyed the king by failing to arrest his uncle Sir Thomas Mortimer for the latter's part in the 'Lords Appellants' attack on the royal army in 1387, and the acclaim of the populace as he arrived for the Coventry Parliament in 1398 may have alarmed the increasingly autocratic Richard as implying potential support for a coup. He died young in a minor skirmish at Kells, in Meath, in July 1398, removing one major contender from the forthcoming struggle for the childless king's throne – his son Edmund was only seven at the time, which put him at a disadvantage when it came to claiming the succession. His cause could however call on his uncle Sir Edmund Mortimer and his aunt Elizabeth's husband Henry 'Hotspur' Percy (1364?–1403), son of the Earl of Northumberland.

Richard staged a major reassertion of royal power in 1397–9, following his humiliations in 1387–8 when he had had to submit to the superior force of the coalition of 'Lords Appellant' and allow the execution of his closest supporters. Having arrested and probably murdered the leader of the 1387–8 revolt, his youngest uncle Thomas, Duke of Gloucester, he proceeded to target the other appellants one by one. He took advantage of the quarrel between his first cousin Henry of Bolingbroke, the youngest of them and either a few months older or younger than himself, and Thomas Mowbray, Duke of Norfolk and Earl of Nottingham (and lord of Gower in the Marches), to require them to fight a rare judicial duel at Coventry in 1398. Instead of allowing the duel to proceed he cancelled it when they were already horsed and about to fight, and announced that they were both exiled. This quarrel, which aided Richard's plans, indeed hinged on the allegation that Richard was planning revenge on them despite all his solemn promises to forgive them for their earlier actions – something they clearly thought only too likely. (Thomas was alleged to have personally killed Gloucester on the king's behalf and could reveal this to embarrass him, so Richard had reasons to discredit and silence him.) Henry was banished for ten years, later extended, and Thomas for life. The Earl of Warwick, Guy de Beauchamp, was arrested and exiled to the Isle of Man for his actions in the earlier revolt; the Earl of Arundel, and lord of Clun and Oswestry in the Marches, Richard Fitzalan, executed; and the latter's brother Thomas deposed as Archbishop of Canterbury. Arundel argued with his judges about his earlier pardon still being valid. Popular reaction was shown by rumours that Arundel's head had been miraculously reunited with his body, i.e. that he was a saintly victim of unjust royal murder. Parliament was intimidated by the king's large bodyguard of Cheshire archers into passing whatever legislation Richard desired, and the king seemed to be invincible. It was now made treason to coerce the sovereign, all past councils, now deemed 'controlling', such as that of 1310 and 1388–9 were roundly condemned, and all new peers and office-holders had to swear to approve and uphold Richard's recent legal reforms. He attempted to make it treason to reverse the actions of this Parliament, a misunderstanding of the powers available to him to restrict his successors, and was supposed to be intending to reverse the posthumous pardon of Thomas of Lancaster under which his lands had passed down through his family to John of Gaunt, who could thus be stripped of the duchy of Lancaster. His methods implied that nobody who had acted against his authority in the past was safe from a long-meditated vengeance, and people made comparisons with the behaviour of Edward II in 1322 – with the unspoken reminder of what had happened to Edward. The king's desire to stress his legal rights and achieve constitutional support for 'autocracy' suggests that Richard, isolated in a hierarchical court where flattery not plain speaking was the order of the day, mistook the image of power for its reality. His father and grandfather had never made that mistake, governing more by the consent of their senior nobles than by legal theory; they had also led the aristocracy in traditional – that is, military – pursuits, acting as the personal focus of a chivalric ethos in competitive sports (e.g the tournament). Once Henry was exiled Richard even refused to allow him to succeed his father John of Gaunt as Duke of Lancaster, thus threatening normal legal rights of inheritance.

As Henry illegally returned from exile with a small band of supporters and landed in Yorkshire in summer 1399, Richard was absent in Ireland leading his second expedition there to overawe the semi-autonomous Irish lords nearest the English 'Pale' around Dublin, particularly those in Leinster such as the MacMurroughs of the Wicklow mountains. The local royal commanders in Yorkshire, the Percies of Alnwick Castle led by the veteran Henry, Earl of Northumberland, stood aside and accepted Henry's claim – and reputedly his sworn oath – that he had only come to reclaim his dukedom of Lancaster, which he had illegally not been allowed to inherit when John of Gaunt had died in February 1399. Richard was caught by surprise but despite urgent messages from the regent he had left behind, his uncle Edmund, Duke of York (next brother to John of Gaunt), he delayed his sailing home from Ireland for a crucial two weeks or so, while his position in England collapsed as the unhindered Henry crossed the Midlands. The Duke of York, unable to raise an army around Gloucester and Bristol, gave up and came to terms with him at Berkeley Castle on 27 July. (The choice of that site by York was probably a deliberate echo of the fact that the last king to be deposed, Edward II, had been imprisoned there – a hint to Henry that he accepted the likelihood of history repeating itself.) The leading Ricardian ministers were seized and executed as Bristol, the main port in the West of England and key to the South-West, defected, and tenants in the Welsh Marches failed to muster for the king. By the time Richard returned directly to Pembrokeshire on *c.* 14 July – and landed in an isolated part of Wales, far from the centres of power in England – Henry had already gained control of most of England. The king advanced east to reach Whitland on 29 July and Carmarthen on 31 July, and according to the monastic chronicler Thomas Walsingham was initially looking forward to fighting Henry. But lack of local support condemned him to abandon a direct march against Henry's positions around Bristol, probably bolstered by news of the fall of that port. Instead he made a slow advance north through difficult country along the Welsh coast to attempt to link up with remaining loyalists under the third Earl of Salisbury. According to the Dieulacres Abbey chronicler, he abandoned his army to travel with only fifteen companions, possibly for speed or else through fear of betrayal. One writer who was with Salisbury claims that Richard disguised himself as a priest, suggesting that fear of arrest was his main motive. He was out of touch with his continually deteriorating position within England, and ended up trapped with Salisbury at Conwy Castle as the superior Percy army blocked his route and Henry arrived at Chester to join them. Arriving at Conwy around 15 August, he agreed to open negotiations although his first envoys (his Holland half-brother, the Duke of Exeter, and his nephew Edward, the new Duke of Surrey and son of the Duke of York) were arrested on arrival at Chester. As of this point, he had an inferior army to Henry's, and Salisbury had suffered desertions, too, so fighting was not an option. Ex-Archbishop Arundel arrived with Henry's terms (probably on 12 August). Richard may well have been tricked into surrendering with a false promise that he would preserve his throne, whether or not the Percies were being honest later in asserting that Henry had told them Richard would not be deposed (they perhaps had negotiated with Richard in good faith at the time). Whether Henry was being honest at the time in his oath is impossible to know. But Henry would have known from experience that Richard was untrustworthy, and he showed a slippery ability to dodge accusations with a flimsy excuse when he later claimed he had not killed Richard.

Northumberland and Arundel apparently swore to Richard that he would preserve his dignities, and the claim by pro-Henrician sources that the king offered to abdicate at this point have been rubbished by modern analysts. The more neutral sources, for example the French eyewitness Jean Creton, claim that Northumberland merely required Richard to accept a Parliament presided over by Henry plus the trials of five leading supporters, including the dukes of Surrey (Edward of Aumale) and Exeter and the Earl of Salisbury. The earl also swore that Henry did not intend any deceit – though as Parliament had required Edward II to abdicate in similar circumstances in 1327, it was obvious that Richard could be deposed later by this means. Richard duly emerged from Conwy Castle to accompany Northumberland to a meeting over dinner at Rhuddlan, east of the river. Only when he was away from the walls did an armed Percy contingent emerge from a nearby valley and take him captive. Confined at Flint Castle, he was said to have realised that he was doomed when he saw Henry's army approaching the walls. Northumberland may honestly have expected a council of senior peers to have been set up to exercise royal power, as had been done in 1264 and in 1310. In any event, it was a disastrous misjudgement: Richard was reported to have boasted that he would not consider himself bound by any promises that he gave to Henry, who would be punished later. This is known to the chroniclers, so it is apparent that Henry was told about it and made the most of it on his arrival at the London Parliament to urge the other peers to depose the unreliable king. Henry had his victim brought to London to abdicate publicly, so that a large group of nobles could witness the act – and possibly so that it could be done quicker than had been possible with Edward II being kept at Kenilworth Castle while Parliament met.

Henry was supposed to have sworn either not to claim the Crown at all or to hand it over to the worthiest candidate – the latter, of course, could mean himself if his peers judged him worthy, and the election by Parliament upon Richard's abdication on 30 September could be judged as an ideal opportunity for this candidate. He also swore not to levy the oppressive taxation that Richard had done, an oath which he more definitely violated under the needs of war in 1401 (with resultant riots). It is possible that some magnates who joined him expected Richard to be removed in favour of Edmund Mortimer, whose father Roger had been the beneficiary of the king's last reasonably clear words on the succession to Parliament in 1385. Keeping Richard under the control of a Council instead of removing him was more problematic; the problem of restraining a monarch with a council given special legal powers could have its predictable complications when the king recovered his freedom of action – as shown by Edward II's recall of the banished Gaveston and his and Richard's hunting down of the nobles who had conducted their humiliation. We know, of course, that Henry was to establish a dynasty that lasted for sixty-one years in September 1399, but contemporaries did not have foresight; it may have seemed to Henry (or to his Percy allies as they accepted his claim to the throne) that if he only became regent he would end up like Simon de Montfort did in 1265. Given that Edmund Mortimer was aged eight, if he was put on the throne there would be a long regency. Henry was the rightful claimant to the regency as the nearest male kin, being son of the next of Edward III's sons to Edmund's ancestor. The previous personal 'governorship' of an underage new king, Edward III, had gone to his nearest male kinsman, Earl Henry of Lancaster.

Edmund of York was an alternative choice as king to the underage Mortimer. Whether or not this apparently sluggish and unpolitical elderly prince decided it was not worth risking execution by defying his nephew Henry's advance, his military inaction as Henry invaded and subsequent journey to meet him on friendly terms at Berkeley Castle was significant, and so he could be counted as an ally to Henry's cause – and safe for Henry to have as his new sovereign had Henry's faction wished this? It is possible the fact that Richard had made him regent gave him hopes of securing the succession, the role of regent normally going to the male heir – though the 'rightful' heir as Richard saw him, Edmund Mortimer, was too young to be regent in 1399 so a substitute had been needed. The next choice of regent after Edmund of York, his son the new Duke of Surrey, Edward of Aumale, had been sent to Ireland in 1398 and so was unavailable. If Edmund of York had any hopes of the throne in 1399, helped by Henry's avoidance of claiming the crown when he landed, these were to be disappointed. The climactic assembly of the lords spiritual and temporal at Westminster Hall on 30 September did see the claims to the throne of York and his sons, Edward of Aumale and Richard of Cambridge, formally raised – but only after the king's abdication had been announced and Henry had made his claim first. According to French witness Jean Creton – more reliable than a Henrican partisan – the lords did not speak up for York and his family, and acclaimed Henry instead; it would have taken a brave man to stand out against the clear intention of the assembly, with the current Archbishop of York (Scrope) and the soon-to-be-restored ex-Archbishop of Canterbury (Arundel) flanking Henry to show the Church's symbolic support for him. It is more significant that Edmund Mortimer's name was not mentioned. It is possible that the York family's hopes and their thwarting led to the equivocal attitude of Edward of Aumale to Henry IV's regime – though Edward had other reasons to revolt as Henry had required him to hand back the dukedom of Surrey that Richard had given him. Edward joined the plot to murder Henry and his sons at New Year 1400, only to swiftly change his mind and inform the king, who thus escaped assassination. He was never charged, and may even have acted as a double agent once he had decided to change sides. Meanwhile Richard disappeared into the dungeons of Pontefract Castle, and in February 1400 was conveniently declared to have died of unspecified causes – which a large number of people refused to believe.

Overthrowing Henry on behalf of Edmund Mortimer – and the Welsh revolt by Owain Glyndwr; a 'Tripartie Alliance' of Mortimer, Percy and Glyndwr considers giving most of Engand to Edmund – and he nearly escapes from royal custody

Owain Glyndwr, lord of Glyndyfrydwy in eastern Powys at the time of his 'national' revolt against the preoccupied Henry IV in September 1400, was not of the direct line of Gwynedd but a descendant of the ruling house of Powys (themselves descendants of Bleddyn ap Cynfyn, d. 1075, half-brother of Gruffydd ap Llewelyn ap Seisyll) and by female descent of Gwynedd and of Dyfed/Deheubarth. His father was Gruffydd, either grandson or great-grandson of Gruffydd Fychan (d. 1289) of Powys, who held lands in the ancestral cantref of Edeirnion and had been steward for the earls of Arundel in the lordship of Chirk. His mother Elen, daughter of Owain ap Thomas of Ceredigion, brought him a half-share in the half-commote of Iscoed Llwch Hirwen and Gwynionydd; both his paternal grandmother (Elizabeth Lestrange) and wife (Elizabeth Hanmer, daughter of a King's Bench judge) were English. Born around 1354, he had succeeded his father at Sycharth in his mid-teens. His initial revolt owed much to the frustrations of the local gentry in Gwynedd and Powys, legally discriminated against and ignored by their English overlords, and immediately to grudges against the new regime of Henry IV for lack of the usual rewards in patronage. Glyndwr himself had had an English legal training in London and probably kept a residual loyalty to Richard II, overthrown by Henry in 1399, who had made much of the soldiery of his nearby county palatine of Cheshire. Glyndwr had served on Richard's Scottish campaign of 1385. The suspicious death of Richard in captivity at Pontefact in February 1400 had not stopped plots against the unpopular new government on behalf of its dynastic rivals, the Mortimer family, who were lords of Wigmore in the middle Marches, and at the time of his revolt Glyndwr was being victimised by a neighbour and Henrician loyalist Reginald de Grey, lord of Ruthin. It appears that Glyndwr expected to be granted the chief forestership of the local forest at Chirkland by the new king in 1399–1400 and was disappointed, and their pre-rebellion correspondence reveals threats by Grey to burn his lands; the latter was ordered to keep the peace by the king, though his foe did not know this.

Even if Glyndwr's decision to revolt was partly due to fear of royal punishment through Grey's connections and was linked to Ricardian plots, it quickly built up into a 'nationalist' movement as Henry's preoccupied government failed to react decisively. The small local revolt that Glyndwr launched on the Gwynedd/ Powys frontiers started with around 270 men sacking Ruthin on 18 September, followed by Denbigh, Flint, and Hawarden, only to meet a potentially disastrous reverse as local Shropshire loyalist Sir Hugh Burnell defeated the attack on Welshpool. Glyndwr had to flee the battlefield within days of proclaiming himself 'Prince of Wales', but he survived the initial English counter-attack in 1400–01 and was aided by the counter-productive paranoia of the militant MPs in the English Parliament of early 1401 banning Welshmen from owning land or holding office in England or prosecuting Englishmen in Wales. (To be fair to Henry IV, the Commons were out of his control and used their 'power of the purse' to remove his principal ministers so he could not intervene.) Rumours next spread that Parliament would ban the Welsh language, and the revolt was further inflamed. Thanks to the adherence of Glyndwr's cousin William ap Tudor and his brothers in Anglesey, a rebel attack seized control of Conwy Castle at Easter 1401 while the garrison were out at Mass – though they feared reprisal from local royal lieutenant Henry 'Hotspur' Percy and secured a temporary pardon and truce, in return for handing over some miltants for execution. Henry's local Marcher lords were unable to suppress the revolt in the North-East – Glyndwr captured Grey in person – and in June 1401 Glyndwr achieved victory against a larger army of loyalist Pembrokeshire settlers and their Flemish allies at Mynydd Hyddgen on the western side of Mount Plynlymon. There, as later, archers were his main resource. The king's own major expedition later that year lumbered ineffectively around countryside alive with guerrillas amidst atrocious weather. A local rebel, Gruffydd Vaughan, promised to lead Henry to Glyndwr but lured him into an ambush instead, so Henry had him hung before looting Strata Florida Abbey and retiring to safety; once he had left Glyndwr sacked Welshpool and tried to storm Caernarfon.

The inability to put down revolts quickly was inevitable, given the lack of a standing army or close supervision of the gentry and magnates – and their possession of private armies of servants and tenants. Armed defiance of the English government and its local officials was nothing new to local lords in the remote Welsh borders, particularly English Marcher lords with their own armed affinities. Individuals or groups of more powerful and obstreperous peers had been plotting against the king since the 1075 revolt of the Earl of Hereford, and judicial orders were sometimes difficult to enforce. A frequent response of the Crown was to rely on one particular local magnate – usually in favour at Court – as a viceroy, as with the younger Despenser in South Wales from 1320–6 and with the chosen nominees of the Yorkist kings, William Herbert in 1461–8 and the Duke of Buckingham in 1483. In 1485–95 Henry VII was to rely on his uncle Jasper Tudor, Earl of Pembroke and a leading actor in the region back in the late 1450s and mid-1460s. This resulted in fears by their rivals that the Court favourites' enemies would not secure justice from a biased king and his nobles – a reason for Glyndwr's action. At the worst, dispossessed lords with a grievance could retreat into the hills and live as bandits until they were caught or pardoned – as famously done by the legendary outlaw Fulk FitzWarin around 1200. This defiance was more common among English than Welsh landowners – and Glyndwr had indeed been educated at the Inns of Court in London and at one time lived at Court. He was acting within an English Marcher tradition, and his defiance in the face of anticipated punishment by his Court-affiliated foe was thus nothing new. It was his dynastic claims and his declaration of a national movement for independence that brought a special danger to the revolt – though, even so, he could have been militarily neutralised quickly by luck or a tip-off in autumn 1400. His revolt would then have had no more than a mention in the history books, alongside all the other abortive plots for a revolt since 1284.

In the anti-English troubles in 1294–5 the revolt in the South had been contained by the long-established Marcher lordship of Glamorgan, held by the de Clare dynasty; in the early 1400s there was no English strongman in this area to help Henry IV hold back Glyndwr as the Glamorgan lands had been ruled by the pro-Ricardian Thomas Despenser, Earl of Gloucester, who was killed in the January 1400 rising against Henry. (His widow Constance, daughter of Edmund, Duke of York, was later to betray Henry by trying to take her ward, the king's rival Edmund Mortimer, to South Wales to join the Glyndwr revolt in 1405.) John of Gaunt, lord of Ogmore in Glamorgan (by inheritance from his first wife's grandfather Earl Henry of Lancaster, d. 1345, heir of the de Chaworths) as well as Duke of Lancaster, had died in February 1399 and thus his lands in central South Wales were under the control of the king's agents in 1399 after being confiscated from Henry. Henry was their nominal lord but had little local experience. (He had been resident in the region earlier at times; his eldest son was born at Monmouth.) The central Marches lands of the Mortimers were also now owned by an unreliable and underage lord, the said Edmund Mortimer. In the north-central region, the lands of Clun and Oswestry had been seized by the king on the execution of their hereditary lord, the Earl of Arundel, in 1397; Gower and Chepstow had been confiscated on the exile of their lord, Thomas Mowbray, the Duke of Norfolk, in 1398, and his son (restored by Henry) was young and inexperienced. Thus as of 1400–05 Henry could not rely on a vigorous and local adult male lord in crucial Marcher lordships to head an army and hold Glyndwr at bay. Mortimer's uncle Sir Edmund was defeated and captured by Glyndwr at the Battle of Pilleth, then defected to him. Did this give the rebels an unusual advantage – and what if Henry had been able to rely on capable and locally accepted Marcher lords in these regions?

Edmund Mortimer, descendant of Edward III's second son Lionel in the female line, was the genealogically senior claimant to the throne after Richard, but was only eight in 1399 and lacked experience or an established magnate clientage to lead a revolt. If his father Roger, a former Lieutenant of Ireland, not died in 1398 he would have been a more viable threat. But now the Percies, probably dubious of the wisdom of trusting a restored Richard to keep his terms regarding an amnesty for them for their actions in 1399 and so far less likely to revolt in 1403 on Richard's behalf than on Edmund Mortimer's, might still have quarrelled with Henry. In the event, they were supposed to have been annoyed at him demanding control of and the ransoms for top-ranking Scots prisoners captured at Homildon Hill in 1402. In addition Henry had handed the justiciarship of North Wales over from Northumberland's son 'Hotspur' to Prince Henry in spring 1402 – a not unreasonable precaution given that 'Hotspur' was brother-in-law to the recently defected Sir Edmund Mortimer. He had refused to reimburse 'Hotspur' for his financial outlay on war against the Scots and Welsh – which he could not do anyway due to popular resistance to new taxes – and had shared out offices on the Scots Marches between the Percies and their local rivals, the Nevilles. One story even had it that Henry had punched 'Hotspur' in a violent quarrel at Court. The Percies' decision to revolt apparently took Henry by surprise, as he was en route north for the latest campaign in North Wales, with the news that 'Hotspur' was raising the men of Cheshire against him for not sending him off in haste to join his son Prince Henry at Shrewsbury. Hearing the news at Lichfield, he was luckily as close to Shrewsbury as 'Hotspur' was and was able to arrive first; when his foe reached the town he found the gates shut (20 July 1403). The catalyst for the Earl of Northumberland, Henry's long-term ally, to join his rebel son may well have been Henry's refusal (or inability) to pay up funds he had promised for the earl's imminent campaign to take Ormiston Castle in Scotland. Once 'Hotspur' had decided to revolt, the earl was in a difficult position of being likely to be suspected of collusion in any case; his son's defeat would inevitably mean the forfeiture of his lands and offices and a major blow to the dynasty. The earl accordingly joined in the revolt, but Henry was at this point closer than him to Shrewsbury so the king could link up with his son in time. As a result, Henry and his son were able to win the battle, albeit after heavy losses and the prince nearly being killed by an arrow in the face; 'Hotspur' was killed. The Welsh did not intervene in time, though a later story had it that Glyndwr watched the battle from afar.

Owain Glyndwr was also aided by Edmund Mortimer's eponymous uncle Sir Edmund Mortimer, a Henrician captain whom he captured at his first major victory at Pilleth in 1402 and who went over to his side. Marrying Owain's daughter, Sir Edmund acted as the agent of the Mortimer family claim of his nephew to England in allying with Owain, who in return was recognised as Prince of Wales. The eventual Mortimer-Owain-Percy 'Tripartite Indenture' of 1405 divided Henry's domains among them, with Owain ruling as far east as the Severn and the Trent. This, an enhanced Wales in full sovereignty, was clearly Owain's aim. In fact genealogically Owain had little claim to Gwynedd, being in the direct male line of the royal house of Powys instead; he relied on female descent for his claim to Gwynedd, but the same could be said of Edmund Mortimer, descendant of Llywelyn ap Iorweth via the latter's daughter Gwaldys. His declaration of himself as prince was more of an consensus election by popular acclaim. The 'triple alliance' between Percies, Welsh, and Mortimer partisans of March 1405 looked forward to a division of England between the three allies, but its potential was somewhat spoilt by Mortimer being safely in royal hands, though he had temporarily escaped a few weeks earlier. Given the need to muster a viable military challenge to the English royal army, the input of French troops was vital – about 10,000 seem to have landed in Pembrokeshire that summer. Having taken the town of Haverfordwest, they marched as far as eastern Herefordshire – the first French incursion into England since 1216 – without achieving much. They were said to have encamped on the hills above Abberley and Great Witley, within Worcestershire and a few miles north-west of Worcester. But this attack was too late in one respect: it would have had far greater impact in 1403 when 'Hotspur' Percy had an undefeated army at large in the northern Marches and his father Northumberland had an army of his tenants ready in north-east England. The French raid occurred once the Percies' northern power base had already been wrested from them as a result of their defeat at Shrewsbury by the king in July 1403, and Northumberland's part in the 1405 plan consisted of revolting from his remaining lands (graciously returned to him by Henry in 1404 in return for grovelling for mercy) without his confiscated wardenship. He had the support of Archbishop Scrope, who added the Church's prestige to denunciations of Henry as a tyrannical usurper who had broken his pledges on lower taxes and nailed up rebel manifestoes on York's church doors. But Ralph Neville defeated Scrope and his ally Lord Nottingham's (the late Thomas Mowbray's son) army at Shipham Moor by luring the two commanders to talks with a pretence of sympathy and telling their men falsely that agreement had been reached so they could go home. Scrope and Nottingham were arrested and later executed by Henry, and Northumberland (crucially absent from the Shipham incident) had to flee to Scotland as his castles of Alnwick and Warkworth were attacked. (For the first time, cannon were used to encourage the garrisons to surrender.) After this, Northumberland was a landless 'broken reed' and his arrival in Wales in 1406 to help Glyndwr was of little use; his only use was as a rebel envoy to France, in which capacity he persuaded Charles VI to hurry up his expeditionary force. Moving on to Flanders in search of men and then back to Scotland, he was largely ignored by the regent, the Duke of Albany, and the latter's good relations with England thereafter make it likely that he was seen as an embarrassment. The double-dealing regent may have colluded in the English capture of his nephew Prince James, soon to be king, in spring 1406. The state of affairs in Scotland rendered Northumberland's capacity to invade his home county marginal, and in 1407–8 he was to be lured into a desperate invasion and end up killed.

The plot to arrange the escape of Edmund Mortimer and his brother from protective custody at Windsor Castle in February 1405 meant that there would be a pretender available to take the throne in the event of success, albeit one too young to fight in person. Luckily for Henry, when the boys' governess Constance, Lady Despenser (*née* Holland), sister of the Duke of Exeter, secured duplicates to the castle keys and fled with them on horseback on 13 February, Henry was quickly informed. His half-brother John Beaufort then led the pursuit. A gallop west along the main road for South Wales ended with the royal posse catching the escapees up in a wood near Cheltenham; their rescuers were overpowered or killed, and they were taken back to Windsor. Had the boys had a few more hours' leeway, they would have reached Glyndwr's rebel area and their uncle Sir Edmund Mortimer, who was shortly to agree a division of England between the young Edmund, Northumberland, and Glyndwr. The agreement may have been planned in anticipation of the boys' arrival to act as a focus for the rebel campaign, and would have had more force had its main beneficiary been at liberty. As it was, the plan was given seeming supernatural weight by another of the current crop of prophecies, this time one predicting the overthrow of the sixth king after John (i.e. Henry) by a triple alliance from West (Wales), North (Northumberland), and Ireland (where the Mortimers had lands).

Edmund continued in royal custody after the failed attempt to rescue him, and his wardship and the right to choose his wife was transferred to the increasingly dominant Prince of Wales, the future Henry V. He remained loyal to the House of Lancaster through Henry IV's declining years, but soon after Henry V's accession in March 1413 went behind the new king's back in secretly arranging his marriage to Anne Stafford (d. 1432), a cousin, for which he had to obtain papal dispensation. She was the daughter of the Lancastrain loyalist Ralph, Lord Stafford, who had been killed fighting for the late king at Shrewsbury in July 1403, by Anne of Gloucester – daughter of Richard II's murdered uncle Duke Thomas and so with a distant claim on the throne. Henry was furious at the marriage and fined Edmund the massive sum of ten thousand marks, which may have lured him into joining a rather vague and impractical conspiracy to murder the king and start a rebellion by his sister Anne's husband, Earl Richard of Cambridge (younger son of the late Duke Edmund of York). Richard was not the current holder of the Yorkist claim to the throne, via Duke Edmund who had been next younger brother to Henry V's grandfather John of Gaunt, as his elder brother the new Duke of York was still alive – though he was soon to be killed at Agincourt. But Richard seems to have had a grudge against the king, possibly over not being given enough land to sustain his new title as an earl, and joined ex-Treasurer Lord Scrope of Masham and a Northumberland knight, Sir Thomas Grey of Heton, to plot to put Edmund Mortimer on the throne as Henry V was assembling his army at Southampton for the expedition to France in July 1415. The official accounts had it that Henry was to be assassinated, then Edmund would escape to the New Forest and somehow lure dissident parts of the army to join him while other plotters in the Welsh Marches (possibly the refugee proto-Protestant, Lollard heretic Sir John Oldcastle) and a gathering of fellow persecuted Lollards staged a military revolt. The Scots would then march south to join in; possibly the French, keen to stop Henry's invasion, were involved, too. The combination of all these parts of the plot succeeding was unlikely, and apparently Edmund had second thoughts about it and at the end of July went to the king and told him all the details. He was pardoned a few days later, but Cambridge (the prime mover), Scrope and Grey were all tried and executed at Southampton (hence the term 'Southampton Plot' for this event). The whole episode was murky and questions remain unanswered about how serious or practictable it was, but Cambridge was clearly serious in planning to remove the king and probably appealed to the brooding Edmund's sense of anger about his being fined to lure him with promises of a crown. Once Edmund had had time to think about the plan, he wrote it off as hopeless and saved himself, though due to he and his wife having no children it was Cambridge's son by Anne Mortimer, Duke Richard of York, who was to succeed to the Mortimer estates and to his claim to the throne. Edmund himself remained loyal to Henry and served faithfully through his French campaigns, and after Henry's death in August 1422 was appointed as Lord Lieutenant of Ireland, like his father and grandfather. This may have been to remove him from court by Henry V's younger brother Duke Humphrey of Gloucester, head of the regency council to the infant Henry VI. In the event, Edmund died of the plague at Trim Castle, chief seat of the Mortimer (ex-Lacey) lands in Meath, on 17 or 18 January 1425, ending the male line of Mortimer.

9

THE MORTIMER HEIR
BECOMES KING

Richard of York seizes the regency under Henry IV; Henry's army attacks York at Ludlow; York flees to Ireland but returns to take the crown.

The final thirty years of the Plantagenet dynasty – a surname for the family incidentally invented by Richard, Duke of York and his supporters in the 1450s to emphasize their superior dynastic lineage to their rivals – was an unprecedented era of political instability in England. In previous centuries the smooth (or not) transfer of power from each monarch to his son or brother, usually his own choice as heir, had been broken only once when childless and autocratic thirty-two-year-old Richard II was overthrown in an invasion by his cousin Henry of Bolingbroke (Henry IV) in 1399. Henry had claimed to be Richard's rightful heir, as son of the next-senior male offspring of Edward III to leave a male heir, Edward's third surviving son Duke John of Lancaster (John of Gaunt). But his election by an assembly of nobles excluded the rights of Edmund Mortimer, the grandson – daughter's son – of Edward III's second son Duke Lionel of Clarence, who was only a child at the time so his accession would have led to the instability of a regency. Indeed, Edmund's claim was not even tested at the election; the Salic Law theory that a woman could not inherit or transmit rights to a throne did not apply in England. The feeling that Edmund had been cheated by the illegal usurpation of Henry's

Lancastrian line led to assorted plots and rebellions in his name under Henry IV and later an attempt to murder Henry V, but then faded away as the Lancastrian throne became more secure and led a successful war to pursue its rights to the throne of France (which ironically relied on the legality of succession via a female line, namely via Edward III's mother Isabella).

But the incapacity and misjudgements of the unwarlike and allegedly unworldly Henry VI and his coterie of favourites in the 1440s led to renewed dynastic challenges after the humiliating loss of France in 1450–3. This was largely stimulated by the exclusion of powerful nobles from decision-making at Court and the fruits of office by Henry's clique, led by the junior Lancastrian line of Beaufort, and was thus politically opportunistic. Dynastic luck and the shifting sands of politics resulted in the current heir of Edmund Mortimer's line, his sister Anne's son Duke Richard of York (1411–1460), being the leader of the politico-military opposition to Henry VI's disastrous governance in the 1440s and early 1450s, excluded from power and seemingly under threat of elimination like the King's late uncle Duke Humphrey of Gloucester (who died while under arrest at the Bury St Edmunds Parliament in 1447 after being targeted by the king's favourite, John de la Pole, Duke of Suffolk, and the Beauforts). Duke Richard duly led one relatively successful expedition to Normandy in 1436–7, though he arrogantly delayed leaving on time so he could negotiate better terms from the Council and so missed his chance to coordinate his war with Duke Humphrey's attack on Artois, and a more successful campaign in Normandy as governor in 1441–2. He could thus pose as the successful warlord who had held onto Henry V's lands in France but been 'betrayed' at home by cost-cutting and greedy Court rivals and recalled too soon. A mixture of ambition and self-preservation determined his struggle for influence with the king's favourites in 1450–5, a political bid for power over an increasingly feeble and once catatonic king rather than a dynastic challenge, although his role as a potential heir also implied the latter.

York united the lines of Edward III's second and fourth sons, Lionel (d. 1368) and Edmund (d. 1402), in opposition to the line of the king's third son, John of Gaunt (d. 1399) in the person of the usurper Henry IV (John's son)'s grandson Henry VI. He had inherited his mother Anne Mortimer's extensive Marcher lands, centred on Ludlow and Irish lands in Meath, and her claim to the throne via Edward III's second surviving son Lionel. Richard II had recognised the March line as his heirs in 1385, and its descent via the female line was not an insuperable legal problem – after all, the English kings claimed the French throne by that means. This genealogical seniority to the House of Lancaster (descended from John of Gaunt, the third surviving son of Edward III) made York more of a threat than his father Richard, Earl of Cambridge (descended from the fourth son, Edmund of Langley), had been. The latter had already been executed in 1415 for plotting to murder Henry V before the Agincourt campaign. To add to the danger, York had made a name for himself as a reasonably successful military commander and had opposed the Duke of Suffolk's unsuccessful policies of accomodaton and surrender there. He was a magnet for returned captains and soldiers disgruntled at the inadequate support they had received from Suffolk's regime at home in the final years of Henry V's Continental empire. The popular anger at this betrayal and its focus on Suffolk and his cronies as the villains was shown in Parliament and the popular Kentish revolt led by the enigmatic rabble-rouser Jack Cade in 1449–50. Cade claimed to be from York's Mortimer family – so was he an ally of the duke?

The alienation of York from the dominant faction at Court, sent out of England by Suffolk's government to carry out the (usually titular) titular governance of Ireland in person in 1449, thus continued after Suffolk's death. Far from solving the conflicts by removing the perceived chief evil counsellor attacked in Parliament in 1450, the politically dangerous monopoliser of royal patronage, Suffolk's flight and execution by 'vigilantes' only led to new problems. There were allegations at Court that the exiled York had been behind the popular outbreaks of 1450, and that they were aimed at removing the childless Henry from the throne in his favour. (The Cade rebels denied this.) Whether or not this finally alienated the threatened Queen Margaret from York, the duke was not trusted with any major office or role at Court after his return from his successful years as Lord Lieutenant of Ireland in the late 1440s. Indeed, amidst the continuing factional confrontations York's leading supporter Sir William Oldhall (in trouble at Court as a leader of Parliamentary action against the Suffolk regime) was ostentatiously dragged out of sanctuary at St Martin's-le-Grand in London by the Duke of Somerset's men in a blatant sign of official ill-will to the duke. A first military confrontation between York's armed supporters and the king occurred at Dartford in March 1452, though on this occasion the greater numbers of the royal faction's troops enabled the mediating senior clerics to persuade York into a formal submission.

The Cade revolt, as in 1381, focussed on Kent and led to a march on London and a lynch-law by the armed protesters in the streets. (Henry, unlike Richard II in 1381, hid in the Midlands.) The extent of the anger and violence seems to have been unexpected, and probably Suffolk was too preoccupied with the danger from dissident magnates of royal blood that the Crown had faced in 1387–8 and 1399 – a problem seemingly warded off by sending York to Ireland. The popular anger was bound to focus on Suffolk, given his visible monopoly of patronage and policy. But this raises the question of why an adult king had allowed one minister such a free rein, and thus Henry's culpability for the crisis. Already in the 1440s the evidence of popular rumour, recorded in the chronicles of Harding and Capgrave, spoke of Henry being scorned by his most outspoken subjects as a simpleton. The probability is that he was easily led by unscrupulous courtiers into giving them excessive grants rather than judiciously buying support from a wider constituency. The land-grants that Henry had been making since his effective majority (1437) were subject to a sweeping review and cancellation by Parliament in the early 1450s, an indictment of nationwide perceptions of their fair distribution of assets among the landed gentry and nobles. Like Edward II and Richard II, the king was perceived to be the tool of a greedy and politically disastrous faction. It was however symptomatic that there was no political generosity towards York by the king. He had used a progress through York's Marcher lands in 1452 not to display forgiveness to his errant subjects but hold judicial tribunals for ex-rebels and require miscreants to appear before him wearing halters to beg pardon – not even staying with York when he visited the duke's principal residence at Ludlow, an evident snub. He also endeavoured to hand over a disputed part of the Despenser inheritance in Glamorgan from York's nephew and ally, Richard Neville, Earl of Warwick (1428–1471), the later 'kingmaker', who had inherited his Warwick lands via his wife Anne Beauchamp and held Glamorgan by fully legal wardship, to its rival claimant the Duke of Somerset. Warwick was refusing to obey and holding onto the disputed castles, while in the North another armed magnate dispute saw his relation Sir John Neville fighting the pro-Beaufort Percy cadet, Lord Egremont. It was while on progress in the West Country, rather than preparing for his promised expedition, that Henry suffered his mental collapse.

York attacks the king from Ludlow and takes over the government, 1455

The king's first mental collapse in 1453 led to him spending months in a catatonic state, unable to speak or move and being kept in seclusion away from the London area (mostly at Clarendon near Salisbury, where the illness began in August 1453). At the time, shock at the news of the final English defeat in Aquitaine at Castillon was supposed to be the likeliest cause. Losing the last of his ancestral Continental possessions but for Calais was a profound humiliation, and could have stimulated a depressive stupor. The main symptoms of his illness were complete loss of awareness and movement – by contrast, his maternal grandfather Charles VI's mental illness had involved delusions and bouts of violence. As the next legal adult heir, York assumed the regency as 'King's Lieutenant' to open the next Parliament by request of the Council, as it became apparent that feuding great lords (particularly in the North) were taking advantage of the lapse in personal royal rule to wage private war. Rather than seeking reconciliation with his foes and broadening his support as the government was paralysed, he was still issuing bitter complaints about Somerset. Ironically, the birth of a son to Henry and Margaret in the interim, in October, meant that York was no longer heir apparent and so would not take the throne if Henry died – which may have induced his fearful enemies, led by Somerset, to go along with granting him regency powers. To make matters worse, Archbishop and Lord Chancellor Kemp died on 22 March 1454, so there was no official licensed to operate the Great Seal and legalise administrative measures – the catatonic Henry could not appoint or approve a successor. York had not endeared himself to Parliament by his vindictive arrest of its Speaker, Thomas Thorpe, a personal foe, but there was no option to granting him the power to run the government if chaos was to be avoided. On the 27th he was named as 'Protector' of the realm – like Duke Humphrey in 1422, military leader and first among equals on the Council but not regent. York led the Council – minus the arrested Somerset – until Henry was demonstrably capable again in early 1455. His monopoly of power meant the inevitable dismissal of his rivals from office to secure control for his nominees, but he made no attempt to come to an agreement with Somerset and used his power to place the latter in the Tower. This escalated the already toxic distrust of Beauforts and allies for the York faction, and once Henry regained his senses they arranged the dismissal of York's appointees (led by his brother-in-law the Lord Chancellor, the Earl of Salisbury) and a formal absolution of Somerset from all charges. Somerset's ally the Duke of Exeter, who had been arrested by York in summer 1454 for assembling an armed force in Yorkshire and claiming that he should be both Duke of Lancaster (as a descendant of John of Gaunt's daughter Elizabeth) and the rightful Protector during

Henry's incapacity, was released from custody and the accusations made against him declared groundless. This was legally dubious, as Exeter had been defying the legally appointed Protector by armed revolt and so was as guilty as York had been in 1452. Exeter was a close ally of the Percies and had been disputing the inheritance of some of Elizabeth of Lancaster's estates with the pro-York Lord Cromwell, whose daughter was married to Salisbury's son. York and Somerset were bound over to keep the peace until their disputes were to be resolved in June. The duke's withdrawal from Court under threat of prosecution returned matters to the uneasy stand-off of 1452, with York unable to answer summonses to Court for fear of arrest and execution. In spring 1455 the Court faction arranged alleged 'arbitration' of the York/Somerset dispute, which was expected to come down heavily in Somerset's favour and legalise punitive measures to ruin York's power. This was to be dealt with by a 'Great Council' (dominated by the Beaufort faction) at Leicester – well away from turbulent London, which could riot in York's favour – on 21 May. The royal entourage of Household and armed Court nobles set out with its army for the meeting, and York decided to intercept it en route and prevent himself being punished. As shown by the outcome, if he could not secure 'justice' from the king (which would entail removal of his enemies from Court) he intended to fight to regain physical control of the sovereign. Not since 1387 had a group of alienated major subjects decided on this course, and not since Simon de Montfort's revolt in 1264 had a king been attacked in person.

The king's worst miscalculation was probably to pardon both Somerset and Exeter, which renewed the impression that he was an unjust tool of a faction and so boosted York's support. York's envoys demanded that the Chancellor, Archbishop Bourchier (another royal cousin), excommunicate Somerset and Exeter and summon a more representative, i.e. pro-Yorkist, assembly than the one which was due to meet at Leicester. But the royal army moved on and early next morning received supposed assurances of their opponents' goodwill and desire to 'protect' Henry from his 'evil counsellors' from York's confessor and envoy, William

Willeflete. The option of returning to London once they knew York's proximity on 21 May was not followed; nor was the option of halting at Watford when Willeflete arrived and daring York to attack. The armed attack on the royal army as it advanced north on 22 May turned political confrontation into bloodshed. The king himself seems to have hoped to negotiate a truce with the defiant rebels, as in 1452, not least as his army outnumbered theirs, and replaced the confrontational royal commander/'Constable' Somerset with the more conciliatory Duke of Buckingham. Henry took up his position in warlike mode by his standard in the town centre of St Albans after a failed meeting of envoys. York and his brother-in-law the Earl of Salisbury launched an attack on the king's camp – not so much a traditional battle as a series of assaults by York's troops on the barricaded streets. A succession of skirmishes ended with the principal Court lords in flight and Henry, hustled from house to house, being captured. Somerset was deliberately cut down as he tried to hold out at an inn, and the Earl of Northumberland – as the head of the house of Percy, principal Northern rival of the Earl of Salisbury's Nevilles – and Lord Clifford were killed in more dubious circumstances. The Duke of Buckingham, lord of Brecon, who had taken sanctuary in the abbey, was arrested in violation of its right of sanctuary but spared, and the Earl of Wiltshire (the new royal appointee as Treasurer) escaped; most of the forty or so royal troops killed were from the king's household and so would have been defending him and his standard. Other royal troops were despoiled by the victors, an example of blatant illegality and disrespect to men who had been defending their sovereign. Henry was escorted to London, with official honour but effectively as a prisoner, and York resumed his Protectorate as the king suffered another bout of his illness. Wiltshire was replaced as Treasurer by the Chancellor's brother Lord Bourchier (who was to continue off and on in this role under Yorkist regimes to his death in 1483 so was clearly capable and trustable). The physical incapacity of the sovereign made a formal regency by his captor legally defensible. But how long would this last, and what of the situation if or when Henry recovered? Was his mental condition likelier to save him from deposition (as a useful puppet and guarantor of legality for whoever held real power) or lead to his removal?

The Lancastrian versus Yorkist confrontation at Ludlow, York's exile, and his seizure of power: 1459–60

Henry was able to cancel the 1455 grant of the Protectorate to York in a personal appearance in Parliament in February 1456. Apparently the majority of lords opposed to the Act brought him in to overrule York. Although Henry was probably prompted he was clearly seen by all to be capable of a formal role in governance. His physical capacities were probably limited thereafter, however, and he spent long periods of the next few years away from the dangers of unruly London with his queen taking the lead in building up her clientele in the North Midlands. He spent much of his time visiting monasteries, and significantly it was the queen (whose castle at Kenilworth was his main secular residence) who took part in a ceremonial entry to Coventry. The withdrawal of the Court from the London area was prolonged (three-and-a-half years) and unprecedented for a mediaeval English sovereign resident in England. But was it prompted by a French queen used to Valois practices of long periods of residence taken at large chateaux away from the capital? Special arrangements were made to provide Westminster central funds for the Court, and more were raised by use (or abuse?) of the Crown's hereditary revenues – as was to be done again in 1629–40 with similar results. While the French mounted raids on the Kent coast, as in 1377, the government made no effective reponse – despite the levying of archers for war in 1453. There were apparently paid troops in existence in 1457, as after 1459 the Yorkists were to allege they had been raised to terrorise the king's subjects. But no more was heard of endeavouring to regain the king's French dominions, even in Bordeaux. Possibly the main royalist military preoccupation was fear of another rising by York as in 1452 and 1455 – particularly after the blatant dispossession of Carmarthen

Castle and imprisonment of the king's new choice as his local lieutenant, his half-brother Edmund Tudor (1430?–1456), the new Earl of Richmond, by York's South-East Wales allies Sir Walter Devereux and Sir William Herbert in August 1456. This incident led to Edmund's death in prison at Carmarthen before his son by Margaret Beaufort (1443–1509), the just-teenaged heiress of the late John Beaufort, Marquis of Somerset (d. 1444), was born. The Beauforts of Somerset's role as the descendants of the children of John of Gaunt's third marriage, to Chaucer's sister-in-law Katherine Swynford, made them the genealogical next heirs of the Lancastrain dynasty after Henry VII and his sons, Henry's uncles (the brothers of Henry V) all having died without children – but as John's and Katherine' s children had been born while he was married to other women, they had been born illegitimate and their subsequent legitimization by Parliament in 1396 had barred them from the throne. Margaret was the only child of the eldest Beaufort son's eldest son, the Marquis of Somerset, so she was a catch for the ambitious Edmund Tudor, although her father's Somerset title had passed not to her but to his younger brother Edmund (killed by York at St Albans in 1455) – and he had hurried to get her pregnant when only thirteen. This suggests ruthless political ambition with no regard for his wife's health, given her age, and she was not to bear any more children to her subsequent husbands, which is suggestive. The removal of one major future prop of the House of Lancaster by the early death of Edmund after this Marches showdown and the resulting fatherless upbringing of his son Henry (VII), brought possible long-term psychological effects on the ultra-insecure founder of the House of Tudor, and political effects from the lack of any brothers or sisters for his family.

The semi-mutinous Yorkist allies Herbert and Devereux in the southern Welsh Marches could easily have formed the nucleus of a new rebel army, and York's wife Cecily Neville's brother Salisbury's son, Richard Neville (1428–1471), had inherited the earldom of Warwick and its lands – including the lordship of Glamorgan and the honour of Ogmore – by his marriage to Anne Beauchamp, sister and heiress of the childless Henry Beauchamp,

Earl of Warwick (d. 1446). However, a showdown was delayed as York was still recognised as the king's principal councillor and military stand-in, in which capacity he was able to take a royal expedition north to Yorkshire in summer 1456 to force the invading James II of Scotland to withdraw from Northumberland. Also, his wife's nephew Warwick was now finally admitted to his governorship at Calais by the mutinous garrison, by royal command. The eventual dismissal of Lord Chancellor and Archbishop Bourchier, half-brother of the relatively conciliatory Court magnate Duke Humphrey of Buckingham, and other York-appointed ministers was apparently the work of the queen. She was also accused of wanting to deal with York at the Council meeting of October 1456 and being stopped by Buckingham. The meeting of a 'Great Council' at Coventry in 1457 may have seen another requirement on York to swear an oath of loyalty and an appeal from Buckingham to make this the last time York would be pardoned for his part in unnamed disturbances, though this is uncertain. Parliament did not have to meet for over three years due to the customs and subsidies having been given to Henry for life. Only Court-allied magnates were allowed onto a legal commission of 'oyer and terminer' into the Devereux-Herbert activities in South Wales in 1456 during Henry's progress to Hereford in summer 1457, and the opposition's misdemeanours were duly punished by a one-sided enquiry.

In this atmosphere, York chose to defy the Court's next moves to arraign him in 1459. Local land disputes, such as that between the Earl of Warwick, York's nephew, and the Beauforts over the lordship of Glamorgan, and the Courtenay versus Bonville feud in the West Country, continued unabated; the deceased Duke Edmund of Somerset's son Duke Henry (d. 1464) was claiming that as John of Gaunt, his great-grandfather, had inherited the Glamorgan lands from his father-in-law, the Duke of Lancaster, they should now come to him as the nearest male heir after the king. Disarming the rival magnates in the counties required a bolder king than Henry – who had no personal army anyway except the garrison at Calais. Nor did Henry manage to secure an even nominally stable government involving men from both factions, with a division of patronage which might have temporarily bought off the great lords. Attempts were made to remove Warwick as commander of the large and well-trained garrison at Calais, and when he refused to resign he was supposed to have suffered a murderous attack in Westminster. Possibly the emergence now of a story that the Prince of Wales was not Henry's son was deliberately sponsored by York as a way to remove the danger of Margaret as regent for the boy if the king died or was deposed – and so caused her obsessive hatred of him? Accordingly, as the subsequent indictment of York makes clear, he and his closest allies refused repeated summonses to Court in mid-1459. Apparently a repeat of the armed defiance of 1452 and 1455 was planned, with a summons for loyal subjects to meet the king at Leicester on 10 May armed for two months' campaigning and a reinforcement of the royal supplies of arrows for a large body of archers. A great council then met at Coventry towards the end of June, which York, Salisbury, and others did not attend in defiance of their summonses. This time the queen's faction struck first. As the Earl of Salisbury, York's brother-in-law, started to advance south from Yorkshire, the royal army moved quickly forwards to Nottingham to deny him the castle, and he was forced to march south-west to join York at Ludlow. The queen's army – many of them Cheshire levies, last used as a royalist 'private army' by Richard II – intercepted Salisbury at Blore Heath on 23 September, but was routed; the royal army then pursued him to Ludlow. Henry was again paraded at the head of the royal army in the advance on York's Marcher base, and proved a major psychological weapon as the Court propagandists played up the treason of fighting against the king and his standard. York's men had had no such scruples in 1455, but this time Andrew Trollope, commander of the Calais troops, declared that he had not known he was being brought along by Warwick to fight the king in person and deserted after the encounter at Ludford (across the Ludford Bridge). Apparently outnumbered, York and his older sons Edward and Edmund, Salisbury, and Warwick (all of whom could face execution for treason) fled Ludlow overnight across the Teme Bridge upstream from Ludford Bridge – with the royal commanders too incompetent (or too sympathetic to want York killed like the Queen may have done?) to guard all the bridges and trap them. The crucial role in the confrontation, for the final time, was played by Henry in person as a talisman of his queen and her allies, used to show that resistance to their army would be treasonous. For the moment the queen was able to assert her faction's power after her military victory, and at the quickly summoned Parliament at Coventry York, his elder two sons, Salisbury and his son Warwick, Salisbury's wife (as heiress of the earldom of Salisbury), and their principal adherents were attainted and all their lands seized. Pardon was possible if the accused submitted, but the sweeping and legally dubious nature of the conviction aroused support for them and was as counter-productive as York's killing of the Court leadership at St Albans had been. Worse, the means used implied that Parliament could be used for legal pillaging of any Court critic in future, an implicit threat to the entire social elite's safe possession of their property. Such a sweeping purge of 'traitor' nobles had only been seen before by the restored regime of Henry III in 1265 (later wisely modified) and by Richard II in 1397–9. This politically unwise triumphalism therefore can be seen as a factor in the failure of the majority of the peerage or landed gentry to rally to the king and queen as York's heir, Edward, Earl of March, and Warwick led an expedition back from their refuge at Calais to Sandwich on 26 June 1460. A papal legate joined them, and so did Archbishop Bourchier – Sandwich, pillaged by the queen's countrymen the previous year, was hardly likely to hold out on her behalf. The expedition entered London unopposed on 2 July, with only the Tower holding out, and marched on to encounter the king's army near Northampton on 10 July. Crucially, the warlike queen was not with her husband, and heavy rain accompanied Warwick's assault on the royal army, which crumpled in half an hour. From now on the king was a prisoner in the hands of York's faction, and his removal from the throne with his supposed consent became one way to counter the control his wife and her party had over him. But support for his right to remain king was strong enough to make his threatened deposition in autumn 1460 by York's clique unpopular with a majority of the lords – and the well-informed French observer Jean de Wauvrin believed that non-partisan peers had been reassured by Warwick's group swearing not to depose him as they invaded. To the fifteenth-century mindset, the importance of keeping sacred oaths of allegiance outweighed such practical considerations as the king's competence. At the time, the queen and her army in the North were still a major factor, with their advance on London expected. The infant Prince of Wales was with them, so deposing Henry would not neutralise the Lancastrian dynasty. Ludlow had been sacked for assisting a rebel after its fall to the royal army in autumn 1459 – would it be London's turn next if the king was deposed and his wife returned? Fear of the possible revenge to be expected on Lancastrian deserters by Queen Margaret meant that self-preservation should induce those nobles supporting her dynasty's displacement to grant York, their champion, what he wanted and prevent their enemies securing a compliant king again. The scale of courtier reprisals against the York faction in 1459 seems to have altered the balance of support by uncommitted nobles, though not to the extent of enthusiasm for Henry's immediate deposition. York's bold legal claim to depose Henry, made to the House of Lords on 16 October 1460, was promptly passed on to Henry himself as a weighty matter that only the king could rightfully decide; and as Henry refused to abdicate, the question was passed to the senior judges, who also equivocated and preferred to leave it to the decision of the nobles of the 'blood royal'. It was also pointed out that York claimed the throne now as direct heir of Edward III's second son Lionel, Duke of Clarence (senior to Henry VI's ancestor John of Gaunt), but until this he had displayed the arms of, i.e. relied on the claim of, Edward's fourth son Edmund, Duke of York. He was thus changing the rules of the game to suit his current position. Eventually the king agreed to a compromise put by Warwick's brother Bishop George Neville: he would remain king until his voluntary abdication or death, but his son would be disinherited. This gave York the role of heir apparent and its estates (the principality of Wales, duchy of Cornwall, and earldom of Chester) plus legal immunity from prosecution, as stripped from Prince Edward. Quite apart from the excuse of apparent rumours of the late Duke of Somerset being the boy's real father, nobody had taken any oaths of allegiance to the prince yet, and disinheriting him removed the threat of Margaret seizing power if Henry died leaving an underage successor. Despite his failure to gain the throne, York had secured the succession, legal immunity, and vast estates to reward his family and friends – always a major inducement for a semi-royal medieval magnate.

The drama of York's killing in December 1460 added to the notion of the political conflict over patronage and the succession being a 'blood-feud', with elements of treachery that the Yorkists could play up. York had gone to his South Yorkshire residence, Sandal Castle, to raise troops against the gathering Court/Percy army based at nearby Pontefract, but had not taken the offensive; instead the enemy advanced by surprise to blockade him and cut off his supplies. A sortie into Wakefield to gather supplies was then ambushed in dubious circumstances and the Yorkist leadership targeted for killing. In fact, contrary to Shakespeare's story, Margaret was not present at the battle or the executions, though she exulted in them afterwards; the surprise attack on

York's force – possibly at a time of truce – was led by the dukes of Exeter (who had a distant claim to the throne himself) and Somerset, the Earl of Northumberland, and Lord Clifford. The last three, sons of the principal lords killed at St Albans in 1455, had old scores to settle. Nor was York's seventeen-year-old son Edmund of Rutland a youthful non-combatant, whose killing was seen as unprecedently shocking: he was old enough to fight and be killed by contemporary reckoning. But the killings left York's heir Edward at large in the Welsh Marches, where he had been raising troops, and the local Court force under the Earl of Wiltshire and Jasper Tudor (Henry VI's half-brother) was unable to complete the queen's victory by killing Edward. Instead, the latter took the offensive and destroyed the Lancastrians at Mortimer's Cross on 2 or 3 February before marching on London to link up with the Earl of Warwick. After the battle he executed the king's stepfather Owen Tudor, whose grandson Henry VII was to kill his brother Richard in 1485.

Henry VI's deposition by Edward (3 March 1461) was not carried out with the confirmation of most of the political 'nation', as had been the agreement of October 1460. There was no formal meeting of the lords, though the unsettled state of the war-torn country and the need for speedy action after Edward's arrival in London on 26 February made that impossible in any case. The only major magnates involved in the Great Council at Baynard's Castle, the York residence in the City, that backed Edward were Warwick and the (Mowbray) Duke of Norfolk; the churchmen were led by the Archbishop of Canterbury and the Bishop of Exeter. The latter, Warwick's brother George Neville, was also Lord Chancellor, in which capacity he had set out Edward's genealogical claim and decried the misrule by Henry to a public meeting at St George's Fields on 1 March. The seizure of power was unrecognised in the Northern counties occupied by the queen's forces, and it was only their defeat in a bloodbath of a battle on Towton Moor over Easter that drove her and Henry

VI to flee to Scotland and thus secured the new regime the control of almost all of England.

EPILOGUE

TREACHERY ON THE ROAD
FROM LUDLOW

York's grandson Edward V is attacked en route to his coronation by his uncle, Richard of Gloucester.

A whole historical industry has grown up around the fate of Edward V and his brother Richard of Shrewsbury, Duke of York, the 'Princes in the Tower' – where the former of the two boys ended up after being intercepted by his uncle Duke Richard of Gloucester en route to London from his residence at Ludlow Castle. His father Edward IV had sent him there as titular head of the new 'Council' in autumn 1473, aged nearly three, with the latter arranged as the latest scheme to keep an eye on the Marcher lords with their private armies and fierce defence of their autonomous jurisdictions (which the king's judges now curbed). The establishment of a bureaucratic Council was not however Edward's first plan to control the Marches, centre of his own power as heir of the Mortimers and where he and his brothers had principally grown up (as seen above). As heir of the acquisitive Mortimers (holding twenty-three separate lordships by this right) as well as the dukedom of York, and aided by the fruits of deaths without heirs in battle plus confiscations from Lancastrians, he had had many of the lordships under his direct or indirect control in the 1460s. His first choice as his local strongman was William Herbert (*c.* 1425–1469), a rising Yorkist magnate in Monmouthshire and lord of Raglan Castle, son and heir of the elder Sir William (d. 1445), sheriff of Cardigan and Carmarthen, who had fought under Henry V and married the daughter of the South Welsh magnate Dafydd Gam. Edward IV made Herbert, the man who had aided his father York by defeating and capturing Edmund Tudor in the South Wales clashes of 1456 and had become guardian to Edmund's posthumous son Henry Tudor (later Henry VII), the chief justice and chamberlain of South Wales (8 May 1461) and life constable of Cardigan Castle (2 August 1461). He then became lord of Pembroke, Cilgerran, and Castle Martin as confiscated from Edmund's brother Jasper (3 February 1462), chief justice of Meirionydd and lord of Harlech castle (17 June 1463), steward of Usk, Caerleon, and other duchy of York estates (26 September 1463), chief justice of North Wales and steward of Denbigh and Montgomeryshire (28 August 1467), and constable of Conwy Castle (11 November 1468). To these were added the earldom of Pembroke (8 September 1468), the wardship of the young Henry Stafford, Duke of Buckingham (born 1453?), who was lord of Brecon, and the lordships of Gower and of Chepstow Castle, which the Mowbrays had to transfer to him (September 1468).

This former junior member of the South Wales gentry thus became effective ruler of most of Wales for the king; the only remaining local magnate able to challenge him was the king's cousin and most powerful supporter, Richard Neville, Earl of Warwick, lord of Glamorgan. But the latter, whose reputation and landed power overshadowed the king, who was fourteen years his junior, was at odds with Herbert, and Warwick's alienation from the increasingly assertive king was symbolised by the latter's (initially secret) marriage to the Lancastrian widow Elizabeth Grey, *née* Woodville, while the unaware Warwick was negotiating to marry him off to a French candidate. In July 1469 Warwick rose in rebellion in allliance with the then sonless Edward's heir, his next brother Duke George of Clarence, who Warwick married off to his daughter Isabel in defiance of the king at Calais. As Warwick invaded England Herbert led an army of Welshmen to aid the undermanned royal army, but was caught and routed on 26 July at Edgecote Field near Northampton by Warwick – who captured and executed him to be rid of a rival. The latest Marcher strongman thus ended up the same way as many others, and in March 1471 it was Warwick's turn to die in battle at Barnet against Edward, who he had deposed at the second attempt in autumn 1470 and replaced with Henry VI, but who had then invaded England in turn. The restored Edward's choice as his main governor in Wales, his youngest and loyal brother Richard, Duke of Gloucester (born October 1452), had been put in charge of the region in 1470 after Warwick's exile but was now transferred to rule Northern England. Hence the region needed a new ruler, and Edward first chose to divide it between Hebert's son William, second Earl of Pembroke (d. 1484), as justiciar of South Wales and John Talbot, Earl of Shrewsbury and lord of Goodrich Castle, as justiciar of the North. Their inexperience, inefficiency, and lack of zeal probably contributed to a rising tide of lawlessness, and in 1473 the king had to visit Shrewsbury and summon the main regional lords to make them sign up to cognizances (bonds) for good behaviour on pain of fines and forfeiture. He later intiated a governing council in the name of his infant elder son, who in 1473 was sent to live at the headquarters of his family's ancestral lordships at Ludlow, receiving the lands of the Principality of Wales (he was created prince on 26 June 1471 aged seven months), and in 1479 adding on the earldom of Pembroke, which Herbert had to hand over. As of 1472–3 the Council, of nobles and lawyers, were merely administering the prince's own lands, but their initially sporadic grants of temporary powers to deal with particular disorders were slowly extended to a general and permanent judicial power over the whole region during 1476. The Council was headed by John Alcock, the prince's tutor, and also the bishops of Rochester (1472–6) and Worcester (from July 1476), with the prince's maternal uncle Anthony Woodville, Earl Rivers, as his personal governor and head of his household. This arrangement mixed the traditional control of the vast hereditary estates of the next king, as Prince of Wales and as Mortimer heir, by his Household and

Council with a new administrative and judicial control of a whole region by the latter. But on 9 April 1483 Edward IV died, just short of his forty-first birthday.

Richard of Gloucester had been nominated as 'Protector' of the realm in Edward IV's will – or so he claimed, though the document is not extant and it may be that Edward IV only intended him as personal governor of the new underage king, as normal for his closest male relative. There had been no need of an adult 'Protector' – a formal head of the royal Council with full royal powers – for the fourteen-year-old Edward III in 1327, though his mother and her lover Roger Mortimer had acted as unofficial regents. Alternatively, the role might not have held full powers, merely those of being 'first among equals' on the Royal Council. Richard alleged that Edward IV's mother Queen Elizabeth Woodville and her partisans were planning to get the new king to London for a quick coronation in order to argue that a crowned king did not need a Protectorate. (The precedent was Henry VI, titularly adult from his coronation in 1429, aged seven-and-a-half, though controlled by a Council until 1437.) They would then take over the government for their own benefit, contrary to the late king's intentions. From the propaganda that Richard later put out when seizing power in the *Titulus Regius*, he was allegedly concerned at the Woodville family's immorality, grasping habits, and bad influence on the late king, and feared for their control of the government. Indeed, they were blamed for driving Edward IV to his death by loose living and gluttony – a plausible charge given that Edward was recorded as being noticeably overweight as early as 1475. Edward had not only died at forty but had showed little signs of his old vigour in recent years, most noticeably in the dispute with Scotland since 1480 when his brother Richard had been left to command the invasion of 1482. The royal court was riven by a feud between the king's close friend and chamberlain, Lord Hastings, and the king's stepson the Marquis of Dorset, suggesting that Edward IV could not control his relatives and demanding that they show public respect to each other. Nor was there any indication that Edward was formulating a reponse to the serious diplomatic reverse he had suffered in 1482, when Louis XI – who had effectively bribed him to abandon his invasion in 1475, a disappointment to royal advisers like the belligerent Richard – had abandoned the betrothal of his son 'Dauphin' Charles to Edward's eldest daughter. The unmilitary Louis had been careful to buy off Edward at Picquigny as a serious threat, but now ignored him in his rapprochement with his old enemy, Edward's ally Maximilian of Habsburg (ruler of the Low Countries, England's principal trading-partner).

The new king's uncle and guardian Anthony Woodville, Earl Rivers, evidently did not expect trouble from Richard in April 1483. He did not leave Ludlow with Edward V in a hurry, which should have been the case if he intended to get to London before Richard arrived from the more distant York as advised by the Woodvilles in London. News of Edward IV's death on 9 April reached the isolated Welsh Marches town in five or six days, probably on 14 April – time to move the royal entourage quicker than he did. His delay for ten days to 24 April suggests that, contrary to Richard's claims circulated in London in May, he was not involved in the queen's alleged plan to stage an early coronation (3 May) and avoid the need for a Protectorate. Certainly he was not ready to leave Ludlow in a hurry, which argues against the modern suggestion that he and the queen had slowly poisoned Edward in order to run a lucrative regency. He had to be urged to make haste by her son by her first marriage, the Marquis of Dorset, and was clearly not intending to arrive in London by Dorset's intended date of 1 May. Apparently the queen's attempt on 11 April to get the Council to agree to Edward V and Rivers bringing a large force to London, which other Councillors blocked, so alarmed Lord Chamberlain Hastings that he threatened to withdraw to his governorship of Calais (where he had troops of his own) sooner than cooperate with it. The governor had a large, coherent body of standing troops, unlike the king; at this date there was no regular army, only local retainers raised for specific campaigns by their lords when required. When the plan for a large army of Welsh Marcher retainers advancing from Ludlow was abandoned and the force limited to 2,000 men, Hastings sent in haste to Richard to warn him to hurry to London and stop the plot; from what Richard's partisans circulated in May it seems that there was supposed to be a Woodville plan to ambush Richard en route to London.

Richard set out from Middleham Castle on 20 April, with only 300 men (presumably more could not be collected quickly), but accepted an offer from Henry Stafford, Duke of Buckingham, who was based in his Marcher lordship at Brecon, to meet him en route. Buckingham also had around 300 men, and despite being married off by Edward IV to his queen's younger sister Catherine Woodville, he now deserted the Woodvilles for their rivals, possibly resenting his wife as beneath his social rank. They arranged to meet at Northampton, on the main road south-east across the Midlands, on 29 April – when Rivers was informed he agreed to join the rendezvous. When Richard's and Buckingham's forces arrived on the 29th Rivers had already moved on to Stony Stratford, several miles ahead. If this breach of the agreement was intended to avoid Richard, as the latter seems to have suspected, it was not very effective as Richard could easily catch the royal party up by a forced ride. More likely is Rivers' own explanation sent to Richard, that he did not want all three armed parties to try to secure lodgings in one small town. He did not try to escape or fight, but rode over to Richard's lodgings in Northampton to join him for dinner. Next morning he woke up to find his inn surrounded by troops, and he and other senior Woodville agents – his nephew Richard Grey, the queen's younger son by her first marriage and Dorset's full brother, and the chamberlain Sir Thomas Vaughan, seized on the 30th at Stony Stratford – were arrested by Richard and sent to prison in Yorkshire. The king was secured at Stony Stratford as he was mounting up to ride on to

London, which suggests that, as his party was caught unawares, Rivers had told them to set out on the 30th without waiting for his return. Was Rivers just nervous of the potential for a clash between the two armies, or did he expect the king's party to keep a day or two's ride ahead of Richard all the way to London and enable him to link up with Dorset's men there? The king's party still outnumbered Richard's and Buckingham's by around two to one, but without Rivers' leadership they put up no resistance, and the soldiers obeyed Richard's orders to disperse and go home. Edward had to complete his journey with Richard's men. Richard informed the king that he had rescued him from a plot to take control of the government by the Woodvilles, but was not believed. According to the Italian Dominic Mancini, not a witness but in London in spring–summer 1483 and so able to talk to members of the royal entourage, Richard and Buckingham complained that the Woodvilles had ruined Edward IV's health with riotous living and were not fit to take charge of his son. Buckingham also sneered that a woman, namely the queen (his wife's sister), should not take charge of a regency as Elizabeth was proposing to do. Edward defended his right to rely on his mother's family, to no avail. On news of the capture of Edward and his Woodville escort the queen and her remaining children took refuge in the sanctuary of Westminster Abbey, apart from her eldest son Dorset who with her brother Sir Edward Woodville fled the capital. Woodville had seized part of the late king's treasure and control of the fleet, at least according to what Mancini heard. If the money raised to wage the intended Scottish campaign in 1483 was meant, this was not the 'royal treasure', a phrase suggesting Edward's personal fortune. Was the implication that the Woodvilles had embezzled the king's personal fortune a piece of post-coup Ricardian propaganda?

When Richard arrived the Lord Chancellor, septuagenarian Archbishop Rotherham of York, had some explaining to do about why he had handed over the Great Seal to the queen in sanctuary rather than kept it ready to give to Richard; he was over sixty and may have been confused but was clearly amenable to Woodville pressure. He changed his mind after a night to consider it and retrieved the Great Seal, but when Hastings wrote to Richard informing him Richard promptly had him dismissed. The Archbishop of Canterbury, Thomas Bourchier (Richard's great-uncle and also related to Buckingham), took the Seal until a new Chancellor was appointed. The royal party arrived in London for a State entry on 4 May, and the new Protector displayed cartloads of alleged weaponry and armour seized from Rivers' force on his arrival in London to demonstrate the latter's warlike intentions. Mancini wrote that the explanation for the weaponry was not accepted by the public, and that the arms had been stored in London for use in the next Scots war; Sir Thomas More's account of *c.* 1513 alleged that people said that the arms would have not been sealed up in barrels if the Woodvilles anticipated using them. (If it was a Woodville stockpile, why had Sir Edward not removed most of it on his twenty ships?) According to the 1486 Croyland Chronicle, Richard led the taking of oaths of fealty to Edward V by the lords spiritual and temporal, and on 10 May the Council confirmed Richard as 'Protector'. The Chronicle and Mancini agree that there was relief in London at the peaceful outcome, and that Richard treated Edward with all due respect as his sovereign. But as events were to show, the truce was not to last and Buckingham was to aid Richard to depose Edward in June and then try to overthrow him in the autumn. The coup on the road from Ludlow was the final major political clash involving a Marcher army in the turbulent world of medieval England. Though one might have occurred later that year had Buckingham's own revolt not collapsed in the heavy rain.

BIBLIOGRAPHY

Primary

Adam of Usk, *Chronicon*, ed. and trans. E Maunde Thompson (1904 edition)

The Anglo-Saxon Chronicle, ed and trans. Michael Swanton (Phoenix Press edition, 2002)

Annales Cambriae, ed. J Williams ab Ithel (Rolls Series, 1860)

Annals of the Four Masters, ed. J. O'Donovan (Dublin 1854)

'Annales de Margam 1066–1232', *Annales Monastici*, vol. I, ed. H. R. Luard (Rolls Series, 1864)

Annales Monastici, ed. H. R. Luard, 5 vols (Rolls Series 1864–9)

The Annals of Roger de Hoveden, vol I: AD 732 to 1154, trans Henry Riley (1853, reprint by Llanerch Press 1994)

The Annala of Ulster, ed. W. M. Hennessy and B. MacCarthy (Dublin, 1887–1901)

Welsh Genealogies AD 300–1440, 8 vols, ed. P. C. Bartrum (University of Wales Cardiff 1974)

Brut y Tywysogion or the Chronicle of the Princes, Peniarth MSS 20 version, ed. and trans. T Jones (University of Wales Press, Cardiff 1952)

Brut y Tywsyogion, Red Book of Hergest version, ed. and trans. T. Jones (University of Wales Press, Cardiff 1955)

Calendar of Close Rolls, 1272–1422 (HMSO, 1900–32)

The Chronicle of Bury St Edmunds 1212–1301, ed. Antonia Gransden (1964)

Chronicles of the Reigns of Stephen, Henry II and Richard I, ed. R Howlett 4 vols (Rolls Series 1864–9)

Chronicles of the Reigns of Edward I and Edward II, ed. W. Stubbs, 2 vols (Rolls Series, 1882–3)

Chronicon ex chronicis, ed. B. Thorpe, 2 vols (English Historical Society, 1848–9)

Close Rolls 1227–1272 (HMSO, 1902–38)

'Cronica de Wallia and other Documents from Exeter Library Mss. 3514', ed. T Jones, *Bulletin of the Board of Celtic Studies*, No. 12 (1946–8) pp. 27–44

J. C. Dickinson and P. T. Ricketts, 'The Anglo-Norman Chronicle of Wigmore Abbey', *Transactions of the Woodbridge Field Club* Vol. 39 (1969) pp. 413–46

Gesta Regis Henrici Secundi, ed. W. Stubbs, 2 vols (Rolls Series 1879–80)

Gesta Stephani, ed. and trans. K. Potter and R. H. C Davis (Oxford UP, 1976 edition)

History of Gruffydd ap Cynan (1054–1137), ed. and trans. A. Jones (Manchester UP 1910)

Matthew Paris, *Chronica Majora*, ed. H. R. Luard, 7 vols (Rolls Series, 1872–83)

Ralph of Diceto, Opera Historica, ed. W. Stubbs, 2 vols (Rolls Series, 1876)

Roger of Wendover's Flowers of History, trans. by J. A. Giles: Volume One, Part One: 447 to 1066 AD (reprint by Llanerch Press 1993); Volume One, Part Two: 1066 to 1170 AD (reprint by LLanerch Press 1994)

Scalacronica: The Reigns of Edward I, Edward II, Edward III and Richard II, as recorded by Sir Thomas Gray, ed. Sir Herbert Maxwell (Glagow 1907)

Vita Edwardi Secundi, ed. N. Denholm-Young (1957)

Thomas Walsingham, *Historia Anglicana*, ed. H. T. Riley, 2 vols (Rolls Series, 1863–4)

Annales Ricardi Secundi et Henrici Quarti, ed. H. T. Riley (Rolls Series, 1866)

Walter of Guisborough, Chronicle, ed. H. Rothwell (Camden Society, 1957)

Secondary

M. Altschul, *A Baronial Family in Medieval England: The Clares 1217–1314* (Baltimore, 1965)

Frank Barlow, *Edward the Confessor* (Methuen, 1970)

G. Barraclough, *The Earldom and the County Palatine of Chester* (Oxford UP, 1953)

T. H. Bound, *History of Wigmore* (1876)

Art Cosgrove ed., *A New History of Ireland: Vol II, Medieval Ireland* (Oxford UP, 1987)

D. A. Crouch, 'Oddities in the Early History of the Lordship of Gower, 1107–1166', *Bulletin of the Board of Celtic Studies*, Vol. 31 (1984), pp. 133–42

G. P. Cuttino and T. W. Lyman, 'Where is Edward II?', *Speculum*, No. 53, Vol. 3 (1978), pp. 522–3

J. Conway Davies, 'The Despenser War in Glamorgan', *Transactions of the Royal Historical Society*, 3rd series, Vol. 9 (1915), pp. 21–64

R. R. Davies, *Lordship and Society in the March of Wales, 1282–1400* (Oxford UP, 1978)

'Henry I and Wales', *Studies in Medieval History Presented to R H C Davis*, ed. R. Mayr-Harting and R. I. Moore (1985), pp. 132–47

Conquest, Co-Existence and Change: Wales 1063–1415 (Oxford UP/ University of Wales Press, 1987)

J. G. Edwards, 'The Normans and the Welsh March', *Proceedings of the British Academy*, Vol. 42 (1956), pp. 155–77

Bibliography

Michael Faraday, *Ludlow 1085–1660: A Social, Economic and Political History* (Phillimore, 1991)

N. Fryde, *The Tyranny and Fall of Eward II 1321–6* (Cambridge UP, 1979)

R. A. Griffiths, 'The Norman Conquest and the Twelve Knights of Glamorgan', *Glamorgan Historian*, Vol. 3 (1966), pp. 153–69

The Principality of Wales in the Later Middle Ages: The Structures and Personnel of Government, vol 1: South Wales (Cardiff, 1972)

R. M. Haines, 'The Afterlife of Edward of Carnarvon', *Transactions of the Bristol and Gloucestershire Archaelogical Society*, Vol. 116 (1996), pp. 65–86

C. Warren Hollister, *Henry I* (Yale UP, 2001)

P. A. Johnson, *Duke Richard of York 1411–1460* (Oxford UP, 1988)

Edmund King, *King Stephen* (Yale UP, 2012)

J. D. Cathcart King, 'Henry II and the Fight at Coleshill', *Welsh History Review*, Vol. 2 (1984–5), pp. 367–75

'Pembroke Castle', *Archaeologia Cambriae*, Vol. 127 (1978), pp. 75–121

J. L. Kirby, *Henry IV of England* (1970)

F. R. Lewis, 'A History of the Lordship of Gower from the missing cartulary of Neat Abbey', BBCS, Vol. 9 (1939–40), pp. 149–54

J. E. Lloyd, 'Wales and the Coming of the Normans', *Transactions of the Cymmrodorion Society (1899–1900)*, pp. 122–79

A History of Carmarthenshire, 2 vols (University of Wales, Press 1935–9)

The Story of Ceredigion (400–1277) (University of Wales Press, 1937)

A History of Wales from the Earliest Times to the Edwardian Conquest (3rd edition, 1939)

J. F. Mason, 'Roger de Montgomery and his sons 1067–1102', *Transactions of the Royal Historical Society*, 5th series, vol. 13 (1963), pp. 1–28

J. R. Madicott, *Thomas of Lancaster 1307–22* (1972)

Simon de Montfort (Cambridge UP, 1994)

J. Meisl, *Barons of the Welsh Frontier: The Corbet, Pandulf and Fitzwarin Families 1066–1272* (Lincoln, Nebraska, 1980)

J. E. Morris, *The Welsh Wars of Edward I* (Oxford, 1901)

Ian Mortimer, *The Greatest Traitor: The Life of Sir Roger Mortimer, Rule of England 1327–1330* (Pimlico, 2004)

L. H. Nelson, *The Normans in South Wales 1070–1171* (Austin, Texas, 1966)

J. R. S. Phillipps, *Aymer de Valence, Earl of Pembroke 1307–24: Baronial Politics in the Reign of Edward II* (Oxford, 1972)

Michael Prestwich, *Edward I* (Methuen, 1988)

T. B. Pugh, *The Marcher Lordships of South Wales, 1415–1526* (University of Wales Press, 1963)

W. Rees, 'The Medieval Lordship of Brecon', *Transactions of the Cymmrodorion Society* (1915–16), pp. 165–244

A. C. Reeves, *The Marcher Lords* (Llandybie, 1983)

I. W. Rowlands, 'The Making of the March: Aspects of the Norman Settlement of Dyfed', *Proceedings of the Battle Conference*, Vol. 3, ed. R Allen Brown (Boydell and Brewer, Woodbridge, 1981), pp. 142–57

'William de Braose and the Lordship of Brecon', *Bulletin of the Board of Celtic Studies*, vol. 30 (1982–3), pp. 123–33

Nigel Saul, *Richard II* (Yale UP, 1997)

J. B. Sherborne, 'Richard II's Return to Wales', *Welsh Historical Review*, Vol. 7 (1974–5), pp. 389–402

J. B. Smith, 'The Lordship of Glamorgan', *Morgannwg*, Vol. 9 (1965), pp. 9–38

'The Middle March in the Thirteenth Century', *BBCS*, Vol. 24 (1970–2), pp. 77–93

'Owain Gwynedd', *Transaction of the Caernarfonshire Historical Society*, Vol. 32 (1971), pp. 8–17

'Edward II and the allegiance of Wales', *Welsh History Review*, Vol. 8 (1976), pp. 137–71

'The Treaty of Lambeth, 1217', *English Historical Review*, Vol. 94 (1977), pp. 562–79

'Llywelyn ap Gruffydd and the March of Wales', *Brycheiniog*, Vol. 20 (1982–3), pp. 9–22

L. B. Smith, 'The Death of Llywelyn ap Gruffydd: The Narratives Reconsidered', *Welsh History Review* (1982–3), pp. 200–14

D. Stephenson, *The Last Prince of Wales* (Buckingham, 1983)

'Llywelyn ap Gruffydd and the Struggle for the Principality of Wales, 1258–82', *Transactions of the Cymmrodorion Society*, 1983, pp. 39–61

T. F. Tout, 'Wales and the March in the Barons' War, 1258–67', *Collected Papers*, Vol. ii (Manchester UP, 1933), pp. 47–100

D. Walker, 'Miles of Gloucester, Earl of Hereford', *Trans. of the Bristol and Gloucestershire Archaelogical Society*, Vol. 77 (1958–9), pp. 66–84

'William FitzOsbern and the Norman Settlement in Herefordshire', *Transactions of the Woodhope Field Club*, Vol. 39 (1967–9), pp. 402–12

'The Lordship of Builth', *Brycehiniog*, Vol. 20 (1982–3) pp. 23–33

'The Norman Settlement in Wales', *Proceedings of the Battle Conference*, Vol. 1, ed. R Allen Brown (Boydell and Brwerr, Woodbridge, 1978), pp. 131–43

Ian Walker, *Harold: The Last Anglo-Saxon King* (Sutton, 1997)

W. L. Warren, *Henry II* (Methuen, 1973)

W. E. Wightman, 'The Palatine Earldom of William FitzOsbern in Gloucestershire and Herefordshire', *English Historical Review*, Vol. 77 (1962), pp. 6–17

The Lacey Family in England and Normandy (Oxford UP, 1966)

Bertram Wolffe, *Henry VI* (Methuen, 1981)

INDEX